Joint Investigation in Child Protection

Working Together – Training Together

Liz Davies

and

Debbie Townsend

Russell House Publishing

First published in 2008 by:
Russell House Publishing Ltd.
4 St. George's House
Uplyme Road
Lyme Regis
Dorset DT7 3LS

Tel: 01297-443948
Fax: 01297-442722
e-mail: help@russellhouse.co.uk
www.russellhouse.co.uk

British Library Cataloguing-in-publication Data:
A catalogue record for this book is available from the British Library.

ISBN: 978-1-905541-32-4

Typeset by TW Typesetting, Plymouth, Devon
Printed by Bell & Bain, Glasgow

Russell House Publishing

Russell House Publishing aims to publish innovative and valuable materials to help managers, practitioners, trainers, educators and students.

Our full catalogue covers: social policy, working with young people, helping children and families, care of older people, social care, combating social exclusion, revitalising communities and working with offenders.

Full details can be found at **www.russellhouse.co.uk** and we are pleased to send out information to you by post. Our contact details are on this page.

We are always keen to receive feedback on publications and new ideas for future projects.

Contents

Preface

This is one of two manuals by Liz Davies and Debbie Townsend to help with:

- **Joint investigation in child protection**
  - by police officers, social workers and any other professionals who have responsibilities to work together to safeguard and protect children
  - by showing how training together can help everyone involved to understand: what constitutes 'significant harm'; how to focus on the children involved; how to improve investigative skills . . . and understand the roles of people from all other agencies sufficiently well that they can work with, and if necessary, challenge them.
- **Investigative interviewing of children: achieving best evidence**
  - by police officers and social workers
  - by showing how training together can make sure that the investigative interviewing of victims and witnesses in possible child abuse cases is undertaken to the highest possible standards . . . in ways that build on and can be applied to the investigative interviewing of children in other contexts as well.

The other manual, *Investigative Interviewing of Children: Achieving Best Evidence (RHP, 2008)*, is closely linked to this one. But it can be used independently, as indicated immediately above by the somewhat different readership for the two manuals.

Important advice for anyone who works with LSCBs

This *Joint Investigation in Child Protection* manual has as its primary purpose the joint training of specialist police officers and social workers; but it:

- Can also help all LSCB-linked agencies achieve their performance objectives.
- Is available at a price commensurate with the budgets of even the smaller organisations that are involved in this work.
- Challenges and goes beyond existing government guidance in ways that can significantly improve safeguarding and protecting work with children and young people.

It contains a wealth of material that can be used in the training of anyone whose responsibilities for safeguarding and protecting children and young people is linked to Local Safeguarding Children Boards, including:

- health workers in PCTs and hospital trusts
- teachers and education staff in formal and informal education
- social workers in children's and adults' services and other local authority workers such as housing staff
- probation officers, and staff in the prison service, secure provision and youth offending teams
- police officers who work with children
- staff in the voluntary and private sectors delivering services for children and adults
- religious leaders and volunteers providing services to children within faith communities.

Working together, training together

These two manuals:

- Have been developed by police officers and social workers, working together.
- Have been extensively tested with London-based police officers and social workers, training together.
- Contain high-quality and extensively tested material that directly addresses major current gaps in the training that is available to police officers and social workers. The goal is to enable them to work together on the investigation of possible child abuse in ways that can meet concerns that have been raised – but not yet addressed – during high profile inquiries of the last two decades.
- Contain photocopiable handouts.
- Contain a full and clearly explained assessment of the urgent need for this training, with full reference to these inquiries, legislation, policy and practice guidance, as well as critical thinking about them. This is contained in the *Introduction and Overview*.
- Provide an opportunity to develop analytical skills and reflective child-centred practice in the context of multi-agency working.
- Will help police officers and social workers meet and exceed their performance objectives.
- Have been developed and extensively tested by Liz Davies and Debbie Townsend who have worked together since 1997. **Liz Davies**, who has many years experience as a social worker and child protection manager and trainer, now teaches social work at London Metropolitan University. At the university she also delivers post qualifying courses to police and social workers with **Debbie Townsend**, a former Metropolitan Police detective specialising in child abuse investigation and also a child protection trainer. Debbie now works as a consultant designing and delivering child protection courses. Liz

Davies is widely published, and regularly works with the media on child protection issues.

Support for trainers

To help anyone wanting to incorporate the Handouts into their teaching or training, purchasers of each manual can subsequently purchase these trainer's materials as PDFs, available only from the publisher.

Each of the two manuals includes information on how the material in them can be used to create a 2-week course for validation as Bachelors and Masters Modules.

Why is the thinner manual more expensive?

The publisher's decision on pricing is based on costs being spread across the two manuals, and reflects:

- The must-have, highly specialist nature of the training for police officers and social workers in *Investigative Interviewing of Children: Achieving Best Evidence*.
- The similar need for high-quality in *Joint Investigation in Child Protection* training, not only for police officers and social workers, but also for all other professionals who have responsibility to work together to safeguard and protect children.

In the interests of making *Joint Investigation in Child Protection* affordable across its widest possible audience, its price has been kept as low as possible.

Joint investigation: working together – training together

Addressing work done by police officers, social workers and any other professional linked to safeguarding children boards, the

Joint Investigation in Child Protection manual can help everyone involved to:

- **understand and recognise what constitutes 'significant harm'**
- **focus on the children involved**
- **develop suitable investigative skills**
- **understand the roles of fellow professionals from all other agencies sufficiently well to work effectively with, and if necessary, challenge them.**

Workers from all of these backgrounds, with varied levels of experience, knowledge and prior learning can benefit from this training's approach to child-centred interviewing.

The *Joint Investigation in Child Protection* manual:
- Challenges and goes beyond existing government guidance in ways that can significantly improve safeguarding and protecting work children and young people.
- Contains a wide range of 23 presentations and 34 activities, which specialist police and social work trainers – working and training together, demonstrating their flexibility and expertise across disciplines – can pick and choose from to design their own

5-day course, depending on participants' experience and needs, including those whose needs may be at an introductory level. And trainers will still have further materials 'left over' for use at other times: this is a rich and extensive resource. The manual includes a wide range of materials suited to adult learning such as role plays, carousels, storytelling and quizzes.
- Is available at a price commensurate with the budgets of even the smaller organisations that are involved in this work; or of agencies of any size for whom this work may be crucial, but perhaps not their principal undertaking.

Applicability in Scotland and Northern Ireland

This book follows English and Welsh statutory guidance, and is adaptable for use in Scotland and Northern Ireland. For Scotland, *Guidance on Interviewing Child Witnesses in Scotland – Supporting Child Witnesses Guidance Pack 2008* is available on www.scotland.gov.uk. In Northern Ireland, *Achieving Best Evidence in Criminal Proceedings (Northern Ireland) Guidance for Vulnerable or Intimidated Witnesses including Children (2003)* is available on http://www.nio.gov.uk.

About the Authors

Liz Davies is a Senior Lecturer in Social Work at London Metropolitan University teaching 'Safeguarding Children' and 'Communication with Children' modules at both undergraduate and post-graduate levels. She also delivers, with Debbie Townsend, the post-qualifying training, in joint investigation and investigative interviewing skills, to social workers and police. In 2007, with the publisher Akamas, she published introductory online child protection training and a resource book entitled *Protecting Children*. *Proactive Child Protection* (Davies, L. and Duckett, N. 2008) is a text book for social work students published by Learning Matters.

Liz provides consultancy to the media and writes widely on child protection issues. In 1972, she began her social work career in mental health services and later whilst a team manager in Islington she exposed extensive abuse within the care system. In the 90s as a child protection manager and trainer in the London borough of Harrow, Liz developed her specialism in child interview skills and the investigation of organised abuse networks. In 2005 she was the expert witness for Lisa Arthurworrey, social worker to Victoria Climbié, in her successful appeal to the Care Standards Tribunal. She is currently writing a PhD through prior output entitled *Protecting Children: A Radical Contribution to Policy and Practice Development*.

Debbie Townsend is an independent child protection trainer and consultant. She contributes to the social work programmes and delivers the post qualifying child protection training at London Metropolitan University. She began her police career in 1975 and worked in East London on major investigation teams which included the investigation of organised and institutional abuse. As a detective with the Metropolitan Police, she worked in a child abuse investigation for 16 years and took the lead in designing and delivering single and multi-agency child protection training in 10 north London boroughs. In 2005, she contributed to a resource book for law enforcement officers on good practices in combating child trafficking, published by the International Organisation for Migration and the European Commission. Debbie is also involved in the development of a national police training programme for child abuse investigators at foundation and advanced level and is a recognised expert in investigative interviewing of child witnesses. For the last 23 years she has organised holidays every year for 60 vulnerable children from east London authorities through her work with the charity 'Police Summer Camp Project'.

Acknowledgements

We would like to thank all the police, social work, health, education and probation trainers who have contributed so much energy and expertise to the development of these courses, in particular Pat Rackind, Wendy Thorn , DS Jeff Boxer, Michael Hames, Dr Ximena Poblete, Dr Claire Sturge, DI Mick Cooper-Bland, DC Chris King, DS Debbie Moore and DS Kevin Smith. We have learnt so much also from Demetrious Panton, Peter Saunders, Teresa Cooper and Phil Frampton who have provided their experiences and knowledge as survivors of abuse to many of our courses. Lisa Arthurworrey deserves special mention for assisting our understanding of the Victoria Climbié case and in reminding us of the importance of these courses, which she did not have the opportunity to attend. A number of experts in child protection have helped to develop our comprehension of this complex subject and have been there to guide us along the way, namely Martin Calder, Terri Dowty, Eileen Munro and Sarah Nelson. We especially thank Brian Douieb, Liz's partner, who has given his time, expertise and support based on many years of children's social work experience. Thanks also to Angus Stickler and Eileen Fairweather, two investigative journalists dedicated to the protection of children who have persistently kept children's safety firmly in the public arena. We thank Roger Stoodley who played a major role in Debbie's choice of a career path in child protection and for his support and guidance. We also acknowledge the commitment of Stephen Fox, head of social work at London Metropolitan University, to the continued delivery and development of these courses which enables us both to continue our teaching and to learn about current practice from the participants who attend. Finally, Liz's sons, Corin and Tiernan, and Debbie's 12 godchildren, nieces and nephew for continually reminding us that there is childhood without abuse.

Dedication

To the children

About this Manual and the Training Course

The two training contexts in which this material can be used

As noted in the Preface:
- This *Joint Investigation in Child Protection* manual has as its primary purpose the joint training of specialist police officers and social workers.
- But it can also help all LSCB-linked agencies achieve their performance objectives; and contains a wealth of material that can be used in the training of anyone whose responsibilities for safeguarding and protecting of children and young people is linked to Local Safeguarding Children Boards.

Use of this material in any context

Workers from all of these backgrounds, with varied levels of experience, knowledge and prior learning can benefit from this training's approach to child-centred interviewing.

It challenges and goes beyond existing government guidance in ways that can significantly improve the safeguarding and protecting of children and young people.

This material can help everyone involved to:
- understand and recognise what constitutes 'significant harm'
- focus on the children involved
- develop suitable investigative skills
- understand the roles of fellow professionals from all other agencies sufficiently well to work effectively with, and if necessary, challenge them.

The manual contains a wide range of 23 presentations and 34 activities, all suited to adult learning such as role plays, carousels, storytelling and quizzes. Trainers can pick and choose to design training that is adapted to participants' experience and needs, including those whose needs may be at an introductory level. There is enough here to deliver a full week's training; and you will still have further materials 'left over' for use at other times. This is a rich and extensive resource.

The material is not prescriptive, but rather takes the trainers from one aspect of the subject to another through the prompting of some short presentations, which are in no way exhaustive.

Whilst recognising the sensitive nature of the subject of child protection, some activities included are designed to lighten the atmosphere and provide some relief from the intensity of the material.

Appropriate surroundings and equipment

The provision of a suitable learning environment cannot be over-emphasised.

Comfortable chairs should be arranged in a horseshoe shape and be easily moved to accommodate the varied activities. Some of the activities are role plays which will involve participants sitting at a table to replicate practice. Otherwise there should be no physical barriers between the trainers and the participants in the form of tables.

This is not a manual that covers detail such as telling trainers that they will need flip chart, paper and pens; but they do need to be totally familiar with the equipment – video, DVD, projector and computer. Certainly, when the material is used to deliver a formal course, trainers will find that it moves swiftly between the different methods of delivery.

Joint training with police and social workers

The content of the course

When used in this specific context, this training manual takes the reader on a journey through a five day course which we would recommend as an essential prerequisite for the Achieving Best Evidence investigative interview course (as presented in the companion manual *Investigative Interviewing of Children: Achieving Best Evidence*) and prepares participants in their approach to a child-centred interview. A wide range of activities are offered to appeal to different levels of skill and knowledge which the trainer can use as a 'pick and mix' of resources. There is no possibility of achieving the delivery of all this material in the course of a week. It is up to the discretion of the trainer which activities and content are chosen from the key themes as outlined within the framework of the five days.

In general, courses have a maximum of 14 participants with, as far as possible, equal representation from police and social workers. It is acceptable to have a higher number of participants on the Joint Investigation course given that not everyone will progress to the Investigative Interviewing course.

The background to joint training

This joint investigation course is based on a blend of two courses which the authors have delivered separately since the early 1990s. When they first met to train together in 1997 they were amazed at the similarity of course content, derived from years of child protection practice.

The course has now been refined and is delivered several times a year at London Metropolitan University to social workers and police from the London Boroughs and social workers in SSAFFA who respond to the needs of children of those in the armed forces. As well as police officers from Child Abuse Investigation Teams, participants also include police from domestic violence units, schools involvement officers, local CID, Public Protection Units, Complex Abuse Investigation Teams and those responding to serious sexual and organised crime. Social workers often include those working in specialist teams such as for disabled children, unaccompanied minors and child and adolescent mental health. A recent development has been the validation as post-qualifying training of the two week courses at both undergraduate and postgraduate levels.

Participants prior knowledge requirements

Police and social workers will be of varied levels of experience, knowledge and prior learning. It is not unusual to be training an officer newly appointed to the police child abuse investigation team with no knowledge at all of the current legislation or policy in this area of work. Initially, the participants needed to have undertaken a two day introductory child protection training course but this unfortunately can no longer be a prerequisite because these courses are now largely unavailable, and it would be unreasonable to insist on this requirement. We have therefore included some content of an introductory level in this course.

The background and qualifications needed by trainers

This is not a pack that a trainer from another discipline can take off the shelf and deliver to police and social workers.

When used in this context, it is absolutely essential that the trainers are highly experienced and skilled child protection practitioners from both police and children's services. They should adapt the material to suit their needs, responding to any recommendations about practice or training derived from the findings of both local and national serious case reviews.

The trainers should model working together by being flexible in the delivery of the content and demonstrating their expertise across disciplines. The police trainer may, for instance, present training about the child's needs and the impact of abuse whereas the social work trainer may cover legal and procedural issues. This approach supports the credibility of the trainers with both police and social workers, as well as promoting and validating learning across professional boundaries.

The forms of training used

Trainers need to adopt a facilitative approach which draws on the experience of the group and allows maximum contribution with didactic delivery kept to a minimum. It should be noted that police officers may not be as familiar as the social workers may be with style of delivery. The activities are designed to enable participants to question and challenge at every stage creating a mutual and safe learning process. Given the complex nature of the course content, it is important that participants are informed that trainers operate a 'walk-out' policy which means it is acceptable for them to leave the room for a short break should it be necessary. Trainers need to be flexible and open to changing the programme in response to the learning needs of the group.

Responding to the diverse backgrounds of the participants

Because the participants may have very different background experience and training, the trainers will be faced with a number of dilemmas. At an early stage of the course the qualifications possessed by the participants are clarified. Entry requirements for social workers and police differ. Social workers in order to qualify and attain registration have to have completed a degree in social work (previously diploma) whereas police have no such academic entry requirements. However, police working in a Child Abuse Investigation team complete a specialist child protection professional development programme over and above their initial police training. Some participants will have already been in child protection work for many years and others will be completely new to the subject. As well as a wide range of skill and knowledge base there are commonly obvious differences in ethnicity and gender. On one occasion, 6 white male police officers and 6 black female social workers attended a course and issues of prejudice and value systems evident in both groups had to be addressed.

Applicability in Scotland and Northern Ireland

This book follows English and Welsh statutory guidance, and is adaptable for use in Scotland and Northern Ireland. For Scotland, *Guidance on Interviewing Child Witnesses in Scotland – Supporting Child Witnesses Guidance Pack 2008* is available on www.scotland.gov.uk. In Northern Ireland, *Achieving Best Evidence in Criminal Proceedings (Northern Ireland) Guidance for Vulnerable or Intimidated Witnesses including Children (2003)* is available on http://www.nio.gov.uk.

Photocopying Permission for Use of the Handouts

1. Permission to photocopy the 38 handouts is only given to **individuals or organisations who have bought a copy of the book** and then only for distribution at the local level within their organisation. The price of this book has deliberately been kept affordable to smaller organisations. It is therefore expected that, as a matter of honour, larger organisations – for example national or county-wide statutory or voluntary organisations – who might want to use the photocopiable material in numerous locations, will buy a copy of the book for use in each locality where they are using the material.

2. If a **trainer or an educational organisation** wants to copy and distribute these handouts to assist their work with clients in organisations where they are training, it is expected that they will buy a copy of the book for each organisation where they undertake such training and – in line with the principles set out in point 1 (above) – a copy for each locality when they are training in a large organisation at multiple locations. This expectation is based on respect for the author's copyright and the view that providing manuals in this way will add to the benefits delivered in the training. The publisher and author therefore seek trainers' active support in this matter.

3. Under no circumstances should anyone sell photocopied material from this book without the express permission of the publisher.

If in doubt, anyone wanting to make photocopies should contact the publisher, via email at help@russellhouse.co.uk.

Other photocopying permission

Anyone wishing to copy all or part of the handouts *in any context other than set out here* should first seek permission in the usual way:

- either via Russell House Publishing
- or via the Copyright Licensing Agency.

Anyone wishing to copy any other part of this book in any context, beyond normal fair trading guidelines, should first seek permission in the usual way:

- either via Russell House Publishing
- or via the Copyright Licensing Agency.

Electronic Supply of the Handouts

A PDF of the 38 handouts of this manual is available free, by email from RHP, to purchasers of the book who complete and return the licence request at the end of the book.

Please note that anyone who is reading this in a copy of the book from which the tear-out coupon has been removed would need to buy a new copy of the book in order to be able to apply for the electronic materials.

The following terms and conditions for use of the electronic materials apply in all cases:

Terms and conditions for use of handouts from *Joint Investigation in Child Protection*

1. Buying a copy of *Joint Investigation in Child Protection* and completing the form at the back of this book gives the individual who signs the form permission to use the materials in the PDF that will be sent from RHP for their own use only.
2. The hard copies that they then print from the PDF are subject to the same permissions and restrictions that are set out in the 'photocopying permission' section at the front of this book.
3. Under no circumstances should they forward or copy the electronic materials to anyone else.
4. If the person who signs this form wants a licence to be granted for wider use of the electronic materials within their organisation, network or client base, they must make a request directly to RHP fully detailing the proposed use. All requests will be reviewed on their own merits.

- If the request is made when submitting the form at the back of the book to RHP, the request should be made in writing and should accompany this form.
- If the request is made later, it should be made in an email sent to help@russellhouse.co.uk, and should not only fully detail the proposed use, but also give the details of the person whose name and contact details were on the original application form.

RHP and the author expect this honour system to be followed respectfully, by individuals and organisations whom we in turn respect. RHP will act to protect authors' copyright if they become aware of it being infringed.

Introduction and Overview

This introductory chapter is intended to provide an overview of the historical context and underlying *raison d'être* for writing the ensuing and timely text. It also appears in the companion volume *Investigative Interviewing of Children: Achieving Best Evidence: Working Together – Training Together.*

Trained staff will be better staff. The quality of care will be improved and the children will be safer.

(Utting, 1997: 12.7)

The lack of emphasis on joint training in recent inquiries and policy documentation

Lisa Arthurworrey, Haringey social worker to Victoria Climbié, had completed a multi-agency 'working together' awareness course but Detective Sergeant Cooper-Bland, who had delivered this course, said in his evidence to the Care Standards Tribunal (Lisa Arthurworrey v Secretary of State) that:

I cannot see how the Haringey course could equip a social worker to carry out an investigation. It was not the aim of the course to provide that level of instruction.

Judge Pearl concluded in the hearing that:

Without training at an advanced level I would not expect Ms Arthurworrey to have understood how to properly investigate an allegation of child abuse. I would not expect her to have understood her role as a social worker in relation to that of the police, the detailed function and purpose of strategy meetings and conferences or

how to assess and confront parent or carer responses in relation to child abuse allegations.

(CST, 2005: 91–3)

One of the key recommendations, from the tragedy of the death of Victoria Climbié, should have been that police and social workers conducting Section 47 investigations and video recorded interviews of children must receive specialist training at advanced level. Yet, there was no such recommendation and there remains no such statutory requirement. Reder and Duncan (2004: 112) with reference to the Climbié case, commented that:

. . . since the findings of any next inquiry could reasonably be predicted before it has taken place, we would like to propose that no further public inquiries are commissioned before all training and resource deficiencies identified over the last 30 years have been remedied.

Lord Laming, however, did state that Arthurworrey, 'was not trained in the Memorandum of Good Practice and could not therefore see a Section 47 child protection inquiry through to its conclusion' (Laming, 2003: 6.10), but failed to address the importance of both joint investigation and child interview training. This view contrasted with the statement of Judge Pearl who concluded that the basic social work training she was given did not prepare her for the responsibilities she had in Victoria's case (CST, 2005: 111). Training gained much mention in the Victoria Climbié Inquiry recommendations for social workers but included only general references to the need for training for 'effective joint working', 'inter-agency working', 'appropriate training' and 'continuing training' (Recommendations 14, 15, 20 and 31). It also stated that managers were to ensure that no case should be allocated, 'until his or her manager ensures he or she has had the necessary training to deal with it properly' (Recommendation 52). The only more detailed recommendations about training (Recommendations 37 and 100), stated that social workers and police must be trained to equip them with the confidence to question the opinion of professionals in other agencies and the police recommendation (103) solely stressed the importance of single agency skills in criminal investigation (Laming, 2003).

The key mistake in the case of Victoria Climbié was that she was responded to as a child in need and not a child in need of protection. Lisa Arthurworrey had been trained in the assessment (sometimes called the family support) approach and thought child protection was only for emergencies. She had no understanding of how to conduct a Section 47 investigation jointly with the police. Lord Laming commented that in the case he had 'heard no evidence of what I would term a Section 47 inquiry ever being carried out by Haringey Social Services' (Laming, 2003: 6. 217). Reder and Duncan in their review of the case stated that, 'A referral received by social services which indicated the likelihood of non accidental injuries to Victoria was labelled from the outset as 'child in need'. This framed all of that departments' subsequent activities on the case' (Reder and Duncan, 2004: 104).

Importantly, this approach led to a lack of joint investigation. Given the professional expertise which informed the Victoria Climbié Inquiry, and the substantial influence of the recommendations in shaping the future of child protection work, it was astonishing that joint investigation training did not gain a mention.

A similar omission was evident in the Bichard Inquiry following the conviction of Ian Huntley for the murders of Holly Wells and Jessica Chapman (Bichard, 2004). Neither Lord Bichard nor Sir Christopher Kelly, in his serious case review, mentioned advanced level child protection training. Kelly, in examining professional responses to the 13 cases of young women sexually exploited by Huntley, concluded that practice had fallen below an acceptable level. He identified inexperienced staff with poor supervision, yet his comment about training was solely that it should be adequate to support processes in 'Working Together' and the handling of child protection cases (Kelly, 2004).

Working Together to Safeguard Children (DfES, 2006) stated clear responsibilities on Local Safeguarding Children Boards (LSCBs) to identify training needs, use this information to plan and commission training and evaluate training to ensure that it meets local needs. The procedures recommended that training sub groups should be established to include people with sufficient knowledge of training needs and processes to enable them to make informed contributions to the development and evaluation of a training strategy. Yet, the inspection report *Local Safeguarding Children Boards – A Review of Progress*, made no comment about the implementation of training programmes. The report did state that police involvement in the LSCBs ranged from excellent to marginal, but did not evaluate the level of involvement of the police role in training (DCSF, 2007). The Boards were urged to shift from 'an operational child protection board to a strategic safeguarding board' which gave an emphasis on broadening the task before there was any indication that essential child protection training was actually in place (DCSF, 2007: 9.6). The inspection report, *Narrowing the Gap*, again paid little attention to child protection training other than to state that, 'safeguarding arrangements are supported by good quality multi-disciplinary training and there is a demonstrable commitment to training from all partner agencies *through the local safeguarding children board*'. It offered no detail of what level of training was being provided to exactly which professionals or agencies (Ofsted, 2007: 13).

In order to understand why this essential training has been virtually ignored in such key recent inquiries and policy documents, it is necessary to explore the range of requirements specified in different editions of *Working Together* and to examine this in the context of the changing nature of child protection work since 1995, when the prevention or 'child in need' agenda first came to notice and when 'assessment' replaced 'investigation'. The history of both the joint investigation and the child interview courses will be explored in this context.

The development of joint training

In 1984, a working party was set up by the Metropolitan Police to review methods of conducting and recording interviews with victims of child sexual abuse. This became known as the Bexley experiment and was the beginning of a seven day training course to address the emotional content of the investigation process.

> *The first two days were wholly devoted to developing an atmosphere within the group that would be conducive to building trust and interdependence. The trainees felt that they were able to get*

> *to know and trust each other and share their feelings and ideas openly which is the foundation on which successful joint investigation depends.*
>
> (Metropolitan Police and
> London Borough of Bexley, 1987)

The training promoted social work and police involvement jointly at all stages of the investigation even, if agreed, during the interview of a suspect. It was said that joint work enabled a flow of information between the criminal investigation and the therapeutic work (Metropolitan Police and London Borough of Bexley, 1987 and Wattam, 1990: 23).

Prior to the implementation of the first *Working Together* arrangements, police and social workers struggled to work together effectively as the following case study illustrates:

In 1988, Liam Johnson, age 18 months, died from multiple injuries. He was said to have been dead for about 6–12 hours before his father arrived with him at the hospital. There were two key professional tasks. The police were pursuing criminal investigation particularly in relation to the father. The social workers were assessing the father and other family members as future carers for the seven year old sibling. Both investigations took place in parallel. The police did not share the witness statements with the social workers although these contained much information that would have assisted the assessment. The social workers did not share their findings with the police to assist the criminal investigation, yet the social workers were meeting regularly to interview the accused father, and they were also interviewing the sibling about events preceding the child's death. The sibling was made a Ward of Court and material gathered for the criminal proceedings was not available to the hearing. Attitudes to the father's contact differed between the civil and criminal proceedings and important medical evidence, reserved for the criminal trial, was not available to the civil case. The sibling remained in long-term foster care and the father received a sentence of 10 years imprisonment for manslaughter. The social workers had not realised that they themselves may have been at risk, whilst working with the father, because information about him, known to police, was not shared with them (Lawson, 1989).

This division, between the work of the statutory agencies, is in stark contrast to the joint working of the late 1980s and 1990s that led to many investigations of familial, institutional and organised abuse, the prosecution of perpetrators and the protection of hundreds of children. Initially, police and social workers were very reluctant to work together. In fact, the authors of this book probably found themselves on opposite sides of the barricades in the demonstrations of the 1970s. The early training needed to address stereotypes and fears about working together. Yet, when both police and social workers worked together, a powerful combination of knowledge and skills did enable excellent practice to take place to protect children. However, early developments relating to joint training mainly focused on the investigation of sexual abuse. The Report of the Inquiry into Child Abuse in Cleveland stated that:

> . . . *we regard training as an issue of central importance in ensuring that the special needs of children who have or may have been sexually abused are properly recognised and met . . . it was our overwhelming impression that the training provided nationally is inadequate . . . many social workers experienced difficulty in responding to sexually abused children because they had not received the training to the task they were undertaking.*
>
> (Butler-Sloss, 1988: 15.2 and 15.6)

The report recommended that training should be properly coordinated and validated on a national basis.

In response to this Inquiry, the National Children's Bureau published a detailed resource about training entitled *A Positive Model. Standards for the Development and Evaluation of Materials for Training in Child Sexual Abuse* (Armstrong and Hollows, 1989). This provided an excellent analysis of the dilemmas and difficulties in such training. 'Different professional groups have different cultures and that extends to learning too . . . training must develop strategies for dealing with groups of individuals with very diverse experience and expectations of training' (1989: 2). The authors emphasised the importance of sensitivity training specifically related to personal feelings about abuse:

> . . . *training packages should carry explicit reference to the fact that training activities in the field of child sexual abuse stimulate a range of intense personal reactions. These may include disclosure by members of the course, anger at the trainers, heated controversy within the group over issues like gender and power, fresh perspectives on management and supervision issues and powerful responses to the plight of children.*
>
> (Armstrong and Hollows, 1989: 13)

The training pack provided extensive advice to trainers about how to build a supportive training environment, allow participants to progress at their own pace and enable exploration of difficult emotional subjects. The authors recommended that the trainers should model their approaches to working with children and suggested the involvement of two trainers because of the probability of disclosure from some participants, either of their own or others history of child abuse. This pack significantly influenced the content of joint investigation courses at the time.

The recommendations of the Report of the Inquiry into the Removal of Children from Orkney, in February 1991, repeated the Cleveland statement that child witness interviews should 'be undertaken only by those with some training experience and aptitude for talking with children' (Butler-Sloss, 1988: 12.34.2). It stated that interviewers should have a high calibre of professional skill. Joint training for social workers with police was specifically recommended as:

> ... the cooperation of the two agencies cannot be undervalued ... workers who undertake joint interviews should train together ... common training can help to improve trust between them and help towards their mutual cooperation to the greater benefit of the children ... in particular the importance and difficulty inherent in the work of interviewing children in cases of alleged sexual abuse requires to be more fully appreciated by the police force.

> (Clyde, 1992: 19. 12–22)

Both inquiries stemmed from the investigation of numerous allegations of child sexual abuse and much public criticism of the 'overzealous' approach of the professionals involved. Whilst much was learnt from both inquiries about improved methods of investigation, both police and social workers in these cases were providing a message that the public was unwilling to listen to at the time, about the extensive prevalence of child sexual abuse.

Since the publication of *Working Together* (DoH, 1991) police officers and social workers have been tasked with working jointly in conducting child abuse investigations, and police forces began to set up specialised child protection units which by 1996 were implemented throughout England and Wales. In 1991, the Department of Health published

Working with Child Sexual Abuse. Guidelines for Trainers and Managers in Social Services Departments, and Chapter 3 specifically concerned training in investigation skills (DoH, 1991). The aim of the training was to 'equip staff to carry out a competent investigation of a child sexual abuse referral, taking action as necessary and making an informed contribution to case conferences' (DoH, 1991: 3.2.1). Much detail was specified as to the course content and it was clear that this advanced level training must build on an introductory level foundation course. Four specific competencies were included. Those:

- Built on an understanding and knowledge of normal child development and various aspects of sexual abuse.
- Built on an understanding of the law, agency policy and procedures.
- Associated with good communication skills.
- Related to an ability to interpret behaviour and weigh information, in order to reach conclusions and make decisions based on knowledge, facts and experience.

In particular, the guidance differentiated between a risk assessment and a needs assessment (DoH, 1991: 4.3.3). Risk assessment was to focus 'principally on those factors which are predictive of future abuse'. Training, it was said, should address what evidence or other information there is that the abuse has stopped, how far the abuser is acknowledging responsibility for the abuse and recognising the consequences, and how far the mother or an abusing carer acknowledges the abuse and recognises the consequences. It should also teach a risk assessment of the particular circumstances of the abuse and the impact on the child. If the abuse had ritualistic elements then staff were advised to focus on the issues of possible sexual, emotional and physical abuse to the child. Also in 1991, Detective Sergeant Williams wrote of the need for training in investigations concerning the ritual abuse of children, as the police had some cases, but no-one qualified to conduct the training (Williams, 1991).

When the *Memorandum of Good Practice* was published in 1992, joint training courses for police and social workers were delivered by the Area Child Protection Committees (Home Office, 1992). The Open University had been commissioned by the Department of Health to produce a training package which was available from 1993 (Stainton Rogers and Worrel, 1993). The training was known to be variable in length and content, but initial research of interviews conducted with children showed them to be of good quality. However, a need for 'an agreed curriculum and properly accredited national standards for trainers and training courses' was still important (Davies et al., 1995). Respondents stated their need for training in the interviewing of children with special needs, those children whose first language was not English and familiarity training for managers. They also requested increased practice in conducting the interviews.

In 1994, a Metropolitan Police survey of joint work in *six* local authorities concluded that 'it was worrying that many child protection staff (two thirds of whom had over *two* years experience) appear to have had no training in fundamental areas of child protection work' (Smith and Clarke, 1994). The survey identified agreement between police and social workers about the need for joint training in the identification of child abuse, assessment of significant harm, preparation for and participation in child protection conferences, child development, anti-oppressive practice, direct work with children and work with disabled children. Birchall and Hallett also studied post qualifying child protection training in London and found it 'very limited and unevenly

spread' with 49 per cent of a range of professionals surveyed having undertaken no training at all in child protection and 37 per cent who had completed less than one week of training. 14 per cent of the sample had received over one week of training and this was generally received most positively (Birchall and Hallett, 1995: 45). Holton and Bonnerjea (1994: 33), in a survey of 91 social services departments, found that 84 per cent had no formal assessment of competence following the child protection training programme. Hughes et al. (1996) interviewed police in ten forces and found that they mainly lacked knowledge about child development, the behaviour of perpetrators, and training in the interviewing of suspected perpetrators. A national training programme was once again proposed.

By 1995:

> . . . *it was clear that there has been considerable growth in the number of people employed specifically to provide inter-agency child protection training. These posts were funded by the Area Child Protection Committees, social services or the voluntary sector. Those providing the training need to be able to command respect from different agency representatives, the facilitative and diplomatic skills need to be complimented by an extensive technical knowledge base and up-to-date information.*
>
> (Hendry, 1995: 227–9)

When social services training mainly became contracted out to the private sector some of these local, specialist training posts were no longer in place.

Following many child protection investigations of organised abuse within residential care establishments, Sir William Utting, in *People Like Us, The Report of the Review of the Safeguards for Children Living*

Away from Home, recommended the importance of training for child care professionals in knowledge about the:

> ... *profiles and methods of perpetrators of child sexual abuse. The sexual abuse of children living away from home occurs in circumstances in which the abuse often goes undetected and is not disclosed, sometimes for many years. For this reason, if abuse of this sort is to be detected in time to help the child victim, reacting to allegations is not enough and proactive approaches to discovery are needed. This requires attention to be directed to the behaviour of the potential perpetrator. Training is necessary to raise awareness of how perpetrators behave and their methods of abusing children.*
>
> (Utting, 1997: 12.35)

Davies et al. concluded that: 'joint training is not only an efficient way to deliver training, but also promotes effective working practices between the police officers and social workers (Davies, 1998: 10). In an analysis of 12 police forces, the research showed that courses were between five and ten days duration. The feedback received from a debrief of the video recordings of training interviews was found particularly useful. Nine areas of knowledge to be covered by joint training were identified:

- Inter-agency working, Section 47 procedures and child protection conferences.
- Law and legal issues; civil and criminal law.
- Technical aspects of interviewing.
- Phased interview approach, including planning and preparation.
- Child development, including memory, suggestibility, use of language, and children's fears.

- Information about sexual abuse, sexual behaviour and perpetrator tactics, grooming and behaviour.
- Evidence gathering and investigation, including that of organised abuse, medical and forensic issues.
- Working with children and families, including disability, trauma and ethnic minority issues.
- Job stress and coping.

Respondents also expressed a need for refresher training, a point which has been restated recently by Davidson et al. who showed that police generally completed child interview training only once and that no update courses were offered, despite regular updates on guidance from the Home Office (Davidson et al., 2006: 251).

By the mid to late 1990s, joint investigation training had generally developed into a two week course with the second week focusing on investigative interviewing. The courses were delivered to police and social workers by local, specialist police and social work trainers employed by their agencies under the remit of the local Area Child Protection Committee. There had been considerable research and analysis of the required content of the training developed from the recommendations of inquiries and the training packages provided by the Department of Health and Home Office. Police and social workers were trained to work in specialist teams, sometimes sharing the same office. The NSPCC established some joint investigation teams and skilled practitioners investigated many cases of complex child abuse, protecting the children and bringing abusers to justice (Wolmar, 2000). This model of working was also promoted by Spence and Wilson (1994: 13), who suggested that, 'by working together, the team can accomplish the goals of all investigative agencies in a more efficient manner and with enhanced results'.

Working Together **as a policy document: examining developments**

The first edition of *Working Together* in 1988 recommended joint specialist training for:

> social services staff, the NSPCC, the health services and police who will be involved in the investigation of cases and subsequent intervention . . . specialist training should include child care law, the concept of child protection and the assessment of danger and alternative forms of intervention'.
>
> (DHSS, 1988: 8.3–5)

It was suggested that social services should take the lead role in the provision of this training and recommended that staff investigating child sexual abuse needed specialist training.

The 1991 edition of *Working Together* more specifically referred to police and social work joint training to:

> . . . enable members of each service to understand one another's role fully, to learn how to work together on a joint interviewing team on cases which may lead to criminal proceedings and above all how to interview children who may have been badly abused by other adults in such as way as to encourage them to provide information without further hurting them. Interviews must always and only be conducted in the best interest of the child.
>
> (DoH, 1991: 7.2–3)

It was the role of the Area Child Protection Committee to scrutinise the provision of inter-agency training (DoH, 1991: 2.12).

In 1999 the title of the guidance significantly changed from *Working Together to Protect Children* to *Working Together to Safeguard Children*. Three levels of training were required to promote *Working Together*:

- Introductory training for those in contact with children and parents.
- Foundation level training for all staff working with children and parents and carers.
- The third level for staff working together who, 'co-work on complex tasks or particular areas of practice that have specific knowledge or skill requirements e.g. joint enquiries and investigations, investigative interviews, complex assessments'. At this level training should 'establish and maintain partnerships of mutual trust and respect' and should include 'understanding of legal frameworks and levels of accountability of decision making in other agencies' (DoH, 1999: 9.15).

It was the role of the Area Child Protection Committee to help improve the quality of child protection work and of inter-agency working through specifying needs for inter-agency training and development and ensuring that training was delivered. The role included 'to encourage and help develop effective working relations between different services and professional groups based on trust and mutual understanding' (DoH, 1999: 4.2).

The revised edition of *Working Together*, published in 2006, restated the three levels of training required. Introductory and awareness training for those in regular contact with children and those who work regularly with children should be in place. A third level was for 'those with a particular responsibility for safeguarding children, such as designated or named health and education professionals, police, social workers and other professionals undertaking Section 47 enquiries or working with complex cases, including fabricated and induced illness' (DfES, 2006: 4.19). These levels were reflected in the London Child Protection Committee document *Competence Matters. A Multi-agency Safeguarding Children Training Framework for London* (Jacob and Hobbin, 2006), which based the three levels of training on those specified in an NSPCC publication, *Training Together to Safeguard Children* (Charles and Hendry, 2000). Level three training, described in *Competence Matters* for those working together on particular areas of practice, was therefore aimed at a wide range of professionals, but differed from the 2006 national procedures by retaining the need to establish and maintain partnerships of mutual trust and respect, and by specifying the need for this advanced level training for those conducting joint enquiries and investigations, investigative interviews and complex assessments.

The subsequent NSPCC training package, *Safeguarding Children, a Shared Responsibility*, which was the government recommended package to accompany recent policy changes, separated the training package into three levels. Level C, the most advanced, was for:

> . . . *social workers, police, paediatricians, senior nurses with particular responsibility for safeguarding children, operational managers and designated or named safeguarding managers. People who hold particular professional/ organisational authority and a substantial degree of personal responsibility and autonomy to act on child welfare concerns including those where a child is or may be suffering significant harm. They work extensively within an inter- or multi-agency context.*
> (NSPCC, 2007: 1, Trainer Guidance)

In Chapter 5 of the accompanying reader, *Working Effectively in a Multi-agency Context*, Horwath advises that

multi-disciplinary training should take place at every level, but makes no mention of specialist joint investigation training: just as in the same chapter, her description of the social work and police role noticeably omits any concept of joint investigative work (Horwath, 2007: 24).

Working Together (DfES, 2006) specified that the detail of training for specific levels should be decided locally, and there was therefore no requirement on LSCBs to provide specialist advanced level training (DfES, 2006: 4.22). The specific need for police and social work training in investigation and joint interviewing was thus omitted. Inter-agency specialist child protection training had now been replaced with generic skills in safeguarding for a wide range of professionals. The role of the Local Safeguarding Children Boards shifted from 'improving the quality of child protection work' (DoH, 1999: 4.2), to that of ensuring both single and inter-agency training, on safeguarding and promoting welfare, was provided to meet local needs (DfES, 2006: 3.22). It stated that relevant training must be provided by organisations to reach relevant staff, but no reference was made to the specific need of police and social workers to train together at an advanced level. It was also stated that the LSCBs did not have to deliver the training themselves, but should establish a sub-group to identify training needs and must ensure that trainers have sufficient knowledge, including that trainers on complex cases should have the relevant level of knowledge and skills (DfES, 2006: 4.23). There is no detail provided of who should conduct the level three training and what qualifications they might need. The purpose of broad based inter-agency training was outlined as aiming to achieve better outcomes for children:

- A shared understanding of the tasks, processes, principles and roles and responsibilities outlined in procedures and local arrangements for safeguarding children and promoting their welfare.

- More effective and integrated services at both the strategic and individual case level.
- Improved communication between professionals including a common understanding of key terms, definitions and thresholds for action.
- Effective working relationships including an ability to work in multi-disciplinary teams.
- Sound decision making based on information sharing, thorough assessment, critical analysis and professional judgement.

(DfES, 2006: 4.3)

Training to assist the co-ordination of separate services had now become training to make integrated services more effective. Improved working relationships now concerned only training to provide staff with an ability to work together in multi-disciplinary teams, and there was no continued emphasis on the importance of building trust and mutual understanding which had previously been a central learning objective. Employer's responsibilities were defined as ensuring that staff were confident and competent to carry out their responsibility for safeguarding and promoting the welfare of children, rather than the former responsibility to carry out child protection responsibilities. Although stating that employers must provide adequate resources, support training and release staff to attend courses, the procedures provided no clarity about which partnerships or bodies were responsible for delivering training, and did not address the thorny issue of which organisation should finance the training of police and social workers in investigative and interviewing skills (DfES, 2006: 4.5). There

had always been a difference between those areas where the ACPC had financed and delivered the training and those where, because this specialist training only involved two agencies, it was seen as a local authority responsibility. This dilemma remained unresolved, leaving a gap in provision.

Delivery of the specialist training was formerly by a police officer from the local Child Abuse Investigation Team (CAIT) and a local authority social work trainer. These professionals developed skills based on experience which reflected the recommendations of local serious case reviews. As with other council services, local social service training became outsourced under 'best value' policies with training largely becoming the responsibility of the local authority human resources teams. The role of experienced, specialist social work child protection trainers, who possessed local knowledge, was lost. Commissioned trainers were of varied competence and were rarely locality based. The police child abuse investigation teams became reduced in size across the country and their specialist training role also diminished. In London, for instance, the Metropolitan Police which had 32 police child protection trainers, one for every Borough, set up a central team of three officers who could not respond to the training needs of the London Boroughs children's services. The resourcing of police CAITs nationally is not known. Tony McNulty, Minister of State, Home Office, in a response to a parliamentary question stated that, 'the number of police officers employed specifically in child protection work is not collected centrally and is an operational matter for involved police forces and their child protection partners' (McNulty, 2007). *Working Together* (DfES, 2006), contained only broad generalisations about the quality of trainers and did nothing to address these serious deficiencies.

The introduction of training standards

Working Together stated that all work in this field should be consistent with *The Common Core of Skills and Knowledge for the Children's Workforce*, which became the broad base of knowledge required throughout single and inter-agency training and included:

- Effective communication and engagement with children, young people, their families and carers.
- Child and young person development.
- Safeguarding and promoting the welfare of the child.
- Supporting transitions.
- Multi-agency working.
- Sharing information.

(DfES, 2005: 4)

Following the green paper *Every Child Matters* (Treasury, 2003) and commissioned by the Department of Health with the involvement of the General Social Care Council, Shardlow and colleagues from the Salford Centre for Social Research published *Education and Training for Inter-Agency Working: New Standards*. The concept was to have the same standards applicable to each occupational and professional group. They recommended a core curriculum to be mandatory at each professional level for all staff on inter-agency working. These standards were to be incorporated into professional standards and the LSCBs were required to provide financial provision for inter-agency training based on the standards. The Salford team identified eight key operational standards with related training standards:

- Roles and responsibilities: Be clear about own roles and responsibilities in relation to those of others.
- Critically evaluate and challenge: Respect, critically evaluate and when necessary challenge the views of other practitioners.

- Consult and communicate: Consult and communicate effectively with other practitioners.
- Evaluate: Evaluate the judgements and conclusions made by themselves or other professionals about particular clients or cases.
- Ethics and confidentiality: Use and communicate relevant information with due regard for the preservation of the client's confidentiality as is appropriate.
- Collaborate with others: Collaborate with other practitioners to enhance the effectiveness of decision making.
- Review: Review the progress of inter-agency collaboration at regular intervals at strategic and individual case levels.
- Recording: Record inter-agency communication and assessments.

(Shardlow et al., 2004)

These standards did acknowledge the need for advanced level training and Shardlow's team emphasised that: 'all training in relation to inter-agency work at a specialist and advanced practitioner level should take place with practitioners from other relevant disciplines and organisations' (Shardlow, 2004: 3). There is also mention of the standards being inclusive of minimum standards of work 'as suggested by legislation and guidance' (e.g. *Best Evidence* and *Working Together*) (Shardlow, 2004: 12). However, 'suggested' should have been 'required', and the formulation of broad, generic standards did not further a recognition of the importance of the need for specialist training of police and social workers conducting Section 47 investigations.

The Shardlow report was a response to the recommendations of the Victoria Climbié Inquiry report which had, in Recommendation 99, undermined the concept of joint working (Laming, 2003). This called into question the social work role in joint work with police by stating that:

> ... *the Working Together arrangements must be amended to ensure the police carry out completely and exclusively any criminal investigation elements in a case of suspected injury or harm to a child including the evidential interview with a child victim.*

This recommendation essentially focused police work on the investigation of crime rather than involvement in making joint enquiries about actual or likely significant harm. As a result, when a level of crime cannot be proven or is not able to be pursued through criminal proceedings, social workers now investigate much child abuse as single agency. This recommendation also exacerbated a policy shift away from joint working imposed since the publication of the *Framework for the Assessment of Children in Need and Their Families* (DoH, 2000). Detective Chief Inspector Bird reflected this difficulty when he expressed concern that, 'social workers are reluctant to be identified with the investigation process ... they are present at an interview as spectators but take no part in putting questions to the victim'. He advocated a return to joint police/social work teams and the need for some social workers to specialise in this area of work (Bird, 2002).

The impact on training of the policy shift from investigation of risk to assessment of need

This split between the police investigation of crime and the social work role became further entrenched in *Working Together* where a Section 47 enquiry was wrongly redefined as a core assessment (DfES, 2006: 5.60). An initial or core assessment may inform an investigation but is a distinct and separate process which should always involve

consultation with police and a decision as to whether the investigation is conducted by a single or joint agency. Assessment involves a tick box approach to completing a triangle of three components – the child's developmental needs, parenting capacity and family and environmental factors. The change in approach was summarised by Stevenson who wrote that:

> ... *the forensic approach to significant harm with its emphasis on concrete physical evidence and hard facts may be quite incompatible with the acceptance of the concept of developmental harm.*
> (Stevenson in Charles and Hendry, 2000: 12)

This model of practice now forms the basis of all government protocols for children – the Common Assessment Framework, Initial and Core Assessments and all the Integrated Children's Systems with standard forms including those for child protection conferences and Section 47 strategy meetings. It is essentially a mechanistic, performance management tool and does not replace a child protection investigation. Assessment focuses on the needs of children and their families and not on targeting perpetrators of child abuse and/or seeking justice for children. An investigation of actual or likely significant harm conducted jointly with police, must always involve a focus on strategies to target perpetrators and to assess risk to the child. Initial and core assessments are not assessments of risk and the prescribed timescales required for their completion cannot be applied to a joint investigation, as 'to gain an abused child's trust, collate information about an alleged abuser, gain the cooperation of a non-abusive parent and have multi-agency debate and analysis of the risk of harm to a child may take months of complex work' (Davies, 2007). Munro and Calder, in their article, *Where has Child*

Protection Gone? discuss how in current policy:

> the very words of 'child protection', 'child abuse' and 'risk' have virtually disappeared from the language and how within this agenda victims of abuse are in danger of being lost . . . They are being merged with all other groups of children in need.
>
> (Munro and Calder, 2005: 439)

The current emphasis on assessment protocols brings with it certain risks that:

- There may be delay in the immediate protection of abused children whilst the seven-day initial assessment is processed.
- Key information in the possession of the police is not obtained soon enough to protect the child.
- Because an assessment of need requires parental permission for all checks there is a risk that parental consent is sought to interview a child who has made an allegation and the child may be at increased risk of harm as a result. A Section 47 investigation allows checks to be made without parental consent if it is thought that to do otherwise might place the child at risk.
- Without a prompt response of a Section 47 strategy meeting, and decisions being made about the method of investigation, an assessment of the child and family's needs will not be effective in evaluating the risk to the child of actual or likely significant harm. The skills of questioning, challenging, confronting and understanding the concepts of professional dangerousness – the blocks to professional recognition of child abuse which are essential to effective child protection work, may not be evident in an assessment process.
- The assessment process is too prescriptive and may interfere with the exercise of

professional judgment. Assessment involves excessive professional time spent on data entry and there is managerial emphasis on surveillance of computer input rather than professional supervision. Skilled, trained professionals working in safe working environments protect children effectively, whereas social workers inputting data will not alone protect children. Social workers ticking boxes will not protect children. Managers counting the ticks will not protect children. Government officials awarding stars for the right number of ticks will not protect children.

- The strict application of timescales may lead to premature closing of a child protection case when for example, children retract initial allegations in response to threats or through fear or when there is not thought to be sufficient evidence and a proactive investigative approach is not implemented.
- Because every Section 47 is required to be a core assessment, which is very demanding of professional time for every child in the family, there is a likelihood that, because of scarcity of resources, cases will be kept at level of Section 17. For instance, if a child makes an allegation of abuse by a teacher how relevant is it to conduct a core assessment on every child in the family? Whether or not a Section 47 includes an assessment process should not be prescribed but should be a matter for professional judgment and decided at a strategy meeting.

In the context of this confusion in policy, and the move away from proactive child protection, following the introduction of the *Framework for the Assessment* (DoH, 2000) multi-agency training on assessment processes was performance targeted and financially supported by government, whereas *Working Together* (DoH, 1999) received no government funding to assist training. The NSPCC published *The Child's World: Assessing Children in Need. Training and Development Pack*, and through a national initiative, PIAT (Promoting Inter-Agency Training) played a key role in training child protection trainers to refocus their training towards assessment processes and away from reactive interventionist strategies to protect children. At a number of conferences trainers were encouraged to move away from joint police and social work courses to a much wider audience, thus implying that the specialist requirements of these agencies were no longer relevant in the context of the implementation of the *Framework for the Assessment* (DoH, 2000).

> *Whilst training cannot do it all, it has a crucial part to play in effecting these changes and is able to do so by adjusting training content and through purposeful attention to audience, thus changing the shape and boundaries of the core inter-agency territory.*
>
> (Charles and Hendry, 2000: 40)

Glennie and Horwath wrote of the need to continue and accelerate child protection being seen as part of the broader provision for children in need:

> *Existing training strategies have been adapted, audiences retargeted and training programmes adjusted to ensure that inter-agency child protection training is not focused narrowly on safety and protection issues but takes a more holistic account of the developmental needs of children.In other words, if inter-agency training is to be effective in the current climate, it must be broadened conceptually to take account of both safeguarding and promoting the welfare of children.*
>
> (Glennie and Horwath, 2000: 148–9)

In the transition from the old to the new the essential need for police and social workers to gain specialist training gained little mention and the suggestion that a focus on 'safety and protection issues' was in any way '*narrow*' went unchallenged at the time.

However, the *Achieving Best Evidence: Guidance* subsequently reaffirmed the joint working relationship by stating that:

> *. . . having responsibility for the police criminal investigation does not mean that the police should always take the lead in the investigative interview. Provided both the police officer and social worker have been adequately trained to interview child witnesses in accordance with the guidance set out in this document, there is no reason why either should not lead the interview. The decision as to who leads the interview should depend on who is able to establish the best rapport with the child.*
>
> (CJS, 2007: 2.12)

The guidance also states that:

> *. . . a special blend of skills is required to take the lead in video-recorded interviews. The lead interviewer should be a person who has or is likely to be able to establish rapport with the child, who understands how to communicate effectively with interviewees who might become distressed and who has a proper grasp of the rules of evidence and criminal offences.*
>
> (CJS, 2007: 3.98–3.104)

The guidance also repeated the Association of Chief Police Officers guidance on *Investigating Child Abuse and Safeguarding Children* (ACPO, 2005: 6.2), in stressing the importance of specialist training in line with occupational standards:

> *. . . specialist training should be developed to interview witnesses with*

particular needs This should include interviewing young witnesses, traumatised witnesses and witnesses with a mental disorder, learning disability or physical disability impacting on communication. Such training should include working with intermediaries. Specialist interview training should also be developed in respect of the techniques in the cognitive interview. It is important to note, however, that training alone is unlikely to deliver effective performance in the workplace. Training needs to be set in the context of a developmental assessment regime. Such a regime should deliver a means of quality assuring interviews, while developing, maintaining and enhancing the skills of interviewers. The regime should be supported by an agreed assessment protocol. In the case of police interviewers such a protocol should take account of the National Occupational Standards for interviewers and witnesses developed in Skills for Justice.

(CJS, 2007: 0.4)

The importance of training being within an organisational learning context was also emphasised by Bostock et al. (2005) who advocated the need to learn about the investigation of risk not only from the outcomes of serious case reviews but from 'no harm' incidents where learning could take place outside of a blame culture.

Summary

Since 2000, policy changes post-Climbié have seen a chasm develop between police and social workers in the investigation of abuse which represents a step back to the situation that existed at the time of the Liam Johnson case. The joint investigation of significant harm by both agencies, the complex joint risk

assessment at the stage of initial referral, and the suspicion of harm, are rapidly sinking into history. The main tool of joint work, the strategy meeting, is now frequently replaced by a discussion on the telephone, which has the effect of excluding key agencies and denies professionals the opportunity to debate and analyse the issues face to face. The child protection register, which was the main multi-agency tool for protecting children identified as at high risk of harm, has now been precipitously abolished. This decision was made on the basis of no research at all. A ministerial response to a parliamentary question confirmed that 'no research has been commissioned by the DfES specifically on the use of the child protection register' (Dhanda, 2007). Specialist Child Abuse Investigation Team police officers have been replaced at child protection conferences by civilian staff and their access to advanced level training is minimal. Abuse which takes place outside the family fits poorly into a system based on the five outcomes for children which focuses professional attention on issues of social inclusion within disadvantaged families and on children as potential criminals rather than victims of child abuse (Treasury, 2003). By changing the definition of 'at risk of significant harm' to mean 'at risk' of a number of poor outcomes, the government has effectively relegated child protection to a sub-category of a larger concern about children's welfare. This implies that abuse is designated as merely one of a range of difficulties that a child may face, rather than as significant harm or a serious crime against a child.

The vast networks of serious crime against children which joint work began to confront during the 1990s are now largely being ignored. The numbers of children for whom a protection plan is needed has halved in the last five years for those defined as at risk of physical and sexual abuse (DfES, 2007). The current failure of existing child protection systems has led to separate systems being developed for specified forms of child abuse such as domestic violence, sexual exploitation and for trafficked and missing children. Establishing separate systems would not be necessary if the *Working Together* procedures were being fully implemented. Having multitudes of different protocols for separate child abuse circumstances will only lead to confusion and variation in practice between localities and will complicate the systems unnecessarily when, in fact, every form of child abuse can be effectively investigated using *Working Together* procedures.

The need to promote joint investigation training at this time could not be greater. The consequences for children of the gap in this provision has been illustrated by the recent report *An Inspection into the Care and Protection of Children in Eilean Siar* (SWSI, 2005), which criticised an over-emphasis on the family support model in the case and recommended the need for social workers and police to be trained in appropriate and up-to-date courses in joint investigation. During October 2003 in the Western Isles, 13 adults were arrested in Scotland and England in relation to the possible abuse of three girls in one family, and nine adults were subsequently charged with rape, lewd, libidinous and indecent practices and behaviour and making indecent images or pseudo images of children on a computer. The basis of the allegations were statements made by the three girls and their mother. However, there was no trial and there were no convictions. The report described that over 100 professionals had been involved with the family; there had been 29 conferences, 21 statutory reviews and 24 children's hearings about maltreatment of the children. The authors concluded that the three children had experienced severe and prolonged physical, sexual and emotional abuse by the father and his friends, that social workers and managers

failed to protect the children and that they should have acted sooner to protect them (SWSI, 2005: 296).

Other recent reviews of child deaths from abuse make the same point. In the case of Aaron Gilbert, who died age 13 months from head injuries, the serious case review executive summary stated that: 'the social worker did not initiate an immediate child protection investigation . . . the error of judgment could have been identified and the case relabelled as a child protection case' (Swansea LSCB, 2006). Although there was a referral about physical abuse and neglect, the case was defined as family support.

Similarly, in Swindon, in the case of Kimberley Baker who died of starvation at 11 months old, it was said that an initial assessment had been pursued rather than a child protection investigation. The executive summary pointed to the fact that the focus was on the mother's and children's health rather than identifying child protection concerns (Burchall, 2007).

In Newcastle, Alexander Gallon died at the age of four months, following a fire. His mother was convicted of infanticide. The executive summary identified that Social Care Assessment Officers were completing initial assessments and recommended that: 'the identification of any child protection issues should be made by a worker qualified and knowledgeable in this area' (Weightman, 2006).

In another Newcastle case, Baby O, aged three months, died of multiple injuries, and the executive summary concluded that: 'analysis of risk was limited across agencies. This could have been avoided if information sharing and planning between all relevant agencies had been consistent throughout, and a comprehensive risk analysis and protection plan drawn up' (Weightman, 2006).

Brief executive summaries provide very limited information about these tragic cases.

Given the number of recent child deaths from abuse where child protection procedures have not been implemented, there is a very urgent need to review the impact of current safeguarding policy on practice.

Conclusion

Armstrong and Hollows emphasised the need for joint training to start from where individuals find themselves and to build on their current experience and competencies so that they may mobilise a fuller range of skills and personal qualities to do the work in hand:

> ... *we see that process as vesting a value in the worker. It can only take place if value has already been invested in the trainer from within the organisation by managers and policy makers, a value which must be reflected in resources developed for their use by those outside the organisation.*
>
> (1989: 1)

Morrison has written about knowledge and learning being about processes not products, at a time when child protection training is operating amidst radical external change including an erosion of state welfare, competitive market solutions and a devaluing of professionalism. He emphasised that child protection training:

> ... *is to equip staff with the values, frameworks, knowledge, skills, personal discretion and strengths necessary for the exercise of judgements, discretion and decision making which enables the organisation to fulfil its child protection goals and responsibilities.*
>
> (Morrison, 1997: 31)

Importantly, he supported training in which:

> ... *the status quo may be confronted and innovations are attempted. The unresolveable nature of many issues is openly acknowledged and struggled with from which unexpected or creative resolution may come ... this is an agency culture in which* thinking *and* feeling *and not just* doing *are legitimised.*
>
> (Morrison, 1997: 33)

Reder and Duncan (2004: 109) reinforced this view that: 'the key aims of training are to arm practitioners with knowledge, skills and the capacity to think'.

Thinking means questioning and critically examining evidence and this can be uncomfortable for those working to protect children and to challenge powerful child abusers.

There are many police officers and social workers struggling against the current tide of public policy in order to protect children and seek justice for them by prosecution of the perpetrators. The task has become more, not less, difficult, and training to support specialist practitioners, given the lack of government recognition of the task and the scarcity of competent and experienced trainers, has become more inaccessible than ever. Strong commitment to the work of keeping children safe from harm must include a determination at all levels of police and social work child protection practice to make joint investigation training central to their Local Safeguarding Children Board agendas.

Introduction to the Course: Making Judgements in Child Protection

Learning objectives

On completion of the course participants should be able to demonstrate the skills and knowledge required to:

- Investigate child abuse under Section 47 Children Act 1989 and seek justice for children.
- Work together within a multi-agency context to effectively protect children from actual or likely significant harm.
- Analyse and evaluate child protection investigations and interventions.
- Work within the key principles of the child's best interests being paramount, partnership with families and carers and anti-oppressive practice.
- Recognise the emotional impact of the work and the importance of safe working environments.

Pre course information

- It is important to inform participants in advance that they will need to attend the course every day. With the exception of urgent court appearances or sickness attendance is a requirement. It is not uncommon for there to be a divide as social workers wish to arrive later than police who are used to beginning courses promptly at 9 a.m. There is a common myth that social workers are always late for courses. To avoid conflict at an early stage of the course it is very important to make the requirement clear in the pre course information. We find that a 9.30 start and 4.30 finish works well. A useful technique is to begin the day with a brief video such as from a survivor website so that when participants arrive late they realise they have missed something that they would have wished to see and they can be told that they can watch it over the break to catch up.
- Police officers need to be informed that the dress code for the course is informal and comfortable and therefore they should not wear uniform.
- Trainers expect that participants will be clear of work responsibilities during the training week. The course is intense and emotionally as well as intellectually demanding. It is not advisable for participants to be calling into the office prior to the course, during lunch breaks or at the end of the day as this will detract from their ability to focus on the course content.

- Participants should be advised to access a copy of *Working Together to Safeguard Children* (DfES, 2006) and their local child protection procedures.

A safe training environment is established to reflect good practice. Police and social workers share information about child abuse. They examine their personal and professional value systems and the impact these may have on their judgement. They learn the importance of both intuition and analysis in making judgements based on testing hypotheses and applying a sound knowledge base to joint investigations.

Trainers remind participants of the key concepts in *Working Together* (DfES, 2006: 1.16):

- To be alert to potential indicators of abuse or neglect.
- To be alert to the risks that individual abusers, or potential abusers, may pose to children.
- Share and help to analyse information so than an assessment can be made of the child's needs and circumstance.
- Contribute to whatever actions are needed to safeguard and promote the child's welfare.
- Take part in regularly reviewing the outcomes for the child against specific plans.
- Work co-operatively with parents, unless this is inconsistent with ensuring the child's safety.

The United Nations Convention on the Rights of the Child

This convention (United Nations, 1989) is referred to throughout the book and includes key articles relating to children under the age of 18 years:

- **Article 3.** In all actions concerning children, whether undertaken by public or private social welfare institutions, courts of law, administrative authorities or legislative bodies the best interests of the child shall be the primary consideration.
- **Article 19.** States parties shall take all appropriate legislative, administrative, social and educational measures to protect the child from all forms of physical or mental violence, injury or abuse, neglect or negligent treatment, maltreatment or exploitation, including sexual abuse while in the care of parents, legal guardians or any other person who has the care of the child. Such protective measures should include effective procedures for social programmes to provide support for the child and for those who have care of the child, as well as for other forms of prevention and identification, reporting, referral, investigation, treatment and follow-up of instances of child maltreatment and as appropriate for judicial involvement.

Activity 1a: Introductory Quiz: True or False? 40 Questions and Statements About Child Abuse

Aim: To introduce participants to the depth and breadth of the subject and to provide trainers with a litmus test of the level of knowledge in the group.

To enable initial debate of complex issues and for participants to gain interest in the subject matter.

Delivery: If the participants are drifting in late then this is a useful activity to begin with whilst others are arriving. This exercise enables those who have arrived early to begin considering the material. The participants at this early stage of the courses are not asked to mix across professions. They remain in their comfort zones.

Participants work in pairs to respond to the following statements as true or false. They are asked to provide gut feelings rather than intellectualisations as this exercise is a test of the breadth of their knowledge and understanding of the subject. They are then given the answers and are asked to make a note of any surprises or questions.

The activity may then be paused to allow for brief introductions. Those who arrived on time will have completed the exercise. Others who arrived late will leave the exercise unfinished. This conveys a message about the importance of good timekeeping but also means that no-one misses the introductions and training agreement.

Quiz answers – to be given to participants when they have completed the quiz in order to check their responses.

True: 3, 4, 7, 9, 12, 14, 16, 17, 20, 21, 29, 31, 34, 40.

Handout 1: True or false?

1. It is against the law to hit a child.
2. Most neglect of children is in low income families.
3. Disabled children have an increased risk of being abused.
4. Children have to consent to a paediatric assessment.
5. Children are always video interviewed about allegations of abuse.
6. Any child subject to a child protection plan is monitored until they are aged 18.
7. Children exposed to abusive images of children are victims of sexual abuse.
8. Repeated sexual abuse of children is uncommon.
9. Most child sexual abuse is perpetrated by someone who knows and is close to the child.
10. Child sex abusers are usually mentally ill.
11. Most non abusive carers know if their partners are sexually abusing children and do nothing about it.
12. Children very rarely lie about being abused.
13. Child sex abusers can be cured by therapy.
14. Female genital mutilation is a crime in the UK.
15. Children who are abused grow up into abusers.
16. Child sexual abuse victims rarely get justice through the courts.
17. It is against the law to hit an animal.
18. Sexually exploited adolescents are not included within child protection procedures.
19. Children are usually asleep when their parents are fighting.
20. In one child sex abuser's life they may abuse more than 200 children.
21. Most child sex abusers begin offending in adolescence.
22. The Children Acts 1989 and 2004 do not apply to children in custody or to children in the armed forces.
23. Black children are more likely to be abused than white.
24. Social workers and police often take children into care.
25. Religious families are less likely to abuse their children.
26. Sometimes it is better to allow abuse to continue rather than break up a family.
27. If a child does not mind the abuse they are not harmed by it.
28. Any member of the public can make checks about children with child protection plans.
29. Failure to thrive in babies may be due to organic causes.
30. When children go missing they are primarily the concern of the police.
31. Children in care are over represented in statistics of missing children.
32. Parents who misuse drugs always neglect their children.
33. A child under the age of 13 can consent to sexual activity.
34. Parental alcohol misuse is a serious cause of violence to children.
35. If a child tells you about abuse you must ask them to try and explain the abuse to you in detail.

36. If a child tells you they have bruises caused by abuse, you should ask the child's permission for you to look at them.
37. Social workers must gain the parents consent before interviewing a child about alleged abuse.
38. The General Practitioner's confidential records cannot be shared at a child protection conference.
39. Children have a right to attend a child protection conference about them.
40. All forms of abuse include emotional abuse.

Introducing trainers and participants

Aim: To introduce trainers and participants to each other and break the ice.

Delivery: A trainer explains the task and allocates the numbers in turn. This exercise does not take up much time and yet ensures that every participant pays attention to what each other is saying as they do not know if they will be asked to repeat it. It is clarified that each person is responsible for keeping themselves safe and sharing only such personal information as they feel comfortable to share. At the conclusion of the exercise trainers reflect on any embarrassment in sharing personal details and make the link with the fact that professionals commonly expect children to disclose very private information to them.

Content: The trainers first introduce themselves to set an informal tone to the course and encourage the participants to become less anxious. Each person is given a number from 1 to 12. One person begins by stating their name, their role, agency and something about themselves. The trainer then chooses another number at random. This person has to repeat what the first has said as best they can remember. Then they continue the exercise with their own contribution until all have contributed concluding with a return to the first person chosen. The trainer should interrupt to expand on any descriptions of role or agency which need clarification particularly to professionals in a different agency. For instance reference to the CEOP (Child Exploitation and Online Protection Centre) may not be known to social workers or the RAT (Referral and Assessment Team) to the police. If they cannot remember some aspects of what the previous person has said, the person may be asked to be helpful and repeat their contribution.

Training environment

Aim: For participants to receive the message that the trainers are genuinely concerned that the participant's needs are met in this respect.

Delivery: The trainer explains that child abuse is an uncomfortable subject. It is very important that the training environment is comfortable and responsive to the needs of participants. If this is not the case they will be distracted and unable to absorb the complexities of the subject.

Content: Practical information is provided about the house rules, refreshments, fire regulations, facilities for receiving messages and use of mobile phones (agreement for them to be on silent if there is good reason – personal or professional).

The flexibility of timing is explained. There may be some negotiation about the length of lunch hour and the time at which the course finishes each day. However, the intensity of some of the material will necessitate reasonable breaks.

If anyone is expecting to be unable to attend at any time during the course this is clarified for the group from the beginning and arrangements made to inform the participant of what they have missed so that there is minimal group disruption.

Training agreement

Aim: For participants to experience a safe learning environment reflective of good practice.

Delivery: Trainers share in the delivery of this presentation.

Content: The following points need to be covered:

- **Acknowledgment of the sensitivity of the material.** This is such that it may trigger unexpected feelings or reflections on personal or professional issues. Even very experienced practitioners do not fail to be shocked by the horror of the crimes perpetrated upon vulnerable children. Protecting children is a painful and difficult subject. Exposure through training to information about child abuse is also painful and difficult. The trainers explain that they will remain accessible during breaks should anyone wish to speak to them personally. No one should go home carrying the burden of child abuse. It is a contaminating subject.
- **Confidentiality.** Training reflects practice in that information is shared on a 'need to know' basis. As an advanced course it is important for participants to share professional experience. Cases shared must be anonymised and made unrecognisable.
- **Respect for each other.** Reference is made to the concept of 'respectful uncertainty'. It is acceptable and important to challenge views and opinions but to do so with respect. Participants are expected to challenge the trainers if they disagree with their views. This is promoting analytical multi-agency practice. Anti-oppressive practice, including a focus on childism – the oppression of children, will underpin the course.
- **Risk taking.** Participants are encouraged to take risks and it is explained that it is preferable to make mistakes during training rather than in practice. In child protection work there are many unknowns and there is always much to learn from shared experience and knowledge.
- **Acknowledgment of the tension in joint training of police and social workers.** Participants are asked to think about assumptions and stereotypes held about each other and to make use of the course to break down some of the barriers to communication. It is common for the police and social workers to be sitting at opposite ends of the room at this stage. The trainers will reflect on this but not seek to change it at this point.

Activity 1b: True or False Quiz Answers

Options for delivery

How the activity proceeds depends on the needs of the group. If some participants are eager to obtain feedback on particular issues then it is important to respond to their needs. Trainers may:

- Proceed by explaining that all the issues will be addressed during the course.
- Take a sample of questions in order to gauge the expertise of the group and to assist the trainers in pitching the course at the appropriate level.
- Spend the entire morning developing the arguments from the questions raised and make notes of issues covered so as not to duplicate material later.

Feedback: The following responses provide some answers to the questions. It would be very unusual to address all of these at the beginning of the course.

1. It is against the law to hit a child   FALSE

It is not against the law to hit a child. The Children Act 2004: Section 58, allows common assault to be justified as a reasonable punishment for children. It is against the law to hit animals or adults. Children deserve equal protection under the law of assault as adults. The United Nations Convention on the Rights of the Child 1989 states that children have a right to be protected against all forms of violence and have a right not to be punished cruelly. The Children are Unbeatable Alliance campaign group provides some shocking statistics about how often children in the UK are hit by their parents and carers (www.childrenareunbeatable.org.uk).

Physical abuse is one of the main reasons for children running away from home. Those running away under the age of 11 years, and children who run away repeatedly, are more likely to have experienced physical abuse (Social Exclusion Unit, 2002: 1.18).

2. Most neglect of children is in low income families   FALSE

Neglect constitutes the largest category of registrations and has increased from 11,700 in 2003 to 14,800 in 2006, whilst registrations for sexual abuse and physical injury reduced by half (DCSF, 2007). Neglect may take place in any sector of society and is not necessarily associated with poverty. 'Poverty is not a sufficient or necessary cause of child neglect; large numbers of families live in poverty and only some are neglectful' (Crittenden, 1999: 49).

About a third of children who die from child abuse die from neglect and the perpetrators are mainly women as the prime carers. In more serious cases parents may be prosecuted under the Children and Young Persons Act (1933) for the crime of cruelty and neglect. Professionals have to make judgements about seriousness and decide when neglect has reached the threshold of requiring child protection investigation and intervention. This means assessing clusters of indicators and considering the accumulative effect on a child of a number of different types of neglect.

Neglect often coexists with other types of significant harm. According to Stephenson the link between neglect and emotional abuse is particularly strong (Stephenson, 1998: 14). Farmer and Owen found that in a third of cases where neglect was the main concern, there were also physical abuse concerns; in a fifth of physical abuse cases there were neglect concerns, and in a quarter of sexual abuse cases there were neglect concerns (Farmer and Owen, 1995 cited in Tomison, 1995).

3. Disabled children have an increased risk of being abused   TRUE

Disabled children are more likely to suffer all forms of child abuse than non disabled children although there is a lack of research in this important area. The presence of multiple disabilities increases the risk of abuse (DfES, 2006: 11.27). Abuse of children increases proportionately with the numbers of adults involved in the child's care. Disabled children may be cared for by a considerable number of adults thereby increasing the risk of abuse. The care may be intimate thus providing more opportunities for child abusers to gain proximity to the child. Sometimes the signs of child abuse are confused with aspects of the disability. Sexualised behaviour may be wrongly interpreted as a sign of frustration or bruising as a 'normal' consequence of a medical condition such as epilepsy. Of course there may well be explanations consistent with the disability but it is important that checks are made with those professionals who know the child well. Child abusers may think that they are more likely to escape detection if a child has difficulty communicating or is less able to protect themselves.

A comprehensive study of over 40,000 children in an American city found that disabled children were on average 3.4 times more likely to be abused or neglected than non-disabled children (Sullivan and Knutson, 2000).

4. Children have to consent to a paediatric assessment   TRUE

In life and limb cases medical professionals may act against a child's will in order to save life. The 'Gillick competency principle' (House of Lords, 1985) allows that children, under the age of 16 years, of sufficient understanding and intelligence to understand fully what is proposed, may provide informed consent and may accept or refuse medical treatment without the need for parental agreement. However, even a young child can refuse consent by being non-compliant. Children are often offered paediatric consultations to enable them to be fully informed by doctors of the processes.

5. Children are always video interviewed about allegations of abuse   FALSE

Home Office Guidance recommends the use of video interviews for children who are victims of or witnesses to crime. However, children may not wish to be interviewed if, for instance, they were filmed as part of the abuse. A video recorded interview may also be considered harmful to the child if they have mental health problems or are suffering Post

Traumatic Stress Syndrome. Children must consent to the process unless they are deemed compellable because of the very seriousness of a particular crime (CJS, 2007).

6. Any child subject to a child protection plan is monitored until they are aged 18 years   FALSE

Theoretically a child could be subject to a plan until the age of 18 years. However, in practice it will be until they are no longer in need of a protection plan to keep them safe from harm.

7. Children exposed to abusive images of children are victims of sexual abuse   TRUE

The definition of sexual abuse includes the statement that 'they may include non-contact activities, such as involving children in looking at, or in the production of pornographic material' (DfES, 2006: 1.32). Renold et al. (2003) have collated evidence on this form of child abuse. Thousands of abusive images of children have been seized from individual's computers downloaded from the internet in recent years but very few lead to the identification of the child victims of abuse.

8. Repeated sexual abuse of children is uncommon   FALSE

In one study the majority of children who experienced sexual abuse had more than one sexually abusive experience; only indecent exposure was likely to be a single incident (Cawson et al., 2000: 89).

9. Most child sexual abuse is perpetrated by someone who knows and is close to the child   TRUE

The research below confirms this fact. However, it must be remembered that child sex abusers may spend a great deal of time grooming the child prior to abuse and therefore become 'friends' or 'relatives' of the family.

The majority of perpetrators sexually assault children known to them, with about 80 per cent of offences taking place in the home of either the offender or the victim (Grubin, 1998).

In Cawson's study, the children who experienced sexual abuse *in the family* were most commonly abused by a brother or stepbrother whereas the children who experienced sexual abuse *outside of the family* were most commonly abused by a boyfriend or girlfriend (Cawson, 2000: 80–1).

10. Child sex abusers are usually mentally ill   FALSE

Sexually abusive behaviour towards children is not a mental illness. It is not possible to identify a category of men and women who are more likely to sexually abuse children. In fact, there is no 'type' of person who is an abuser – they come from every social class, cultural and religious background. Their sexual preference may be solely for children or they may also be heterosexual or homosexual. They are commonly skilled at manipulating people and situations and at creating trust and respect within their community for example as clergy or youth workers. The prevention group 'Stop It Now' have a useful website about the dynamics of child sexual abuse (www.stopitnow.org).

11. Most non abusive carers know if their partners are sexually abusing children and do nothing about it   FALSE

Some non abusive carers may collude with abuse within the family. However, it is possible that the child sex abuser has deceived their partner and also placed children under great pressure to keep the abuse secret.

Non abusive parents and carers may also be victims of the abuser's strategies of deceit, manipulation and/or violence. The assessment of the non abusive parent or carer is a very important aspect of a child protection investigation in order to assess their capacity to be protective of the child.

12. Children very rarely lie about being abused   TRUE

Very few children lie about child abuse. The small percentage who may do so are generally caught between conflictual parents and may be manipulated by one parent against the other. Of course these children may even then be telling the truth about abuse that is taking place. Many people only speak about suffering child abuse much later on in their lives. The allegations made by children who tell as children must be taken very seriously indeed. Many children retract their allegations swiftly after disclosure through fear or because they are being silenced by abusers. It is important to recognise that retractions do not in any way invalidate what a child said at the beginning about abuse happening.

In a study of 10 young adults sexually exploited as children through abusive images, none had told freely of the events in 28 years. This provided a very different view to the idea that children make false allegations (Svedin, 1996). An NSPCC study concluded that 72 per cent of sexually abused children said they were too frightened to tell anyone at the time of the abuse and 31 per cent still had not told anyone by early adulthood (Cawson, 2000).

13. Child sex abusers can be cured by therapy   FALSE

Psychological therapy can reduce re-offending rates but does not provide a cure. Treatments can control or modify offending behaviour but re-offending rates may increase when offenders feel insecure and isolated and are not provided with the strategies and skills to address their offending behaviour. One in four child sex abusers who had abused children outside the family were reconvicted within six years (Hood et al., 2002: 4).

14. Female genital mutilation (FGM) is a crime in the UK   TRUE

Female genital mutilation has been a crime in the UK since the Female Circumcision Act 1985 although there has never been a prosecution. The act of cutting the female genitalia offends against the right of the child to bodily integrity and is violence against the child with long lasting health and psychological consequences. The Female Genital Mutilation Act (2003) made it illegal to take a child out of the UK for the purpose of genital mutilation. FGM is defined as physical abuse and child protection procedures must be implemented if it is suspected that a child is likely to suffer this abuse, if a child has been subject to the procedure and may be harmed further and if other girls in the family are also thought to be at risk (DfES, 2006: 6.11). Further information on this subject is available in an article by Dustin and Davies (2007).

15. Children who are abused grow up into abusers   FALSE

The incidence of child sexual abuse is said to be as high as one in four women and one in six men. Studies of child sex offenders do show a predominance of abusive childhoods but as the incidence of child abuse is so vast this does not mean all abused children go on to abuse. The vast majority of survivors are very good protectors of children because they understand the impact of child abuse.

It is evident that 'a history of sexual abuse as a child is neither necessary nor sufficient to lead to adult sexual offending'. In the majority of cases people who have survived sexual abuse do not go on to become abusers. A history of family violence is more common than sexual abuse in the background of known child sex abusers (Grubin, 1998: 30).

In one study of 224 male victims of child sexual abuse it was found that 12 per cent subsequently abused children themselves (Salter, 2003: 471–6).

Using prospective studies of abused children, rather than retrospective studies of abusing parents, Kaufman and Zigler (1993) suggested that the best estimate for the rate of intergenerational transmission of physical abuse to children was approximately 30 per cent.

16. Child sexual abuse victims rarely get justice through the courts   TRUE

Stuart and Baines (2004: 8) suggested that only one in fifty sex offences against children result in conviction. One in three children who report child sexual abuse are under the age of eight years and yet a study of four police authorities found that prosecutions were extremely rare for these offenders against young children. Disabled children and children for whom English is not their first language also tend to be excluded from access to justice (Utting, 1997: 20.10). The court system is not child centred. Child witnesses have to undergo cross examination and questioning in just the same way as adults.

17. It is against the law to hit an animal   TRUE

Some may argue that horses are hit during the races but in general it is against the law to hit animals.

18. Sexually exploited adolescents are not included in child protection procedures   FALSE

Child protection procedures must apply to sexually exploited children and child sex abusers must be brought to justice. *Working Together to Safeguard Children Involved in Prostitution* is the statutory guidance on this aspect of child abuse (DoH, 2000).

19. Children are usually asleep when their parents are fighting   **FALSE**

It is now known that children witness a great deal of domestic violence and are deeply affected by it. The vast majority of children are in the same or next door room when violence takes place. They may not always have an understanding of what is happening (Gorin, 2004). Mullender et al. (2003) provide a unique account of children's views about domestic violence.

20. In one child sex abuser's life they may abuse more than 200 children   **TRUE**

The high numbers of children abused by a single child sex abuser is a shocking statistic and some experts place it much higher than 200 per lifetime. If one child is protected from a child sex abuser then many other child victims may also be protected.

One study found that the majority of adult male perpetrators had sexually abused more than one victim. Seventy per cent claimed to have abused 1–9 children, 23 per cent claimed to have abused 10–40 children and 7 per cent claimed to have abused 41–45 children. 6.6 per cent of perpetrators also claimed to have sexually assaulted an adult victim (Elliot et al., 1995).

21. Most child sex offenders begin offending in adolescence   **TRUE**

Young people are about a third of those responsible for sexual offences against children. These young people are frequently victims of sexual, physical or emotional abuse. Young people who sexually abuse must access treatment programmes as soon as possible with the aim of preventing further abusive behaviour.

Children and young people with learning disabilities are over-represented within this group. Bentovim and Williams (1998: 103) state that '. . . despite the paucity of reliable evidence, it is clear that the majority of children who are sexually abused do not become [sexual] abusers. Moreover, we know that around half of all young sexual abusers have not themselves been victims of sexual abuse'. Further information on this subject is available on the NSPCC Inform website:
http://www.nspcc.org.uk/Inform/resourcesforprofessionals/Statistics/KeyCPStats/13_wda48730.html

22. The Children Acts 1989 and 2004 do not apply to children in custody or to children in the armed forces   **FALSE**

The Munby judgement (R v Sec of State All ER 465: 2002) created legislation to ensure that childrens services do have a duty of care towards children in custody under the Children Act 1989. 'Working Together' guidance also applies (DfES, 2006: 11.26).

The Deepcut Review raised the important issue of the application of Children Act legislation to children in the armed services (Blake, 2006). Working Together (DfES, 2006: 2.129) emphasises the importance of safeguarding children as young recruits and those serving in the armed services.

23. Black children are more likely to be abused than white   FALSE

Gibbons et al. (1995) suggest that children from black and ethnic minorities (BME) are over represented in the statistics for physical abuse of children but under represented for child sexual abuse. Thoburn (2000) also found that there were less referrals for sexual abuse, neglect and emotional harm within BME groups in comparison with the White UK population.

However, a report commissioned by the Mayor of London found London's black, Asian and refugee children are three times more likely to be attacked in the street than white children. Of those questioned 10 per cent had been physically attacked, 80 per cent had been racially abused or threatened and more than a third had direct experience of crime in the past year (GLA, 2003).

Children define child abuse as bullying and racial bullying in particular but at the moment this is not, in practice, a recognised reason for implementing child protection procedures. Bullying is not currently a criteria for physical abuse of children and does not trigger child protection procedures. However, Sir Ian Blair, Metropolitan Police Commissioner, following a series of fatal shootings of teenagers in 2007, said that society must protect children at risk of violence from gang members, including children in the families of perpetrators, in the same way as children whose parents are violent and abusive are protected. They should be considered under threat and subject to child protection procedures (Laville, 2007). Twenty-three teenagers were killed in London during the first 10 months of 2007 (McVeigh, 2007).

24. Social workers and police often take children into care   FALSE

Most child protection work involves supporting parents in becoming effective protectors and carers of their children. One of the studies in *Child Protection: Messages from Research* found that in 96 per cent of cases where enquiries are made into the safety of children they remain at home with their families. The majority of those who are separated are swiftly reunited. Forty per cent of children coming into care return home within six weeks and 90 per cent within two years (Leadbetter, 2002). Removing children from their families ultimately requires a court decision.

25. Religious families are less likely to abuse their children   FALSE

Child abuse takes place within every religious denomination. There have been major child abuse investigations within many different faith communities. An example of children abused through parental and community belief systems is the report by Stobart of children accused of possession and witchcraft (Stobart, 2006). Another example is Doyle's description of institutional abuse with a religious context (Doyle, 2002).

26. Sometimes it is better to allow abuse to continue rather than break up a family   FALSE

Survivors provide much information about the damaging impact of all forms of child abuse. It is the exception rather than the rule for children to be separated from their families following allegations of child abuse. At times, it may be necessary for a child abuser to be removed from the household or for the child to be removed to a safe environment. Three survivors websites offer many insights about the impact of abuse. www.no2abuse.co.uk, www.napac.org.uk, www.survivorsswindon.org.uk

27. If a child does not mind the abuse they are not harmed by it   FALSE
Child abusers will often make excuses for their offending behaviour by saying that the child has not experienced the abuse as harmful. A child may minimise the impact of the abuse to protect the abuser or may not understand the harm caused. Because they know no different, sometimes children think all children experience abuse the same as them. The child's perception of the abuse does not alter the fact that the abuse is wrong and must be stopped and the cycle of abuse must be broken. Sometimes there is confusion between respecting the child's wishes and feelings and the fact that this principle in the Children Act 1989 must always be secondary to that of the paramountcy of the child's best interests (CA 1989 S1). It is the responsibility of adults to protect children.

28. Any member of the public can make checks about children with child protection plans   FALSE
The safeguarding manager in each authority decides who has access to such information. Facts about children with child protection plans must be kept highly confidential because it is known that child abusers target vulnerable children and will strenuously try to access this information. Now that the Child Protection Register has been abolished there is concern that information about child protection plans may not be so highly guarded.

29. Failure to thrive in babies may be due to organic causes   TRUE
A paediatrician will always investigate the reasons for a child's failure to thrive and only when organic causes have been eliminated will the social and possible abusive causes be investigated. About half of young children with inexplicable poor growth are found to have a previously undiagnosed illness. The growth patterns of babies are monitored with the use of percentile charts which measure the height, weight and head circumference over time and assist analysis of the causes of failure to thrive. These charts require analysis by a health professional.

30. When children go missing they are primarily the concern of the police   FALSE
Children who go missing are the concern of all agencies. Most children who go missing are visiting friends in their locality and soon return. The risks are greatly increased when children go beyond their local area for long periods of time and at a young age. These children are at very high risk of significant harm. There are no police records of children who go missing and are not found. When a child is missing they tend to become lost to professional view. Each local area has protocols for children missing from home and from care (DfES, 2006: 11.63).

31. Children in care are over represented in statistics of missing children   TRUE
Young people living in residential care are much more likely than other children to run away. These young people are approximately three times more likely to run away overnight compared with young people living in families (Rees and Lee, 2005: 12).

Surveys have found that, while less than one per cent of children are looked after, around 30 per cent of runaways reported to the police are missing from substitute care. Many of those who go missing from care have run away from home before they started to be looked after. A recent study of young people going missing from care found that nearly half had first run from home (Biehal and Wade, 2000: 215). These tended to be adolescent entrants to care, who were more likely to be looked after as a result of relationship breakdown. For these young people, the roots of going missing from care tended to derive from problems they experienced while living in the family home.

It is important to note the patterns in a locality where children run away from particular institutions or foster placements more than others and to investigate the reasons for this as it may be an indication of an abusive environment.

32. Parents who misuse drugs always neglect their children   FALSE
If the parents are on rehabilitation programmes they may be able to be effective parents but the opinion of a drug counselling service must be obtained to inform protection planning. It is the chaotic lifestyle of parents who misuse drugs that exposes children to risk of harm as they place their need for drugs above the needs of their children. Children may also be exposed to health risks from syringes and access to dangerous substances. The newborn child may suffer the effects of withdrawal from drugs and there must always be a pre-birth child protection conference (DfES, 2006: 5.140).

One study found a general sense of neglect pervaded many accounts from young people. Many interviewees said that they had to provide both practical and emotional care for their parents, often from a very young age. In the UK there are estimated to be between 250,000 and 350,000 dependent children living with parental drug misuse which equals three per cent of all children under the age of 16 years (Gorin, 2004).

33. A child under the age of 13 years can consent to sexual activity   FALSE
No child under the age of 13 years can consent to sexual activity (Sexual Offences Act 2003). There is no defence in law that the child consented.

34. Parental alcohol misuse is a serious cause of violence to children   TRUE
About 920,000 children, in the UK, live with parental alcohol misuse which is a factor in 50 per cent of child protection cases. The risk of domestic violence is high and the involvement of specialist agencies in investigation is essential. It is an offence to be drunk in charge of a child under the age of seven contrary to the Licensing Act 1902.

The voluntary organisation Turning Point has published a detailed report on this subject (2006).

35. If a child tells you about abuse you must ask them to try and explain the abuse to you in detail   FALSE

It is the role of the child protection investigators to interview the child formally. At the point of first disclosure it is necessary only to obtain sufficient information to support a referral. However, if the child chooses to provide a full account it would be abusive to prevent them from disclosing and a full record must be made contemporaneously.

36. If a child tells you they have bruises caused by abuse, you should ask the child's permission for you to look at them   FALSE

A child may voluntarily show injuries to a professional or some injuries may be easily visible and these must be recorded. It is not the role of a police officer or social worker to examine injuries. This is the role of a child protection doctor or a medical professional designated by this doctor to conduct the examination or consultation. It is not appropriate for a child to be repeatedly examined as this would be intrusive. This is what is known as secondary abuse – abuse by the investigation systems.

37. Social workers must gain the parents consent before interviewing a child about alleged abuse   FALSE

Parental consent is not required by either police or social workers if they are investigating a case of alleged child abuse. However, it is good practice to work in an open and clear way with families as long as doing so does not place the child at risk of harm. A child might be at risk of being threatened or coerced into silence by a parent or there may be a risk of evidence being destroyed. A child may not want the parent involved and if they are deemed competent to make this decision their wishes should be respected. The police may have reason for not wanting the parents to be informed because to do so could impact on their investigation of an actual or suspected crime (DfES, 2006: 5.65).

38. The General Practitioner's confidential records cannot be shared at a Child Protection Conference   FALSE

Information must be shared as is proportionate to the need for the child to gain protection. If in doubt, confidential records can be shared through the chair of the conference so that the relevance of the information and the need for it to be shared can be assessed.

39. Children have a right to attend a Child Protection Conference about them   FALSE

A child protection conference is not a legal forum. Children do not have a legal right to attend. However, it is good practice to involve children and young people in child protection processes if this is compatible with their best interests. Sometimes they may attend for a short while to present their view or provide a letter or recording. If a child attends, the meeting must take the child's needs into account and provide advocacy and a suitable venue and facilities.

40. All forms of abuse include emotional abuse   TRUE

All forms include some element of emotional maltreatment, but emotional abuse may occur on its own. A child is the subject of a child protection plan under the category of emotional abuse only when it is the sole or main category.

Activity 2a: Exploring Role Perceptions/ Consequences

Aim: To be in an ice-breaker and examine police and social worker stereotypes.

Delivery: Participants work in separate professional groups. As with the child's game *consequences* the police officers draw on a strip of paper the face of the social worker and turn it over for the next police officer to draw the body and so on. The social workers draw a police officer in the same way.

Content: The drawings are completed and then revealed.

Feedback: The stereotypes that have been drawn are discussed.

Activity 2b: Exploring Role Perceptions Through Reflection on a Case Study

Aim: To provide an opportunity for participants to explore their perceptions of each other's roles and values.

Delivery: Trainers arrange each social worker to sit directly opposite a police officer in pairs with a small space between them and their phone in their hand. They are asked to sit quietly, read the case scenario and consider what they will say when making the referral. They are then asked to make a phone call to their colleague in children's services, Referral and Assessment Team or the police Child Abuse Investigation Team.

Just as they think they have to make the call, the trainers stop them from making it and ask them to write down individually their hopes and fears as if they had had to make the call. They should consider their expectations and be honest about any stereotypical assumptions.

Feedback: This activity should support participants in addressing any stereotyping about the different professional roles. Trainers should draw attention to the poor practice in this scenario, i.e. the teacher should not have asked Maria to write a statement as it is an investigative role for police and social workers to decide how to obtain the child's account.

Handout 2: The Case study – Maria

You receive a call from Ms Jenson head teacher of Mayflower primary school. She tells you that Maria, aged 7 years, has told her class teacher that her uncle, Marcus, has been putting his hand into her pants. Maria is in her office sobbing and doesn't want to go home because Uncle Marcus is coming to her house this afternoon to take her skating. She doesn't want her mum and dad to know she told because she says they didn't believe her some months ago when it first happened. Maria has a younger sister, Sophie, who really likes going skating with Uncle Marcus. The uncle is known to the school as he is a volunteer with the school reading scheme. Ms Jenson wants you to come straightaway and interview Maria and put her somewhere safe, as the school has to close in half an hour. She tells you she has already asked Maria to write down what she said has happened.

Presentation 1: Childism

Childism is the oppression of children. Unchildren are the children who are unseen in society, children who don't seem to matter at all. For example, Victoria Climbié was an unchild. She was not defined as a child in need of protection.

In a collation of research findings entitled *Messages from Research* (DoH, 1995: 16) it was said that too many children were becoming caught up in the child protection net and that the threshold for defining a child as in need of protection was being situated too low. The concept was presented as if too many children were being defined into the safety net and families were unnecessarily suffering the impact of child protection investigation. This has greatly influenced child protection practice since the mid-1990s with the view that social workers and police were being over interventionist. 'While there was never an overt instruction for social services to refocus their work away from investigation, it is common knowledge that they understood that this was expected of them' (Reder and Duncan, 2004: 104). More recently there has been some comment that the threshold has now become too high. Lord Laming stated, 'It is clear to me that the agencies with responsibility for Victoria gave a low priority to the task of protecting children' (Laming, 2003: 1.18).This view has been repeated by two key inspection reports, 'councils have unusually high thresholds for responding to child protection referrals and in taking action to protect children' (CSCI, 2005: 2.9) and a comment about weak authorities where 'thresholds to access social care services were set too high . . . too frequently these act as barriers to children's safety and wellbeing' (Ofsted, 2007: 5).

A warning of the policy's impact on future tragedies was given when in 1996 the Director of Social Services in Oxford wrote, following a case involving the manslaughter of two children, that 'It is important the mistakes are seen in the context of the publication of the Department of Health's Messages from Research which promoted the value of family support. These messages were in the forefront of the minds of the workers involved at the time this case was investigated' (Robertson, 1996).

Particularly since the introduction of the Framework of Assessment for Children in Need and their Families (DoH, 2000) social workers were being steered away from working with police in child protection intervention to work at a preventative level with health and education. The use of words such as *risk, protection and investigation* were discouraged and replaced with *need, safeguarding and assessment*. Policy became focused on making enquiries rather than investigation of risk. The timescales of the Initial and Core assessment, (7 and 35 days) altered the emphasis away from intervention and created a dangerous gap in practice when action to protect is swiftly required. Section 47 (CA 1989) is the duty to investigate when there is 'reasonable cause to suspect a child is suffering or is likely to suffer significant harm'. In *Working Together* (DfES, 2006: 5.60) it states that 'the core assessment is the means by which a Section 47 enquiry is carried out'. This is incorrect. An investigation is a different process from an assessment. An assessment may be part of an investigation but an investigation of a child abuse allegation demands a focus on the perpetrator as well as an assessment of the child and family's needs. Also, since Laming's recommendation 99 (Laming, 2003) the police have focused their attention on the investigation of crime and social workers have focused on assessment. There is therefore less attention being paid to the joint investigation of actual or likely significant harm and social workers find themselves on their own making decisions about whether or not an allegation has reached the threshold of crime or not. A child abuse investigation cannot be time limited. The use of the Framework of Assessment as a basis for all new protocols, with tight timescales for intervention, risks interfering with professional judgement in making complex decisions about the safety of children.

The child protection register, which has been the main effective professional tool for protecting children since the early 1980s, was abolished in April 2008. The Commission for Social Care Inspection (CSCI) (2005: 6.35) reported that children whose names were on the child protection register were well safeguarded. Yet, new systems are being implemented with no consideration as to the value of what is already in place. In answer to a parliamentary question by Annette Brook M.P., Parmjit Dhanda (DfES) on 30th January 2007, confirmed that no research had been commissioned by the government on the use of the child protection register. Baroness Walmsley raised this and a number of other concerns about the demise of the child protection systems in a House of Lords debate (Walmsley, 2007).

In fact it is clear that many children requiring protection do not access protective systems. There is no doubt that there are numbers of children who require the protection of a very large child protection net. The vast majority of serious crimes against children are unreported and if they are reported they do not succeed in triggering the child protection protocols with referrals remaining as 'child in need' rather than 'child in need of protection'. Very few children report abuse as children and some children are particularly hidden from view such as those in residential institutions away from protective local communities. Some abuse, such as racial abuse or bullying is not defined as such by current protocols. There is also a lack of attention paid to some groups of children – for instance those in the upper and middle classes and those who are in the older age ranges. The statutory guidance is clear that child protection procedures apply up to the age of 18 years:

> *The fact that a child has reached 16 years of age, is living independently or is in further education, is a member of the armed forces, is in hospital, in prison or in a young offenders institution does not change his or her status or entitlement to services or protection under the Children Act 1989.*

> (DfES, 2006: 1.17)

Reducing numbers of children's names on the child protection register up until 2006

Since 1995, the number of children on the child protection register has decreased by one third. The numbers of children registered for neglect and emotional abuse, since 2000, have increased whilst those for sexual and physical abuse have almost halved with totals of just 2,500 and 5,100 respectively (DCSF, 2007). Comparisons with statistics of known child sex offenders and sexual crimes against children illustrate that the number subject to protection planning is very small indeed when considering the extent of crimes against children (Breslin and Evans, 2004).

The following examples illustrate how some children gain little protection:

- **Child victims of abusive images.** Statistics of the number of child victims of abusive images indicate how few enter the protective systems. Operation Ore involved 7,200 men in the UK accessing a gateway to abusive images of children but few of these led to Section 47 investigations (CA 1989) in relation to the children placed at possible risk. Max Taylor, Director of Combating Paedophile Information Networks in Europe, 'found pictures of 13,000 individual children in 2002. Of these, 25 have been identified in the UK, 50 in Europe and 100 in the US and the rest of the world' (Sunday Herald, 2003). Carr stated that 'the victims of these horrendous crimes – the children themselves – are so often not being found and helped' (Carr, 2004).

- **Child victims of trafficking.** Children trafficked for domestic or sexual slavery are unrepresented in child protection planning. Mende Nazer provides an autobiographical account of being a child in slavery in London until 2002 (Nazer, 2004). Operation Paladin Child analysed the cases of 1,738 unaccompanied minors entering the country at Heathrow airport in a three month period and found that 28 were untraceable. Of these, 29 per cent were under the age of 11 years (Metropolitan Police, 2004). Of course, the majority of trafficked children enter the UK accompanied and are even less likely to be identified than those unaccompanied.

  Of the many children who go missing in the UK there are no police statistics of those children who are not found. In a study based in the north of England 48 illegally trafficked children were missing from care representing almost half the sample. 'As these children have never been traced we cannot know what has happened to them, why they went missing or whether they are still in the UK' (Beddoe, 2007: 5). The Child Abuse and Online Protection (CEOP) report on trafficking found 330 children suspected or confirmed as trafficked in an 18 month period and of these 183 had gone missing from childrens services care. Forty-four source countries were identified. In particular 88 per cent of Chinese children had gone missing. The top source countries were China, Nigeria, Vietnam, Afghanistan and Eritrea. Children had passed through nine airports (CEOP, 2007). A report entitled *Rights here, Right now* provides recommendations and guidance regarding trafficked children (Sillen and Beddoe, 2007) and the Home Office provides a toolkit available on its website (www.crimereduction.gov.uk/toolkits). An excellent video 'More precious than gold' is available online and describes the sexual exploitation of children through trafficking (UNICEF, 2003). Of course many children were trafficked from the United Kingdom during the 50s and 60s to Australia and Canada, many of whom were exploited for domestic labour (Humphreys, 2005).

- **Children in custody.** In 2008 there were 3,037 children in custody in England and Wales; 85 per cent were in Young Offender Institutions. In the Joint Inspector's

Report 'Safeguarding Children' it was stated that they could not be confident of the child protection response to young people in prison (CSCI, 2005: 8.8) and that this was of major concern (CSCI, 2005: 8.1). The review raised particular concerns about the use of certain behaviour management techniques in many settings. These include the use of physical control, strip-searching and single separation or segregation in young offender institutions, local authority secure children's homes and secure training centres. (CSCI, 2005: 2.7).

Since 1990 there have been 29 deaths of young people in prison without serious case reviews or public inquiries being held (Goldson and Coles, 2005). There is also concern about children being treated as adult prisoners, receiving poor education and mental health services and the use of lengthy prison sentences for non-violent crimes in breach of the United Nations Convention on the Rights of the Child (UNCRC) (United Nations, 1989). Lord Carlile, in his inquiry into the conditions in which children are held in custody, said that many of the practices would be regarded as child abuse in any other setting (CRAE, 2006: 21). In December 2007 a minister for children and a minister for justice announced that in the light of recent deaths of children in custody two particular forms of restraint were no longer allowed (Lovell, 2007).

The Howard League website provides information on this subject about the over-use of prison for children, the infliction of pain and injury to control children behind closed doors, child deaths in custody, the lack of physical exercise and the use of segregation blocks. This campaign group considers that the UK government is in breach of at least 10 Articles of the UNCRC (United Nations, 1989) (www.howardleague.org.uk/). Up to 1,000 children are remanded into custody each year because they are homeless (Howard League, 2008).

- **Child asylum seekers.** The 'Safeguarding Children' inspection report also expressed concerns about the care of asylum seeking children in detention centres (CSCI, 2005: 7.43). There is particular concern about the length of time children are detained. In the first quarter of 2006, 460 children were detained in such centres. A quarter of the children were kept between 20 and 112 days (Bonomi, 2006). These children have committed no crime but remain imprisoned with little access to health, educational and recreational facilities. The Chief Inspector of Prisons and Childrens Commissioner have also raised concerns (CRAE, 2006: 24). When parents are denied asylum they are refused access to public funds which has a devastating impact on their children (www.southallblacksisters.org.uk). The campaign Standup 4 Children raises very serious issues about the deportation of children. (www.standup4children.org.uk).
- **UK child soldiers.** Concern can also be extended to the protection needs of UK child soldiers following the Deepcut Review where young recruits died in questionable circumstances (Blake, 2006).

The UK has the largest numbers of 16–18 year olds in any European armed force (about 7,000) and recruits children from the age of 15 years. Children under 18 years may be deployed in active hostilities as the UK exempted itself from the Optional Protocol to the United Nations Convention on the Rights of the Child which prohibited the use of children in armed conflict (United Nations, 2003). It is not known how many children under the age of 18 years have been killed in recent warfare.

- **Disabled children.** The 'Safeguarding Children' inspection report concluded that agencies did not sufficiently prioritise the protection needs of disabled children (CSCI, 2005). The presence of multiple impairments increases the possibility of abuse and yet many Local Safeguarding Children Boards do not collect data about disabled children and their protection needs.
- **Children whose parent suffers mental ill health.** Dr Adrian Falkov's research on children who died from abuse who had a parent with mental illness, confirmed that professional attention was primarily on the parent and not the child and that there was little liaison between agencies focusing on the adult and those on the children (Falkov, 1996).
- **Child victims of assault.** Children physically abused by adults in the name of 'reasonable chastisement' are denied the right of equal protection under the law of assault as adults. The Children Act 2004: Section 58, allows a defense of reasonable chastisement in the crime of common assault. Children's views about being hit are clear:
  - Smacking is hitting – a hard or very hard hit.
  - Smacking hurts physically and emotionally.
  - Smacking is wrong.
  - Smacking upsets children and sometimes makes them want to smack someone else.
  - Adults regret smacking.
  - Adults hit children because of how the adult is feeling and not because of what the child does.
  - Parents and other grown ups, aunts, uncles, grandparents, nannies and babysitters most often smack children.
  - Children often get smacked indoors. The bedroom was the most common place followed by when out shopping. They were hit on their bottom, arm or head.
  - Children don't hit adults because they are scared they will get hit again.
  - Half said they wouldn't smack their children when they were adults.

  (Willow and Hyder, 2004)
- **Child victims of domestic violence.** Children are the hidden victims of domestic violence. The high correlation between parental violence and violence to children is illustrated by a US study of 1000 women in refuges which found that 70 per cent of the women with children said their partners had also been physically violent to the children. The more frequent the violence the more severe the physical abuse of the children (Bowker, 1988: 65). A study of nearly 2000 child protection referrals across seven London Boroughs found that 27 per cent of cases involved domestic violence (Humphreys and Mullender, 1999). One in twenty children are witness to frequent physical violence between parents and children also make up about two thirds of the people staying in refuges (Cawson et al., 2000).

  Where conflictual parents have separated and the children remain exposed to violence during contact, Saunders (2004) found that between 1994 and 2004, 29 children from 13 families were killed during contact arrangements.
- **Abuse of babies.** Children under one year old are the most at risk of abuse and injuries suffered are the most likely to have fatal consequences. Nobes and Smith

(1997) found that 52 per cent of children aged one were hit weekly or more by their parents. All children are at risk even though babies are more vulnerable. Children's Rights Alliance for England (CRAE) quote that the homicide rate in 2005/6 was 38 per million for those under the age of 1 year compared with 14 per million for the population overall (CRAE, 2007: 30).

Presentation 2: Investigative Skills

Munro (2002) writes about the need for child protection workers to be like detectives, making a thorough search for the truth with an open mind that considers different possibilities and tests conclusions. She describes the continuum of analysis and intuition. Analysis is formal, explicit, logical and intellectual and justified by a knowledge base. Intuition is an unconscious process drawing on experience, metaphor, imagination and feelings. The conclusion has authenticity because it 'feels right'. Intuition is steered by evidence based knowledge and analysis relies on intuitive skill in collecting and organising the information. Professional expertise is based on:

- Formal knowledge – theory, legislation, policy and practice guidance.
- Practice wisdom derived from experience.
- Emotional wisdom based on reflection on the emotional impact of the work.
- Reasoning skills to debate, make sense of the whole and to make judgements about the reliability and applicability of the information.

Munro describes how fire fighters make prime use of intuitive skills when making decisions in a crisis and base their judgements on their own prior experience and that of their colleagues (Munro, 2002: 112).

Most professional decisions are based on information that is recent, vivid and emotional and weight is given to first impressions (Munro, 2002: 146). Obviously some decisions must be made immediately for a child's safety but a high standard of decision making is achieved when based on knowledge gained from chronologies. Recent information must be evaluated in context as well as making an assessment of professional opinion over time.

The Bridge Child Care Consultancy devised a useful tool for completing chronologies which is adapted below.

Date	Source	Key events	Content	Health	What the carer says	What the child says	Professional view

In this chronology the date and source of every piece of information is collated and every letter, case record, set of minutes and record of interviews is included. Key events in the child's life provide a timeline for quick reference. These might be the date a child started school or moved home, when someone left the household, separations and hospitalisations. The fourth column includes the main content of the particular entry. This might be the content and decisions of a conference or strategy meeting or a summary of a letter. Health information must include a summary of detail from percentile charts and a similar column may be included for education. This allows an evaluation of health and educational information in terms of what exactly was known at what stage. The carers view is crucial and collation allows analysis of any discrepancies and inconsistent explanations for alleged injuries as well as highlighting parental/carer strengths. The chronology places the child's view as central and allows the child's voice to be heard. The child's own words are highly significant although there is rarely much detail recorded. The final column enables an assessment of change in professional judgement over time (Fitzgerald, 1999).

Activity 3: Defining Acceptable and Unacceptable Behaviour

Aim: For participants to evaluate the impact of personal and professional values on judgements about behaviour towards children.

Delivery: The statements are written on separate cards and divided amongst participants.

Participants sit in a circle with the trainers. On the floor at each end of the circle are two large cards marked ACCEPTABLE and UNACCEPTABLE. Each participant takes turns to place each of their cards somewhere on a vertical line between the two extremes. As they position each card they must state their reasons for their decision and how they reached their judgement. The group may then enter into debate until the position is agreed by consensus. Initially this activity takes some time, perhaps about 5 minutes per statement, but as it moves along it speeds up. Participants may volunteer as they feel ready to put their cards down but the trainers need to be observant of any who are withholding their cards and seem reluctant to position them. This activity may take two hours or a whole afternoon. It is important to spend time on this as it is not uncommon to find participants who are reluctant to take part because of deeply held religious or cultural beliefs. This activity is designed to bring into the open the varying beliefs that impact on making judgements in child protection cases and allow for challenge by trainers and other group members.

The majority of these statements have some connection with actual child protection cases.

Content

1. Girl aged 7 years likes to give her father a wet kiss on the mouth.
2. Parents allow daughter aged 14 years to have boyfriend aged 18 years to stay overnight in her bedroom.
3. Single parent mother has boy aged 11 years in her bed for comfort.
4. Father discovers he has erection when he cuddles his child aged 2 years.
5. Mother takes daughter aged 11 years to the clinic to get her the pill.
6. Children observe their parents making love.
7. Father demonstrates to son aged 13 years how to put on a condom.
8. Mother takes daughter aged 14 years for plastic surgery to make her look more attractive.
9. Mother arranges for daughter to be circumcised.
10. Mother asks teenage son to rub ointment into her back.
11. Mother arranges for son to be circumcised.
12. Father avoids cuddling his daughter as she nears puberty.
13. Father wears boxer shorts in the bath whilst bathing with his daughter aged 3 years.

14. Girl aged 14 years has a termination of pregnancy without her parents knowledge.
15. Older brother aged 17 years and his friend go into his younger sister's bedroom.
16. Parents will not allow girl aged 13 years to go out with her friends to the cinema.
17. Parents encourage their daughter aged 12 years to be more 'naturist' about the house like them.
18. Father wipes bottom of daughter aged 4.
19. Mother pulls back her son's foreskin to clean his penis. He is aged 5 years.
20. Lesbian mother and her partner allow her two young children to share their bed.
21. Gay couple teach their nephew aged 9 years about safe sex.
22. Father makes comments on the development of his daughter's breasts and that she is looking 'sexy'.
23. Parents leave sex education books around the house for their son and daughter aged 8 and 10 years to read.
24. Father and mother watch blue movies.
25. Grandfather cuddles young granddaughter and nibbles her ears.
26. Teenage stepbrother has intercourse with stepsister aged 12 years.
27. Father bathes his son aged 11 years.
28. Daughter aged 13 years gets into bed with parents when she can't sleep.
29. Parents use boy aged 13 years to babysit for girl aged 3.
30. Boy aged 9 years dresses up in his teenage sister's clothes.
31. Boy aged 10 years accesses an internet site containing abusive images of children.
32. Father supports daughter in the swimming pool by holding her under her bottom.
33. Female babysitter massages boy aged 8 years gently on his neck and back to help him sleep.
34. Parents allow their children to have TV in their bedrooms.
35. Parents take their young children to pose as models for advertisements for underwear.
36. Children know their parents both have affairs outside the marriage.
37. Mother shaves daughter's head to make hair grow thicker.
38. Children hear their mother calling their father a 'prick' and their father calling their mother a 'slag'.
39. Grandmother tickles baby's genitalia to help them to sleep.
40. Mother explains to daughter aged 14 years what oral sex is.

Feedback

1. Girl aged 7 years likes to give her father a wet kiss on the mouth
Some adults think that kissing children on the lips is abusive but in many families it is the norm as a sign of affection. Whilst not abusive in itself, it is important that children know that they can control which adults kiss them and in what way. They must feel comfortable. If they are taught that it is acceptable to say NO to a kiss by an adult they will have learnt important self protective behaviour knowing that they can choose which touches are 'yes' feelings and which are 'No' feelings. They will also be confident that their parents support them in making these decisions in keeping themselves safe from harm.

2. Parents allow daughter aged 14 years to have boyfriend aged 18 years to stay overnight in her bedroom

To allow sexual offences to take place in the home is a criminal offence and if these young people are engaging in a sexual relationship they may well be committing offences. A four year age difference may certainly be indicative of an exploitative relationship and the parents in allowing this relationship in their home may be exposing their daughter to possible significant harm. However, the young people may also be having a consensual and healthy relationship and it is important not to criminalise all aspects of teenage sexuality – particularly to ensure that they access relevant health and educational advice.

Professionals will decide when to intervene in adolescent sexual relationships. This will be mainly when there is a clear risk of harm or when crime is being committed. In this case the parent may consider that by allowing the couple to stay in their house they can find out more about the young man and perhaps avoid the risk of the daughter running away from home to be with him. As protective parents they may need help in managing the situation. They may of course be involved in encouraging men to abuse their daughter. Child protection demands an open mind to such possibilities.

3. Single parent mother has boy aged 11 years in her bed for comfort

Parents have different values about children sleeping in their beds. In this case it may be thought that the mother is serving her needs and not the child's – but perhaps there has been a recent trauma. It may be that the young person is pleased to be able to provide some comfort to his mother at this time. However, if the mother is replacing an absent partner with her child then this would indicate that she is not meeting the child's needs and this could be abusive.

Many parents would think it was acceptable for children to come into their beds if the child has nightmares or is unsettled – and some families may only have one bed as can be the case when families are placed in emergency accommodation. Every situation is different and requires careful evaluation.

4. Father discovers he has erection when he cuddles his child aged 2 years

The author Blake Morrison attended the trial of the two young boys convicted of the murder of Jamie Bulger and wrote about the experience. He explored his own childhood and his relationship with his children which included reflection on the fact that he once had an erection whilst cuddling his young child. This did not mean that he was a child sex abuser. He acknowledged the complexity of feelings adults have in relation to children (Morrison, 1998: 183). Child sex abusers will of course have many rationalisations for the fact that they are sexually aroused by children but context and specialist analysis in each case form part of professional judgment about any such behaviour.

Sometimes professionals working in the field of child sexual abuse, particularly with child sex abusers, discover that they are becoming sexually aroused by exposure to the subject matter. This can be a contamination effect of the work to protect children. It indicates the importance of recognising the possible impact of the work and seeking counselling and support.

5. Mother takes daughter aged 11 years to the clinic to get her the pill

A mother may be accessing medical care for her child as the pill is prescribed for health reasons as well as being a contraceptive. If the child is sexually active and the mother is trying to prevent her getting pregnant then the mother would need help to protect her child from criminal and exploitative behaviour. It could however be that the mother is networking her own child to child sex abusers.

6. Children observe their parents making love

This may be an accidental occurrence indicating that the parents need to take more care to maintain privacy or at the other extreme it could indicate involvement of the child in parental sexual activity.

7. Father demonstrates to son aged 13 years how to put on a condom

It is quite appropriate for a father to teach his son about contraception. It would be expected that he would demonstrate the use of a condom without using his own penis. A boy aged 13 years may or may not be interested. It is important to respond to and be respectful of children's own cues as to when they wish to discuss sexual matters with a parent and in what detail. It is also important to consider that child sex abusers, when confronted, will often use the excuse of 'sex education' to justify their abusive behaviour with a child. This may also be part of grooming a child before sexual abuse actually begins. Once again a behaviour may mean many things – an innocent explanation or child abuse – hence the importance of keeping an open and questioning mind.

8. Mother takes daughter aged 14 years for plastic surgery to make her look more attractive

A child cannot have plastic surgery without parental consent under the age of 16 years. However, if there is a medical reason and it is the child's wish, this would be acceptable. There is much pressure on young people to fit an idealised image and it could be abusive to a child if a parent is bullying them into the operation resulting in them having undue influence. The right to bodily integrity is contained within the UNCRC 'the protection of the child from all forms of mental and physical violence, injury or abuse, and maltreatment' (United Nations, 1990: Article19).

9. Mother arranges for daughter to be circumcised

Female Genital Mutilation is the correct term and the procedure is illegal in the UK and defined as physical abuse (DfES, 2006: 6.11). The UNCRC requires parties to take all effective and appropriate measures with a view to abolishing traditional practices prejudicial to the health of children (United Nations, 1989: Article 24.3). Dirie (2005), Nazer and Lewis (2004) and Walker (1993 and 1996) provide three personal accounts giving an in depth understanding of their experience of this abusive procedure. The Metropolitan Police have an excellent website about Project Azure, an initiative to provide a protective response to this serious form of abuse. It covers:

- Stop FGM poster in Arabic, Somali and English
- Information sheet on FGM
- Leaflet – Summer is for Fun, not for Pain
- Prevalence profile of FGM in different communities

Details are available on the Forward website which is the main campaigning group against the practice of FGM (www.forwarduk.org.uk) and on the London Safeguarding Children Board website (www.londonscb.gov.uk).

10. Mother asks teenage son to rub ointment into her back

The son could be a carer for his mother and quite pleased to assist her and this is likely to be a positive and healthy aspect of a mother/son relationship. However, it is important to keep an open mind and viewed in context with other information it may be a breach of boundaries.

11. Mother arranges for son to be circumcised

Non-therapeutic male circumcision is a controversial subject. The campaign group NORM UK (www.norm-uk.org) defines the procedure as Male Genital Mutilation (MGM) and campaigns for genital integrity for men and women. NORM consider MGM to be abusive expressing a view that by removing irreversibly the foreskin and because the child does not and cannot consent, it infringes a child's right to bodily integrity (United Nations, 1989: Article 24.3). The practice is not legally defined as abusive in the UK but there are associated risks of harm such as when the child acquires an infection as a result of neglect, sustains physical or cosmetic damage, suffers emotional, physical or sexual harm from the way the procedure was carried out, or suffers emotional harm from not having been consulted or having his wishes taken into account. There may be harm through the procedure being conducted incompetently or facilities being inadequate or unhygienic (LSCB, 2007).

12. Father avoids cuddling his daughter as she nears puberty

In some cultures when a daughter reaches puberty the father shows affection in ways other than a hug – perhaps patting her on the head. This does not indicate a lack of caring.

13. Father wears boxer shorts in the bath whilst bathing with his daughter aged 3 years

Reactions to this statement usually range from 'what's wrong with that?' to 'that's unusual'. In a child protection investigation where a three year old child had alleged sexual abuse by her father during bath time, he said it could never have happened because he always wore boxer shorts in the bath. The abuse was finally proven. At an initial stage though, a number of professionals just had a feeling that this behaviour was rather strange. This is a useful example to explain the importance of reflection on 'feelings' through multi-agency debate and to test hypotheses through the collation of evidence and fact.

14. Girl aged 14 years has a termination of pregnancy without her parents knowledge

Young people of an age and understanding to provide informed consent may gain access to medical advice and treatment including contraception and termination of pregnancy. This is called the Gillick principle (R v the Secretary of State, 2002).

It is important to consider the risk of harm to a young person in each situation. A child may be at risk of significant harm if a parent did find out they were pregnant or had a termination. However, a young person who has become pregnant is a victim of a crime to which in law they cannot consent under the age of 13 years (Sexual Offences Act, 2003). Each case must therefore be reported to the police to enable joint investigation to take place (CA 1989: S47). Whether and how to inform parents is just one of the complex decisions the professionals have to make in such cases.

15. Older brother aged 17 years and his friend go into his younger sister's bedroom

Each home, family, residential children's home, boarding school or foster home, will have different rules about access to rooms. Commonly there is a 'knock and wait' policy which gives the child control about who enters their room and when. The younger sister in this example may be happy that her brother and his friends go into her room, perhaps to borrow something or to feed a pet, or she may feel invaded and exposed. The behaviour may indicate a family where there are no safe boundaries for the child.

16. Parents will not allow girl aged 13 years to go out with her friends to the cinema

Parents who restrict their children's activities may be acting in a protective way. In some areas children have been kept indoors because their parents feared racist attacks in the locality. When investigating child abuse allegations it is important to consider the community factors which impact on parenting and child safety (Barter, 1999).

17. Parents encourage their daughter aged 12 years to be more 'naturist' about the house like them

Some families are naturist and this is a lifestyle choice. A young person aged 12 years may be quite accepting of this lifestyle or may want to live differently. The important point is that the child's wishes and feelings should be respected within the household.

18. Father wipes bottom of daughter aged 4

It is important for fathers to play a key role in the intimate care of their children. At the age of four years a child may need to be assisted with wiping their own bottom. The child may want to do it for themselves and this is a judgement every parent and carer has to make as to when the time is right.

19. Mother pulls back her son's foreskin to clean his penis. He is aged 5 years.

There are varying views about hygiene for boys and there will no doubt be a range of opinions in the group about what is and is not necessary.

20. Lesbian mother and her partner allow her two young children to share their bed

The issue is not that the couple are lesbian but that of any couple sharing their bed with children. The risk is that in a determination not to discriminate, professionals may not question behaviour which could be abusive. The circumstances in which children share adult beds is often the subject of investigation during child abuse inquiries and circumstances will range from the entirely innocent to that of child abuse.

21. Gay couple teach their nephew aged 9 years about safe sex

In some families it may be more culturally acceptable for relatives other than parents such as aunts and uncles or grandparents to teach their children about sex education. The fact that the couple are gay is of no relevance. Adults of all sexual preferences abuse children and adults of all sexual preferences protect children. As in the other examples the child's own wishes are important. The question must be asked as to whether the child wants to hear this information at this point in time and whether it is in their best interests.

22. Father makes comments on the development of his daughter's breasts and that she is looking 'sexy'

The comments made by a father to his daughter have to be evaluated. The young woman may be deeply embarrassed or the comment may hold little meaning for her. It would be inappropriate to comment on the development of her breasts but he might comment on the fact that she is growing into a fine young woman. The word 'sexy' could have a wide range of meanings from innocuous to indicating abusive attitudes.

23. Parents leave sex education books around the house for their son and daughter aged 8 and 10 years to read

Sex education books left around the home may allow children to read the material when they feel ready to do so. There are many types of books for children and it is important that they are appropriate for the age. Sometimes sex abusers groom children into thinking sexual activity is normal at their age and use books about sex as part of the process.

24. Father and mother watch blue movies

It is abusive if children can readily gain access to adult pornography and the issue in this case is whether the movies are secured and the children protected from exposure to inappropriate images.

25. Grandfather cuddles young granddaughter and nibbles her ears

In some families nibbling ears is defined as similar to kissing children on the lips. It may be viewed as quite acceptable whereas in other families it would not be allowed. It might have a sexual connotation but generally would be a sign of affection.

26. Teenage stepbrother has intercourse with stepsister aged 12 years

Under the Sexual Offences Act sexual intercourse between members of the same household is a criminal offence (2003: Section 27).

27. Father bathes his son aged 11 years

In this case it is possible that the father may be caring for a disabled child who needs assistance with bathing. Also families have many different views about bathing with children at various ages. Obviously if a child is young it would be neglectful not to keep a close eye on them at bath time and many parents will share a bath with their young child irrespective of their or the child's gender. However, a child may reach an age when they decide that they require privacy which should be respected unless they would be in danger if left alone.

28. Daughter aged 13 years gets into bed with parents when she can't sleep

In some homes it is not acceptable for older children to get into their parents bed. However, in others it is quite normal as a form of comfort.

29. Parents use boy aged 13 years to babysit for girl aged 3 years

There is no minimum age for baby-sitting. It is a matter of judgement whether or not a child is being neglected. There would be many factors to consider as to whether or not the three-year-old girl was safe in this situation. The maturity of the 13-year-old, his access to adult help should he need it, access to a telephone, the needs of the three-year-old, provision of food, warmth, clothing and other safety factors need consideration.

30. Boy aged 9 years dresses up in his teenage sister's clothes

There are no age limits for children playing at dressing up and having fun. However, it is not unusual for a sexually exploited child to be dressed up by the abuser from which they derive sexual gratification. The child may be giving the carers a message about something that is happening to them. For instance, sometimes when a child is being sexually abused they try and look unattractive to the abuser and boys may try to look more like a girl or vice versa. In the same way children may become very fat or thin in order to seem unattractive to the abuser and to try and protect themselves from harm. Any child who suddenly changes their self image may be trying to communicate about an experience of harm.

31. Boy aged 10 years accesses an internet site containing abusive images of children

It is not simple to access a website containing abusive images of children. In most cases adults have to contribute many thousands of images in order to become a member and they may also require credit card access. Should a child or adult come across abusive images these must be reported to police. The websites of the Internet Watch Foundation and of the Child Exploitation and Online Protection Centre have information about how to report such abuse (www.iwf.org.uk/and www.ceop.gov.uk/).

32. Father supports daughter in the swimming pool by holding her under her bottom

There are many activities which adults do with children which involve close proximity and sometimes touch such as swimming, learning a musical instrument or riding a bike. When such allegations arise specialist advice is needed as to what is common acceptable practice. Holding a child under their bottom when teaching them to swim may be acceptable for a parent but would not be acceptable for a teacher. However, if a specialist swimming instructor reported a parent who unusually held his daughter in that way for a long time and in a way that seemed abusive, the professionals in investigating the allegation would have to give weight to this specialist view.

33. Female babysitter massages boy aged 8 years gently on his neck and back to help him sleep

Massage can be a caring way of assisting a child to relax and children need to experience safe touches in order to judge those that may be unsafe. However, there have been cases of child abuse within children's homes where staff began to abuse children sexually by getting them familiar with less intrusive touches – a process known as grooming. It is no longer acceptable for residential care staff to massage children in their care. Abusers will use all kinds of means to get close contact with children. Much can be learnt from the experiences of Phil Frampton who was a child in care who wrote about child abuse within the care system (Frampton, 2003).

34. Parents allow their children to have TV in their bedrooms

It is possible to control what children watch and if children have a TV in their rooms it is more difficult for parents to be vigilant that their children are not exposed to sexual or violent programmes.

35. Parents take their young children to pose as models for advertisements for underwear

Children's images are very often portrayed in the media in an abusive way. Babies used in nappy advertisements for instance have not given permission for the public to see their bodies and child sex abusers exploit these images for their own sexual gratification. Parents may be genuinely earning some money by promoting their children as models but there is a wider social issue involved of the exploitation of children when these images are used as commodities to sell products.

36. Children know their parents both have affairs outside the marriage

Secrets in families are not generally healthy for children. Some parents do have other relationships and the children are aware and accepting of this. In other situations it could be emotionally abusive and an example of the parent's needs being placed above those of the child. It is important to consider that people live their lives in many different ways and the children may be very well cared for within a range of family situations.

37. Mother shaves daughter's head to make hair grow thicker

In some cultures children's heads are shaved for specific cultural reasons such as removing hair that the baby had whilst in the womb which may be defined as unclean. This practice may be explained as being fashionable or for hygiene reasons but it also may be an act of shaming a child as a form of discipline and as such is a deeply humiliating means of exerting adult power over the child. Cultural advice would be essential in such cases.

38. Children hear their mother calling their father a 'prick' and their father calling their mother a 'slag'

The use of language within a family may indicate breaches of safe boundaries or may be fairly meaningless and just the words the family commonly use.

39. Grandmother tickles baby's genitalia to help them to sleep

Child rearing practices change over time. It was common in Victorian times for grandmothers or wet nurses to soothe babies in this way just as it was the practice to put whisky or brandy into children's milk. These practices are not defined as acceptable today.

40. Mother explains to daughter aged 14 years what oral sex is

The parent may make a reasonable decision that it is important for the girl's safety that she has an understanding of this sexual activity but, if the girl is disinterested, it has to be questioned whether this information is in her best interests. An open mind is essential in judging the mother's intentions. She could be preparing the child for sexual exploitation. This could be innocent and educational or abusive.

Presentation 3: Defining Significant Harm

The trainer needs to explain definitions of significant harm and the levels of proof required for:

- Criminal proceedings – proof beyond all reasonable doubt.
- Civil proceedings – proof on the balance of probabilities.

Significant harm and likelihood of significant harm are not legal definitions but are decided by professional judgement based on knowledge and research evidence.

Under Section 31 (10) of the Children Act 1989 as amended by the Adoption and Children Act 2002:

- 'Harm' means ill treatment or the impairment of health or development, including for example impairment suffered from seeing or hearing the ill treatment of another.
- 'Development' means physical, emotional, social or behavioural development.
- 'Health' means physical or mental health.
- 'Ill treatment' includes sexual abuse and forms of ill treatment which are not physical.

Under Section 31(10) of the Act where the question of whether harm suffered by a child is significant turns on the child's health and development, their health or development should be compared with that which could reasonably be expected of a similar child.

Activity 4: Making Judgements About Seriousness of Harm to Children

Aim: Participants to explore and analyse, through groupwork, the criteria used when making judgements in child protection cases.

Delivery: Participants work in mixed groups (police and social workers) of four to five to read the list of scenarios and then prioritise them strictly from one to ten in order of seriousness. One is the most serious. They are given ten adhesive notes. They write on each one the letter representing the case scenario and the number representing the perceived level of seriousness. Each group must complete the exercise and post the ten notes up onto a grid to allow trainers to lead a discussion as to the quality of decisions made and the criteria used.

Order of priority	Cases									
	A	B	C	D	E	F	G	H	I	J
1										
2										
3										
4										
5										
6										
7										
8										
9										
10										

It is helpful to have different colour adhesive notes for each group. This exercise may take a group from 5 to 30 minutes. It is expected that participants will be uncertain of the task. Trainers will need to spend some time with each group to assist clarification.

Trainers acknowledge the impossibility of the task and encourage debate by asking participants how they made their judgements. Each of these scenarios is serious and involves a child suffering or likely to suffer significant harm. The ethnicity of the children is not stated in the scenarios in order to encourage participants to consider cultural and religious factors and how these might impact on their decisions.

Handout 3: Seriousness of harm

Prioritise according to the serious of the harm
1 = most serious 10 = least serious

A

Richard is aged 7 years. His parents are wheelchair users. He has missed one outpatient appointment to follow up his treatment following a road traffic accident. Richards' dressings are now filthy and his wounds infected. They have been infected for some days.

B

Shireen is a single parent bringing up two teenage sons, Jason and Darren. Both are feeling depressed and can see no future for themselves. Shireen is struggling to cope. They leave her to do all the work in the house and they both just lie about all day. This morning Darren slashed his wrists and was rushed to hospital. He is severely ill and may not survive.

C

Nazreen is aged 15 years. Today Nazreen's father found out that she had gone clubbing with her friends and had lied to him by saying she was staying with a friend overnight. He has forbidden her to go out again, and says she must leave school as soon as she is sixteen, and he will arrange a marriage for her.

D

Josie is aged 4 years. Both her parents are aged 20 years. The family live in temporary accommodation that is cold and damp. Through lack of experience as parents, and the stress of the living arrangements, the parents fight a lot and the mother gets depressed. Last night after a particularly bad argument, the father left home saying he was never coming back. The mother was on her bed crying when Josie played with the knobs on the gas cooker and was badly burnt.

E

Mandy is aged 8 years and recently her uncle has made her touch his penis and masturbate him. He always tells her she is special and that this is their secret because she is his new girlfriend.

© Liz Davies and Debbie Townsend. *Joint Investigation in Child Protection*. www.russellhouse.co.uk

F
Rashid is the only son in a family of six children. He has to do the family housework and is always called 'idiot' and made to eat his meals in his bedroom. He is not allowed to sit with the family in the living room or go on outings with them. He wears his brother's old clothes and is always unwashed and untidy.

G
Romi is aged 18 months. She is regularly left alone whilst her mother, who is the sole carer, goes to the pub. The mother has some learning difficulties. Romi wakes up at night crying and calling for her mother.

H
Melanie is aged 14 years and has a steady boyfriend. Yesterday her stepfather returned home and found her in her bedroom with her boyfriend. Her stepfather was very angry and hit Melanie with a stick causing marks and cutting through the skin despite her clothing. He wanted to teach her a lesson. The boyfriend had to leave very quickly.

I
Jamie is aged eight months. This morning his father was looking after him while his mother was at work. The father got so frustrated with Jamie's constant crying that he took Jamie out of the pram and shook him until he stopped making a noise.

J
Michael is aged 13 years and goes to an independent school. He has to join the Army Cadet Force even though he is a pacifist and the school will not allow him to wear his Campaign against Nuclear Disarmament badge. His parents, are very committed to the school and do not want to get involved even though he is subjected to school discipline because he is refusing to conform to the rules about the army training.

Feedback: The age of the child is critical. A very young child such as Jamie (I) or Romi (G) has to be considered particularly vulnerable. Adults may not understand the serious harm that may be caused by shaking a baby. One study indicated that 10 per cent of mothers had shaken their babies and 25 per cent had felt like doing so. Half the parents in the survey were unaware of the dangers of shaking a baby. Of those who had shaken a baby or who felt like it 90 per cent said it was because the baby cried incessantly (Shepherd et al., 2000).

Yet teenagers are also at risk of harm. If a homeless young person dies on the street the cause of death will not be 'child abuse' but 'drug overdose', 'hypothermia' or 'assault'. It is known that many homeless young people have experienced child abuse at home but there are no statistics to inform us of how many of those who have suffered abuse have died. Very few serious case reviews are about older children (Brandon et al., 2008: 45).

In the case of Jason and Darren (B) a sibling has attempted suicide and this raises the risk of harm to the other sibling. The Children Act 1989 applies to all young people up to the age of 18 years. In the case of Nazreen (C) it is important to consider whether she is likely to be a victim of forced marriage. An arranged marriage is accepted cultural practice but a forced marriage is child abuse. In some cultures it is known that young women are vulnerable to particular forms of abuse and in such cases specialist cultural advice must be sought to ensure good practice. Cultural assumptions can place children in danger if the cultural or religious context is not understood. Guidance with regard to forced marriage is available on the Home Office website.

Multi-agency working is essential in protecting children. A health visitor, school nurse or doctor would realise that in the case of Richard (A) the child is at risk of septicaemia which could be fatal. Health colleagues must be consulted to allow correct evaluation of the risk to the child. The parents who are disabled may be abusive but they may not be receiving the support they need to parent their child. It would be important to check that they received and were able to access the details of appointments before concluding that they had been neglectful.

In thinking about Josie (D) the fact it was an accident and that the adult did not deliberately beat the child as happened to Melanie (H) might lead to thinking that the level of risk is reduced. Yet in considering Josie (D) there are clusters of indicators of abuse, and the impact on the child was of serious harm. Child abuse may be acts of commission or omission.

In Melanie's case (H) the father 'meant well' but Melanie has suffered serious physical injury which might have even led to her death. It is not uncommon for an adult to provide a rationale for abuse of a child 'to teach them a lesson' or 'to prevent them running away'. In assessing the adult's capacity to change their abusive behaviour it is important to understand their motivation, but ultimately the child has suffered abuse and requires protection. Adults often abuse children because they do not understand the stage of development of the child and have unrealistic expectations. For example, a small child who is not toilet trained urinating on the floor or a baby who will not feed from a bottle may be mistakenly defined by the adult as committing deliberate acts of defiance.

The cases may have been prioritised by a consideration of what action needed to be taken immediately to protect the child in each case.

Mandy (E) is being sexually abused, but it has been going on for some time and it may be thought that she would not die from this in the same way that may apply to other cases such as Jamie (I), Romi (G) or Darren (B). Yet sexual abuse is often correlated with physical violence and neglect and exposure to sexually transmitted infections may expose the child to serious harm. Mandy may not define the sexual abuse as harmful as abusers will often convince the child that they are 'special' and that the abuse is 'normal'. Some young people may even gain some feelings of pleasure from the sexual activity and become confused about what is abuse and what is a loving relationship. The Children Act (1989:1) is clear about the paramountcy of the child's best interests. The child's perception of abuse must be heard but it is an adult responsibility to protect children and sexual abuse is criminal and abusive. It is abuse of adult power with serious consequences for the child.

Rashid (F) presents as a child who is isolated within the family. This is an indicator that suggests a high risk of harm. Children who are treated differently from other children in the family and who are locked in rooms away from sight are children at very high risk. Such risk may be identified at a very early stage even before birth if a parent expresses feelings of rejection towards the forthcoming child. They may not access ante-natal care, make no preparations for the baby's arrival, wish they had managed to get a termination of pregnancy or only desire a boy/girl. The pre-birth history can provide professionals with important information to assist them in assessing risk.

Children in isolated situations are at high risk of harm because they have few means of telling someone if they are suffering child abuse. Children placed in institutions, placements far from their locality or in custody may soon be forgotten to the busy professionals who placed them there. Michael (J) might find it very difficult to tell his parents about his experiences as he knows they are making financial sacrifices to pay for his education. Emotional abuse can result in a child self harming, running away or attempting suicide. The impact must not be minimised. Such young people need clear channels of communication in place for them in order to feel safe.

Trainers should make reference to:

Adcock, M. and White, R. (1998) *Significant Harm. Its Management and Outcome.* London: Significant Publications.

Nelson, S. (2008) *Hear Us See Us. Schools Working with Sexually Abused Young People.* Dundee. Violence is preventable.

Reder, P., Duncan, S. and Gray, M. (1993) *Beyond Blame. Child Abuse Tragedies Revisited. A Summary of 35 Inquiries Since 1973.* London: Routledge.

Reder, P. and Duncan, S. (1999) *Lost Innocents. A Follow-up Study of Fatal Child Abuse.* London: Routledge.

Recognition of Child Abuse, Assessment, Investigation and Intervention

Activity 5: Recognising the Indicators of Child Abuse

Aim: For participants to gain in awareness of how the vulnerable child might be recognised as a possible victim of child abuse within a school environment.

Delivery: The trainer reads out the story printed below. Participants are informed that the story is a chapter from a book written by a survivor of child abuse. It is about the child's school career. They are asked to write down, whilst the story is being read, any indicators of child abuse which might have been recognised at the time. At the end of the story the participants work in small mixed professional groups to compare their lists of indicators. After a short while the trainer provides the checklist to enable comparison. Identifying names have been removed from the text and at the end, the trainers reveal that the story was written by Anne Marie West, daughter of Fred and Rose West, who committed multiple murders, tortured and sexually abused their own and other children and adults (West, 1995).

Content

My School Years
I was never really happy at school. I felt I didn't fit in. Even at infants' and junior school I found it difficult to make friends. My home life made me reserved and I was never allowed to invite other girls and boys home or to go to their houses to play. In later years, at secondary school, my inner anger and frustration emerged as an aggressive, if not delinquent, streak which was not understood by those in authority or by the few friends I did have.

My school reports from my teenage years contained definite pointers to the problem but no-one saw through the tough façade I maintained or bothered to probe further. Teachers then were not as aware as they are today of the behavioural signals from victims of child abuse, but even so it amazes me that some kind of investigation was never made into my background. There were occasions when I was so unruly that one teacher even used to lock me in a cupboard until I calmed down. I never held this against him because he was one of the few I liked. He did it for my own good so that I wouldn't get into even more trouble with the headmaster. To my knowledge my behaviour was not even reported to my parents. I feel sure, if it had been, I would have received a beating for drawing attention to myself.

My home life was often mirrored in my school life . . . Once I found some of my old school reports and looked through them. They reminded me of how hard I tried to fit in with the other children and to please and impress my teachers. These days, with the additional training teachers have, I would hope someone would pick up the signs and realise that there was something wrong. Reading the reports now it's easy to see that they scream 'abused child' – it's all there. Even then it should have registered with someone that I was an unhappy girl growing up into a difficult young woman. Did no-one wonder why?

The earliest report I uncovered, dated 1973, when I was aged eight years eleven months . . . isn't bad. My marks were all Cs except for English, in which I had a B-. There were forty kids in my age group and I was about halfway down in ability. Considering what happened to me at home when I was eight, I was surprised to see that my form teacher had written 'A good year's work. She has worked hard throughout the year. She has been a very helpful member of the class.'

By the following year it was obvious that things were slipping. I was still at about the same position in the class but now there were no Bs. Instead Ds and Es were creeping in. My new teacher summed it up, 'She often doesn't give herself enough time to present thoughtful work. Her presentation is very messy. Her work is often affected by her moods.'

The following year was my last at primary school and I was preparing to go to secondary school. My headmaster, Mr. Martin, described my report as 'quite satisfactory' but the new form teacher had once again noted my behaviour pattern. My marks were a mixture of Cs and Ds and I was still midway down the class. Comments on individual subjects ranged from 'Can do well when she tries' to 'Very interesting when she puts her mind to it'. The general remarks section said more. 'I think she has had quite a good year. Often her work has been quite good, but her moods have not helped her.' If only those well meaning teachers had ever stopped to consider what was causing those wild mood swings.

I don't have the report which followed my first year at secondary school, which is a shame, I tried so hard to make a new start that year. Despite what was happening at home, by then I had been introduced to Mum's clients, I kept battling on at school. The grades at secondary school were applied separately for achievement and effort. Even when I didn't achieve much, my efforts earned As and Bs. But a giveaway sign was my attendance record. I was given a D for below average and the art teacher awarded me a B for effort but commented, 'recent absences have also hindered progress . . .'

By the time I was in the third form it was clear from my report that I was having difficulty in some subjects. Ironically, biology was not one of them. I apparently showed great interest in those classes and got my first ever A for achievement. But other teachers noted that I was struggling despite my obvious abilities. My year tutor recorded that I had been absent on fifty-two occasions and late fifteen times. No one, it seemed, wondered why.

The last report I have . . . was when I was in the fourth form. I had been absent sixty-eight times. It described my conduct as satisfactory, previously it had never been less than good. I'm surprised at this because I was a bit of a bully in the playground and often threw tantrums in class. I have a feeling that perhaps I was given the benefit of the doubt because some of those in authority suspected that things weren't quite right in my household but didn't want to get involved. After all, I was due to leave in the following year.

Only once did anyone become suspicious about my family circumstances and that was when I was in junior school. The PE teacher at school became anxious when yet again I brought in a note saying I could not take part in the games lesson. She insisted I could and I was adamant that I couldn't. Then she noticed the big black bruises on my legs, the real reason why I was refusing and why Mum had written to have me excused. The teacher made me roll down my socks and hitch up my skirt. She gave a slight gasp as she took in the injuries. She frowned and gave me an uncertain look. 'How did you do this? Did you have an accident or did someone do it to you?'

I desperately wanted to say 'My Mum did it. She's always doing it,' but I couldn't find the words. My mouth opened and shut a few times as I tried to tell her, but my fear of Mum was too great. Instead I put my head down and simply looked sullen.

'. . . If someone did this to you, you should tell me. Now, what happened?'

She wasn't unkind. She just didn't know how to deal with the evidence of her own eyes and I wasn't about to help. I continued to look sulky and said eventually, 'I fell over, Miss. I just fell over.'

The PE teacher let me sit out the lesson and nothing more was said. The school day continued as normal and I assumed that was the end of it. But no sooner had I got back home than the doorbell rang. Mum answered it while I was still in the hallway. The smartly dressed woman introduced herself as being from the Welfare Department. She said she wanted to talk to Mum because they were concerned about me. My blood ran cold but Mum kept her cool, invited the woman in and sent me to my room to change. I did as I was told and sat on the edge of my bed, trembling and biting my lip nervously. I wanted to listen in to the conversation but I was too scared to try. When I thought I had been gone long enough I headed back towards the kitchen. The welfare woman was just leaving. I heard her say, 'Oh well, that's fine, Mrs . . .'and she went out of the front door quite reassured and never came back again. Mum had told her a plausible enough tale about me falling downstairs and she didn't even question me on its authenticity. Not that I would have disagreed in front of Mum, of course, or at all for that matter.

Once the woman had gone I received one of the worst beatings of my life. It taught me a lesson about the welfare and those in authority, they couldn't help, and any attempts they made to do so merely rebounded on me.

Going to school got me out of the house so I rarely played truant. The absences occurred when Mum forced me to stay away for some reason of her own. My attendance record wasn't good because she would often invent an excuse to keep me at home. There were always the younger children to look after and housework to be done, or perhaps she had miscalculated and some of my bruises showed. Sometimes I was fit enough to do sport. I remember briefly being in the relay team and I have a swimming certificate. She must have been careful not to do anything that would show until after my school swimming course finished.

But there weren't any lessons I particularly liked. Usually I preferred to wander off on my own at break time and get some peace. I did try hard at school at the beginning. I would have a go at things, but there was always this suppressed feeling inside me. Even though I tried I got so frustrated. Much of this was because I never received praise for anything I did achieve. Eventually it didn't seem worth the effort. I grew disheartened, nobody was going to appreciate anything I did. We had sports days and things like that, but Dad never came and Mum turned up only very occasionally. I wouldn't dream now of missing anything my children were involved in. I know how important those things are to kids.

I had a lot of problems finding my feet. I didn't say much, I was an introvert and by the time I got to my teens I felt under extreme pressure and couldn't cope with the stress. It was difficult trying to be two people. In school I was a child attempting to make friends, learn and pay attention to lessons, and at home there were the men and the beatings. I started to realise that other children had a different sort of life. They went to discos and parties and to their friends' homes. I listened to the other girls giggling about boys and sex in the toilets but I kept my mouth shut when they came out with ridiculous old wives' tales. Inside I was thinking, 'That's rubbish. I know how you do it and what happens', but I never said anything. I just turned away and stayed silent.

In spite of my problems I made a few pals but knowing them began to show me the difference in our lives. They would be out at night playing in the street and I would be in the washroom at the back of the house doing the family's laundry. I could hear them playing and I would sneak out of the washroom and talk to them over the fence. If Mum caught me she would be furious, and to my embarrassment, she would drag me back into the washroom and knock hell out of me with all the other kids watching. The next day they would laugh and say to me, 'Oh, you got a bit of a beating, didn't you?'

Yet I never asked those other children how things were in their households. I just accepted that what I had was what I had. I never had the urge to explore the subject further, I was much too frightened of my family and the consequences.

It was no good pretending that I was the same as those other girls who spent their lives making friends, going to parties and enjoying a busy social life with the blessing of their parents. They might bitch and moan, they were able to sound off safe in the knowledge that they were loved and could love in return. For me it was different. I still yearned for affection from my father and tried to please Mum. The copious reserves of love I had I lavished on my brothers and sisters. But even their responses were governed by fear of Mum. The only physical closeness I had was my father's constant abuse of me, the furtive and shameful attacks when Mum wasn't present, which I longed to resist.

When I was fifteen the inevitable occurred. My father got me pregnant. I suppose in many ways it was fortunate for me that the pregnancy didn't develop properly as it was ectopic, which meant that the embryo was developing in the fallopian tube. It was years before I found out what had been wrong with me, even that I had been expecting a baby. I thought I had simply had something wrong inside me and had had an operation. No one ever explained and it wasn't until I had my first daughter that my doctor's notes revealed the truth.

It took me two full months to tell anybody that I thought there was something the matter with me. My period seemed to be going on for all that time. I did not stop bleeding but I was too worried and ashamed to say anything. I had a dread of anyone examining my body. That might seem strange after all that had been done to me, but those experiences had taken place against my will and I did not want to submit to anything voluntarily. I lay in bed as nurses bustled back and forth, giving me a pre-med and checking my notes. Eventually I was carted off to the operating theatre. Still no one had told me what they thought was really the matter with me and I was afraid to ask. Years later, when I saw my medical records, I understood the attitude of the doctors and nurses. They had been so offhand and unfriendly. It was 1979 and what they saw in the hospital bed was a fifteen year old slut who had got what she had been asking for and didn't deserve any sympathy. It wasn't that they were actively unkind, just businesslike, efficient and decidedly cool.

Well versed in keeping my mouth shut and not asking questions, I didn't press them for information and accepted their manner as the norm. After all, I wasn't used to people being nice to me anyway and I didn't expect it from strangers when I didn't get it at home. Even when the dressing was taken off and I saw the twelve metal pins in my bruised flesh I didn't question them too hard. The matron told me that the operation had been 'something to do with my periods'. I was very frightened and felt so alone. At night I sobbed quietly into my snowy-white pillow, unable to decide which I hated most, the hospital or the home to which I would have to return.

Handout 4: Checklist of possible indicators

delinquent
I didn't fit in
aggressive
tough façade
behavioural signs
few friends
unruly
tried to fit in
wanted to please teachers
wanted to impress – being helpful in class
unhappy
schoolwork deteriorated over time
moods
messy presentation
interested in work 'when she puts her mind to it'
wild mood swings
battling on at school
attendance very poor – hindered progress
works well when in the mood
obvious abilities but underachieving
bully
tantrums
conduct satisfactory – it had previously been good
bruises
had to lie
kept off school by parents – to hide injuries/do housework/care for siblings
wandered out of school to get peace
never got praise for her achievements from parents
secondary school frightening
parents didn't attend school functions
no praise from parents when she got her school badge
introvert
couldn't cope with stress
being two people
feeling different from peers
friends not allowed to visit her home
hit in front of friends
pregnancy
no one told her about the pregnancy
kept her mouth shut

didn't ask questions
sobbing in pillow
knowledge about sexual activities
dread of physical examination
no visits to her in hospital from her family

Feedback: It is important to acknowledge that not all participants will have heard of the case of Fred and Rose West. The serious case review provides a summary of the case (Bridge Child Care Consultancy, 1996). Trainers will encourage debate about the indicators that the groups did not identify and explore the reasons why these were omitted. To conclude trainers can relate the fact that Stephen West, brother of Anne Marie, in an interview was asked why he hadn't told a teacher that his back was bleeding following a very severe physical assault by his father. He sat in the class wearing his large overcoat on a very hot day. He replied that he was the child and it was not up to him to tell what was happening. It was the teacher's job to recognise the signs and to have protected him.

Presentation 4: Definition of Safeguarding and Categories of Child Abuse

Safeguarding definition

Safeguarding and promoting the welfare of children underpins all the five outcomes in *Every Child Matters* (The Treasury, 2003) and in particular is linked to the outcome 'Staying Safe'.

It is defined in a number of ways:

Keeping children and young people safe from harm such as illness, abuse or injury.

(Children's Rights Director for England. CSCI, 2004: 1)

All agencies working with children, young people and their families take all reasonable measures to ensure that the risks of harm to children's welfare are minimised and where there are concerns about children and young people's welfare, all agencies take all appropriate actions to address those concerns, working to agreed local policies and procedures in full partnership with other local agencies.

(DfES, 2003: 1)

Safeguard: protection, safety, security, custody, safe-keeping, anything that offers security from danger, a defence.

(Shorter Oxford English Dictionary 5th edn. 2002, cited by Parton, 2005: 7)

It is also defined as:

- Protecting children from maltreatment.
- Preventing impairment of children's health or development.
- Ensuring that children are growing up in circumstances consistent with the provision of safe and effective care and undertaking that role so as to enable those children to have optimum life chances and to enter adulthood successfully. Child protection is a part of safeguarding and promoting welfare. This refers to the activity that is undertaken to protect specific children who are suffering or are at risk of suffering significant harm' (DfES, 2006: 1.18).

Working Together (DfES, 2006) defines four categories of child abuse. The definitions are as follows:

Physical abuse: May involve hitting, shaking, throwing, poisoning, burning or scalding, drowning, suffocating or otherwise causing physical harm to a child. Physical harm may also be caused when a parent or carer fabricates the symptoms of, or deliberately induces, illness in a child (DfES, 2006: 1.30).

Emotional abuse: Is the persistent emotional ill treatment of a child such as to cause severe and persistent adverse effects on the child's emotional development. It may involve conveying to children that they are worthless or unloved, inadequate or valued only insofar as they meet the needs of another person. It may feature age or developmentally inappropriate expectations being imposed on children. These may include interactions that are beyond the child's developmental capability, as well as over protection and limitation of exploration and learning or preventing the child participating in normal social interaction. It may involve seeing or hearing the ill treatment of another. It may involve serious bullying, causing children frequently to feel frightened or in danger, or the exploitation or corruption of children. Some level of emotional abuse is involved in all types of ill treatment of a child though it may occur alone (DfES, 2006: 1.31).

Sexual abuse: Involves forcing or enticing a child or young person to take part in sexual activities, including prostitution, whether or not the child is aware of what is happening. The activities may involve physical contact, including penetrative (e.g. rape, buggery or oral sex) or non-penetrative acts. They may include non-contact activities such as involving children in looking at, or in the production of, sexual online images, watching sexual activities, or encouraging children to behave in sexually inappropriate ways (DfES, 2006: 1.32).

Neglect: Is the persistent failure to meet a child's basic physical and/or psychological needs likely to result in the serious impairment of the child's health or development. Neglect may occur during pregnancy as a result of maternal substance abuse. Once a child is born, neglect may involve a parent or carer failing to:

- Provide adequate food, clothing and shelter (including exclusion from home or abandonment).
- Protect a child from physical or emotional harm or danger.
- Ensure adequate supervision (including the use of inadequate care-givers).
- Ensure access to appropriate medical care or treatment.

It may also include neglect of, or unresponsiveness to a child's basic emotional needs.

(DfES, 2006: 1.33)

In addition to these four categories of abuse, it is important to have knowledge of the definition of:

Organised abuse: Complex (organised or multiple) abuse involves one or more abusers and a number of children. The abusers concerned may be acting in concert to abuse children, sometimes acting in isolation, or may be using an institutional framework or position of authority to recruit children for abuse. Complex abuse occurs both as part of a network of abuse across a family or community and within institutions such as residential homes or schools (DfES, 2006: 6.7).

Activity 6: Considering the Indicators of Child Abuse

Aim: For participants to begin to define child abuse within the four main categories outlined in the *Working Together* guidance (DfES, 2006).

Delivery: Participants work in mixed professional groups. They make reference to the categories of abuse and consider each scenario. They also consider what other categories may apply.

Handout 5: Indicators of Child Abuse

Referring to the four categories of abuse consider the main category in each of the following cases. There may be more than one category. Then decide any other indicators which might be relevant to each case.

1. **Lesley** aged 6 years has learning difficulties. She has recently broken her arm after falling off the top of a slide. Her parents have not taken her to out-patient appointments for follow up.

Main category

Other indicators

2. **Jamie** aged 14 years has large sums of money which he says he gets in the city centre. He has been seen with older men. One of these men is known to the Probation Service as an adult who presents a risk to children. Jamie rarely attends school and his mother says he is often out at nights. He is having difficulty concentrating on school work and has been cautioned by the police for theft.

Main category

Other indicators

3. **Harmeet** aged 3 years has been in day care for 6 months. She had settled well but over the last two weeks she has cried at home time when her father collects her and she clings to the care worker. She is developmentally delayed and her first language is not English. During a visit to the General Practitioner because of a urine infection the doctor noticed bruises on her inner thighs.

Main category

Other indicators

4. **Sarah** is aged 2 years. She is a hearing child of deaf parents. She arrived at nursery with what appeared to be a triangular burn on her left forearm. Whilst in the home corner she was heard to say, 'Mummy cross'.

Main category

Other indicators

5. **Helena**, aged 8 years, has red marks on her lower back and bottom. She tells her teacher that her mother slapped her for stealing. Her teachers had suspected that she had been stealing at school. It is known that her mother is a victim of domestic violence.

Main category

Other indicators

6. **Ben** is aged 8 months. He has feeding difficulties and the health visitor is concerned because his weight suddenly fell from the fiftieth to the third percentile within a month. He is developmentally delayed and has severe nappy rash. His mother has a history of mental health problems, including hospital admissions, and the family live in cramped accommodation.

Main category

Other indicators

7. **Mohammed** aged 7 years is the eldest of three children and attends school irregularly. He is often smelly, has dental caries and is unsuitably dressed. He often has little food in his lunchbox. He is a bright child but bites younger children when attending the after school club.

Main category

Other indicators

8. **Darren** is aged 13 years. He has a younger brother and sister aged eight and three. The General Practitioner knows that Darren's parents are drug dependent. Darren went to the doctor for his BCG injection and was unusually vague and drowsy. The health visitor has been worried because on her visit she saw syringes on the table and other evidence of drug taking.

Main category

Other indicators

9. **Susan** is aged 15 years. Her friend told the Sunday school teacher that Susan's stepfather has been coming into her room at night for several months and playing with her. Last night her stepfather asked her to have oral sex with him. Susan doesn't want anyone else to know about it.

Main category

Other indicators

10. **Richard** aged 5 years has become progressively quiet and withdrawn and school staff notice that he is losing his circle of friends. Richard's parents told his teacher in front of him that he was an unwanted child. Both parents are professionals, work full time and leave him with a number of different carers.

Main category

Other indicators

Feedback

1. **Lesley:** In this case the participants may have concluded that a vulnerable child has suffered neglect by an adult who was not supervising her properly and did not take the child to medical appointments. This may be the case, however it is important not to make assumptions. Children commonly have genuine accidents even when fully supervised by caring adults. Missed appointments may be due to letters not arriving at the correct address or written in a language not understood by the family. A child with learning difficulties may need more than usual supervision to be safe. It may be that the adults do not have a good understanding of their child's needs which may constitute unintended neglect and this is still, of course, abusive to the child. An investigation would evaluate the consistency of explanations for the injury with the accounts provided by the child and adults.

2. **Jamie:** Jamie is at high risk of sexual exploitation and sexual and organised abuse would be relevant categories. Child sex abusers target vulnerable children. In order to become close to the child they also target the caring adults. The participants may have considered Jamie's parents to be neglectful in not managing his behaviour. However, child sex abusers will betray the trust of the carers in order to entrap the child. It is important for the investigation team to work with the family and to gain their assistance in protecting the child from the abusers. The family may be able to provide details of the abuse network to assist enquiries. The professional task is to help the non-abusive carer to become a proactive protector of the child through empowering them to work alongside the professionals. It may be concluded that the non-abusive carer is not able to be protective and in such a case the child will need alternative care provision.

3. **Harmeet:** This girl is demonstrating possible indicators of child abuse and physical and/or emotional abuse are the relevant categories. Bruising on the inner thighs may be indicative of sexual abuse as it is not commonly found in young children and also urine infections may indicate sexual harm. However, as there may be innocent explanations for both these medical presentations, these medical facts will need to be assessed by the named child protection doctor. This is to ensure that the child receives the most appropriate examination and only one examination. Repeated investigations may be in themselves abusive to children. Abuse of children by professional systems is called secondary or systems abuse. There may be many reasons why a child's behaviour changes and the reason for the change would need to be explored.

4. **Sarah:** The participants may have considered physical abuse in this case. A triangular shaped burn is highly indicative of a burn from an iron which would be more likely to indicate deliberate than accidental harm. If she had fallen onto the iron it would have left a different type of mark. A child protection doctor would be able to provide an opinion on the likely cause of the burn taking into account any explanations provided by the parents and child. The child's comment may or may not be associated with the injury. It is important not to make connections where they may not exist but to also

keep an open mind. Attention must be paid to a child's statement even though the child is aged two years as she may be able to provide an account of what happened. She may need a specialist, such as a child psychiatrist or psychologist, to interview her using play and drawing techniques. As the hearing child of deaf parents it is possible that she called for help and they did not hear her. Disabled parents have the same right to be parents as all parents. They may need assistance in order to be protective parents of a young child. Whilst a sensitive approach would be required, it is also important not to be diverted from the needs of the child. Sometimes professionals over identify with disabled parents and the child's needs remain hidden from view.

5. **Helena:** The relevant category is physical abuse and emotional abuse or neglect may well apply. Sexual abuse cannot be ruled out given the red marks on her back which may be caused through friction. The child's statement may be accurate or may have been made to divert attention away from disclosure of sexual abuse. Expert medical opinion would be necessary to clarify the possible and probable cause of the injuries and to match the findings with the explanations provided by the child and adults. A child may steal in order to gain attention to an abusive situation at home and they may also be stealing food or clothes if neglected. If it is known that a parent is themselves a victim of domestic violence then there is no doubt that the children suffer emotional abuse and commonly physical harm and neglect as well. Police and social workers would interview the child and obtain a formal account of what happened as the injuries are consistent with a crime (assault) having been committed.

6. **Ben:** Health visitors and doctors refer to percentile charts. These record a child's height, weight and head circumference and make comparisons over time bearing in mind cultural and gender differences. A sudden drop in the percentiles is of concern. There may be a medical reason for feeding difficulties. If the child protection doctor concludes that there is no such medical reason then a child protection investigation (Section 47, CA 1989) would be indicated to consider other explanations. Similarly, severe nappy rash may indicate neglect or there may be a medical reason.

   Adults with mental health problems may be protective parents but neglect and emotional abuse may be indicated in this case. Factors such as repeated parental admissions to hospital may be very disruptive to a child's life and professionals need to consider how the mental health problems impact on the adult's ability to be a protective parent (Falkov, 1996).

   Many families live in cramped accommodation and do not harm their children. In child protection work clusters of indicators need to be assessed. When the pieces of the jigsaw of indicators are put together a more accurate picture can be obtained of the risk of harm to the child.

7. **Mohammed:** The main category in this case would be neglect. The reason for Mohammed's non-school attendance needs to be explored because it may be that he is a young carer or working long hours in employment. He may be inappropriately caring for younger siblings and carrying too much responsibility for his age. There are

clusters of indicators of neglect in this case yet each one needs to be explored. What do 'unsuitably dressed' and 'little food in his lunch box' actually mean? Each term may indicate abuse or may have an innocent explanation. Children who bite younger children may be expressing frustration at not being heard, although sometimes biting is associated with an experience of sexual abuse. It is an indication that a child feels out of control and is an emotional response to his situation.

8. **Darren:** The relevant categories are neglect and emotional abuse with possible physical harm from contact with contaminated needles. Parents who misuse drugs can be effective parents if they are cooperating with treatment programmes. The children are at most risk of harm when the parents lifestyle is preoccupied with their drug dependency rather than the needs of the children. Children may be placed at risk from inappropriate visitors to the home as well as access to drugs and equipment. In child protection the needs of **all** children in the household must be considered. In this case it is the health visitor who is able to enter the house and alert other professionals of the risks to the children. It is always important to make sure a professional sees the condition of the home and looks at every room in the house. Parents may keep one room looking very good to impress visitors.

9. **Susan:** Sexual abuse is the correct category. It should not be assumed that a stepfather presents a high risk of abuse to a child. Any adult of any gender in a household may sexually abuse a child. This young woman must be made safe so that the case can be investigated (Section 47, CA 1989). Susan may want to keep the abuse secret but child abusers rely on children remaining silent. Adults have a duty to break this silence, to challenge the abuse and act to make the child safe. Inciting a child into sexual activity is a crime and when interviewed Susan may clarify what has happened. The interviewers (police and social worker) would not make any assumption that abuse has taken place and would know that 'playing with her' might have a range of meanings. They will listen to the child's account in a safe, neutral environment. The Sunday school teacher and the friend would be asked to provide statements which may corroborate the child's account. It is possible that sexual abuse has been continuing for some time and it will not be easy for this young person to speak about what has taken place. If Susan gains protection then other children will also gain safety because child sex abusers commonly abuse many children both within and outside their families.

10. **Richard:** Emotional abuse is difficult to prove and is usually assessed over time. Abuse takes place in all socio-economic classes. It may be damaging to leave children with many different carers. It cannot be assumed that because an adult is a professional that they will not abuse a child. It is essential to always keep an open mind to the possibility of abuse and yet test the hypothesis by thorough investigation, analysis of facts and multi-agency child protection intervention. The impact on Richard of hearing that he was unwanted would need to lead to a specialist assessment of emotional harm.

Activity 7: Record Keeping

Aim: For participants to learn how to correctly record notes of interviews, meetings and home visits to ensure compliance with requirements for civil and criminal proceedings.

Delivery: Both trainers read the role play of an initial interview with a child following a teacher's referral. Participants listen and do not take any notes. They are then asked to individually record all the details of the interaction between the professional and the child, putting themselves in the role of the professional. When the whole group has completed the task, participants are asked to work in pairs and exchange their notes. The trainer asks the group to feedback any discrepancies and adds comment.

Content: The trainer sets the scene by informing the group about the referral as follows:
   Susan Winner is aged 13 years and is in Year eight at Sanford secondary school. Julie is a newly qualified social worker. She has been asked to come to the school by the teacher Ms Hughes to speak with Susan who has shown the teacher a light cut, almost a scratch, across her left cheek and has told her that she is very unhappy at home. The scratch extends diagonally from her cheek bone to her jaw line. The teacher reported that Susan has been unusually quiet in class today, has normally good attendance and is academically achieving well.

Initial interview role play

Julie:	Hi Susan. Ms Hughes said you would like to speak with me. You've been rather quiet today. Tell me what is happening?
Susan:	Well it's not school.
Julie:	It's not school?
Susan:	No, it's my face, it hurts.
Julie:	Your face hurts? Show me where?
Susan:	It's here, can you see? (Susan points to her left cheek).
Julie:	Ms Hughes told me you were fine yesterday.
Susan:	I was 'cos it wasn't there yesterday.
Julie:	When did it happen then?
Susan:	Last night, my mum got upset with me.
Julie:	It looks quite sore. I think we should get the doctor to have a look at it. Is that OK?
Susan:	Yeah, that's alright but I don't want my mum to get into trouble, she's got a lot of problems at the moment.
Julie:	You sound a bit worried about your mum.
Susan:	I am, I don't like it when she gets upset with me. She's been getting upset with me a lot lately.
Julie:	Tell me more about what happened last night.

Susan:	I was staring at my brother and my mum went into one. Mum said I was winding him up, but I wasn't. She just 'wiped' me across the face. (Susan indicates a swipe with the back of her left hand across her face).
Julie:	Is that how it happened?
Susan:	Yeah
Julie:	Has this sort of thing happened before?
Susan:	Yeah, a couple of times
Julie:	I'm sorry to hear about that. How old is your brother?
Susan:	He's two and he can be a right pain.
Julie:	What's his name?
Susan:	Danny.
Julie:	If your mum gets annoyed with Danny what does she do?
Susan:	He doesn't get hit, she only shakes him, it's not fair. I don't want to get her into trouble, she's got a lot of problems.
Julie:	Does anyone else live in the house with you?
Susan:	Not now, my mum's boyfriend Tony was living with us but he left about a month ago.
Julie:	Is there anything else you would like to tell me?
Susan:	I don't think so.
Julie:	Is there anything you'd like to ask me?
Susan:	Yeah, what's going to happen now?
Julie:	What would you like to happen?
Susan:	I just want my mum to be nicer to us, can you talk with her?
Julie:	Yes I will speak with your mum and I understand that you are worried about her but first I will need to get a doctor to have a look at your face. Don't worry I will make sure you know what is going on at every stage. Thank you for telling me all this. It's my job to make sure you and Danny are safe. Is that OK?
Susan:	Yeah.

Feedback: Trainers ask the group the following questions and ensure the correct responses are covered.

Question: What was the first thing that you wrote?

Answer to include: Day, date, time, place. Setting the scene. Who was present?

Question: What did you write next?

Answer: The trainer emphasises the importance of recording the exact account from the child using the child's own words. It is rare for participants to use the exact word 'wiped' they will often insert their own words such as hit/beat etc. The trainer lists the numbers of substitute words recorded by the group and refers back to child's original statement of 'wiped'.

Question: What else have you included?

Answer: The importance of including all detail provided by the child which has relevance to an investigative process. This should include the following:

- Mum – what she said and did.
- Mum's boyfriend/name – relationship with mother.
- Susan's brother – name, age and what happens to him.
- Child's perspective on the situation.
- How the child presented at the interview – to include non-verbal behaviour.

Question: How will the record be concluded?

Answer: Signing, dating, timing. Stating the location of where and when the notes were written and who was present. Remember; 'if it's not written down it didn't happen'.

Presentation 5: Making Accurate Records of an Interview With a Child

Records should use clear, straightforward language, be concise and be accurate not only in fact, but also in differentiating between opinion, judgement and hypothesis.

(DfES, 2006: 5.150)

Follow these guidelines for recording a child's disclosure about child abuse:

- **Written recording during the interview.** Writing a record during an interview can be a barrier. However, it may be important to write down key phrases and words, whilst the child is talking, to trigger recall when the full recording is made.
- **Written recording immediately after the interview.** It is very important to record exactly what the child said using the child's vocabulary even if the meaning is unclear.
- **Recording your own responses.** Your verbal and non-verbal responses should be recorded and it should be clear that a non-leading approach has been used.
- **Recording the context of the disclosure.** The context in which a child chooses to tell about an incident of abuse can provide valuable information to the investigating team, e.g. the child was watching a particular video or was playing with dolls in the home corner.
- **Recording the emotional context of the disclosure.** The emotional context can provide valuable clues to the investigating team. A child may make serious statements in a joking way or may present as tearful and distressed. Children may speak about very serious matters in a matter of fact way which is unfamiliar to adults.
- **Recording repetition.** If a child repeats statements these should be recorded. Consistency in a child's repeated statements adds to the strength of the evidence.

Activity 8: The Fishbowl: A Case Study Tracking a Child Protection Referral Through Assessment, Investigation and Intervention

Aim: For participants to learn from a case study the processes of investigation and intervention to protect children. To provide an opportunity for development of skills in challenging and analysing practice.

Delivery: This case study provides an excellent opportunity for key professionals in the locality to play their own role and to respond to questions making reference to local child protection procedures. As an alternative participants can read from the script. Those reading professional roles wear labels describing their role and sit in a circle in the centre of the room – the fishbowl. Scripts are also provided to observers. Initially participants are given time to read the family composition and family history. They have a copy of the genogram. The script is read out aloud and where STOP is printed there are key issues to be discussed. Trainers should check if any participants have hearing impairment and provide them with a copy of the script.

Content

The roles are as follows:
- Narrator
- Head teacher
- Nursery teacher
- Education social worker
- Social worker
- Social work team manager
- Police officer – Child Abuse Investigation Team (CAIT)
- Police sergeant – CAIT
- Police officer – Public Protection Unit (PPU)
- Probation officer
- General practitioner
- Health visitor
- School nurse
- Paediatrician
- Child psychiatrist

Acknowledgement to Jackie Stroud, Team Manager, London Borough of Barnet Children and Families Service.

© Liz Davies and Debbie Townsend. *Joint Investigation in Child Protection.* www.russellhouse.co.uk

Handout 6a: Case Study – Tracking a Child Protection Referral

History of the Alabi and Jones families

Mrs Felicia Alabi

Felicia left Nigeria when she was aged 11 years to join her mother, a single parent, in the UK. In Nigeria she had been cared for by her maternal grandmother. She works as a night sister at the local hospital.

Mr Joseph Alabi

Joseph met Felicia and they lived in another authority. Mr Alabi misused alcohol and Ady and Carleen witnessed some violent incidents. The relationship ended when Ady was aged seven and Carleen aged 5. Mrs Alabi went to a women's refuge and was later re-housed in this area. Felicia met Frank Jones shortly after she came to this area and Lindy and Dwayne are his children.

Mr Frank Jones

Frank led an isolated life before meeting Felicia. He had been an only child and his father died when he was very young. His mother coped but often got depressed. Frank met Felicia through the local church. He works for this local authority driving a minibus for children with learning disabilities. Work is irregular and he often helps with the care of the children.

Delphine Stewart

Delphine always lived locally with her mother until she got her own flat when Marlene was a baby. Joseph Alabi moved in when Marlene was one year old. They met at the 6th Form College where he works as a librarian. He had been to the Drug and Alcohol Service and no longer misused alcohol. They are both thrilled to be having their own baby now that Delphine is five months pregnant.

Ady Alabi

Ady is critical of his father's violence towards his mother and remembers having to go into the refuge. He does however, value his relationship with his Dad who visits him alternate weekends. He likes it when his Dad takes him fishing. Delphine does not take a lot of interest in him. He is still sore about Frank Jones coming on the scene and felt pushed out when his Mum had the other children. He is close to Carleen and had tried to care for her when times were bad. He is having some problems at school and turns to his mates for support, sometimes misusing substances with them.

Carleen Alabi

Carleen attends school regularly. She feels the same as Ady that her Mum lost interest in her when the other children came along. She hates Frank Jones. She loves her Mum but does not feel she can talk with her openly although she desperately wants her attention. She visits her Dad once a fortnight. He takes her out and they generally have a good time. Delphine can be quite kind to her but sometimes gets cross. She knows Delphine is relieved when it is time for Ady and herself to go back home.

Lindy Jones

Staff at the nursery referred Lindy to the Child Psychiatrist who has seen her once. They were concerned because Lindy had a speech problem, still wets the bed and sometimes has tantrums.

Dwayne Jones

At a recent 18 month check the Health Visitor noted that Dwayne was not yet walking. She heard from a neighbour that he spent too long strapped in his buggy. She also noted him looking tired and lethargic for his age and has not yet heard him talk. His weight was shown to have crossed from the 10th to the 3rd percentile with head circumference remaining on the 10th. This gave rise to concern.

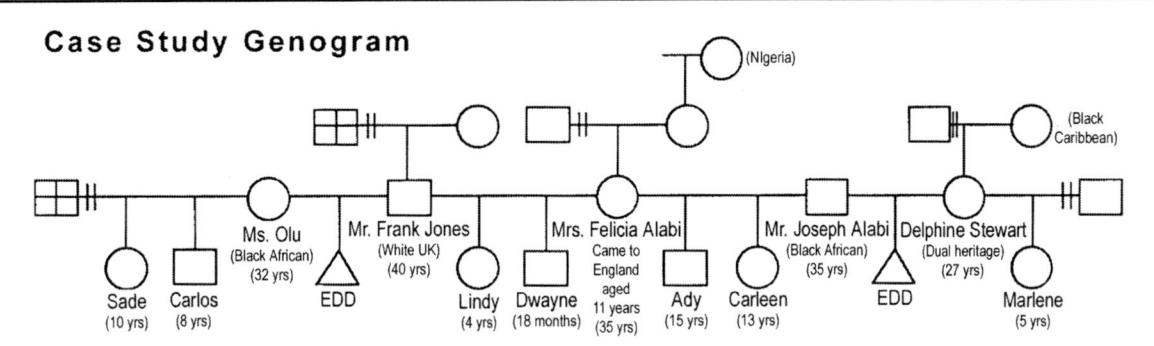

Case Study Genogram

Family Composition

First Household

Mrs Felicia Alabi
Age: 35 yrs
Ethnic origin: Black African
Occupation: Nurse

Mr Frank Jones
Age: 40 yrs
Ethnic origin: White UK
Occupation: Driver

Ady Alabi
Age: 15 yrs
Ethnic origin: Black African
Secondary School

Carleen Alabi
Age: 13 yrs
Ethnic origin: Black African
Secondary School

Lindy Jones
Age: 4 yrs
Ethnic origin: Dual heritage. Black African/
   White UK. Nursery

Dwayne Jones
Age: 18 months
Ethnic origin: Dual heritage. Black African/
   White UK

Second Household

Mr Joseph Alabi
Age: 35 yrs
Ethnic origin: Black African
Occupation: Librarian

Delphine Stewart
Age: 27 yrs
Ethnic origin: Black African
Occupation: Teacher at 6th Form College

Marlene Martin/Stewart
Age: 5 yrs
Ethnic origin: Dual heritage. Black African/
   White UK
Primary School

Third Household

Ms Olu
Age: 32 years
Ethnic origin: Black African
Mr Jones had a relationship with Ms Olu

Sade Olu
Age: 10 years
Ethnic Origin: Black African

Carlos Olu
Age: 8 years
Ethnic Origin: Black African

Handout 6b: Case Study – Tracking a Child Protection Referral

Initial referral two years ago

Head teacher

I am the Head Teacher of the local secondary school. I am also the designated teacher with key responsibility for child protection within the school.

A neighbour, mother of a pupil, told the school secretary yesterday that Carleen had run into her house crying. She said that her Dad's partner, Delphine, had accused her of stealing at the weekend. When she denied it Delphine had twisted her wrist behind her back and called her a 'lying little bitch'. The school secretary spoke to me. Carleen had a bandage on her wrist and had told a teacher it was painful.

I decided to telephone the duty social worker at children's services. I informed her that although English was not Mrs Alabi's first language there was no need for an interpreter.

Duty social worker

I was on duty when the head teacher called. The administrative team made checks and I was aware that children's services had been involved previously. I asked the head teacher to complete an inter-agency referral form. I agreed to speak to my manager, make a referral to the police Child Abuse Investigation Team (CAIT) and telephone her back.

As we had not been directly involved with the family for over a year the file had been archived. Information from the computer indicated a contact from the Education Social Worker who was concerned about Ady. He had been roaming the streets with a group of friends who were into glue sniffing. Ady was also often absent from school.

An initial assessment had been completed a year ago following a referral from a teacher as she was worried about Carleen who had asked to come into care. Carleen had been interviewed and had complained about her mother using her to babysit. Her mother worked nights.

I discussed the referral with my manager and as there was an allegation of a crime we agreed to refer to the Child Abuse Investigation Team (CAIT). I completed a referral form and faxed it to the duty desk.

CAIT duty sergeant

I was the duty sergeant on the referral desk when I received the phone call from the duty team manager. We are a specialist child protection police team and we work closely with children's services and other agencies. There is a small team in every authority and we always have a duty service to respond to referrals but also to provide advice.

Following discussion I thought that we should interview Carleen at school as Carleen had an injury and had provided a clear account of what happened. The duty manager thought we should speak to Mrs Alabi first but, given that the wrist was bandaged, it was thought that Mrs Alabi may have colluded with the person who caused the injury and may not have listened to her daughter's view.

I agreed to make some checks and to allocate the case to a member of the team. The duty team manager agreed to write up the decisions of this call as a strategy discussion which we would both sign.

Police officer CAIT

I met the social worker at the school and we interviewed Carleen. She repeated the information which had been given to the school. She said she hadn't told her mother because she didn't want to upset her father and cause problems. We discussed her options in terms of a possible court case and explained that this would involve interviewing her in a child interview suite. This would be carried out under the Achieving Best Evidence Guidance (CJS, 2007). Carleen said her wrist was painful and we agreed that she needed to see the paediatrician.

Mrs Alabi arrived at the school and initially was angry that the school had not spoken to her first and that Carleen had been spoken to without her consent. She could not understand why Carleen had not told her what had happened. She was afraid that the neighbour, who goes to her church, would spread gossip and it would be all around the neighbourhood. Carleen got very upset too and said that she wanted to stay the night with a friend. Mrs Alabi agreed to this arrangement. We discussed the need for Carleen to see the paediatrician tomorrow as it was now too late in the day. Mrs Alabi agreed to this and as she is one of the parents with parental responsibility she could provide consent.

The family were given details of the telephone numbers of the police and social worker and an emergency number to contact during the night if there were any difficulties. An interpreter was arranged for the following day because whenever English is not the first language an interpreter must be used in all child protection enquiries.

STOP

Key points for the trainer to discuss and clarify

- **The role of the designated/named teacher for safeguarding – explain**

- **The role of the named child protection doctor:** Reference can be made to secondary abuse of children by professional interventions and the importance if appropriate of the paediatrician conducting one definitive medical examination or recommending who is the correct medical expert to conduct the examination.

- **The importance of using an interpreter:** In all child protection investigations when English is not the person's first language an interpreter must be used.

- **The criteria for holding a Strategy Discussion/Meeting** (DfES, 2006: 5.55)

  - Whenever there is reasonable cause to suspect a child is suffering, or is likely to suffer significant harm, there should be a strategy discussion involving the children's services, the police and other agencies as appropriate (e.g. education and health) in particular any referring agency.
  - A strategy discussion may take place following a referral or at any other time.
  - Where a medical examination may be needed a senior doctor from the providing service should be included in the strategy discussion.

- **The purpose of a Strategy Discussion/Meeting** (DfES, 2006: 5.55) is to:

  - Share available information.
  - Decide whether Section 47 enquiries should be initiated or continued if they have already begun.
  - Plan how enquiries should be handled including the need for medical treatment and by whom.
  - Agree what action is needed immediately to safeguard the child and/or provide interim services and support.
  - Determine what information about the strategy discussion will be shared with the family unless such sharing may place a child at risk of significant harm or jeopardise police investigations into any alleged offences.

- **How children tell:** Few children disclose abuse when it happens. Children want the abuse to stop but not for their world to fall apart. It is unusual for a young person to ask to be 'taken into care'. Discuss evaluation of the child's statements.

- **Consent issues within a child protection investigation:** It should be emphasised that in this case the investigating social worker and police officer were correct to speak with Carleen without parental consent.

- **An 'Achieving Best Evidence Interview' – explain**

- **Parental responsibility – define and explain**

- **The importance of gaining the cooperation of the parent/carer thought to be non-abusive in order to gain support for the child:** Initial parent/carer responses may well be confrontational or avoidant because of fear, anger or shock. Given time and an opportunity to ask questions and gain knowledge of the child protection process, a parent/carer may be assisted in becoming supportive to the child. It is therefore important in this case to safeguard Carleen and allow the mother time to process the events. Child abuse is a contaminating subject for all concerned and the mother is afraid of the response from her local community.

- **Police checks:** This is a complex process involving checks with a number of databases. The following information is helpful to police and it is important to provide all possible permutations of names and how they are spelt:

  - Name including middle name/s and aliases
  - Address/former address
  - Telephone number/mobile phone number
  - Date of birth
  - Place of birth
  - Ethnic origin
  - Description – particularly height and distinguishing features i.e. tattoos etc.
  - Employment/previous employment
  - Car make/number
  - Method of offending

Handout 6b: Case Study Continued – Tracking a Child Protection Referral

Social worker

I had agreed the plan with my team manager yesterday so I telephoned the community paediatrician. An appointment was made for the local hospital out-patients clinic as there was probably a need for an X-ray.

Paediatrician

I saw Carleen with her mother and social worker. I took a medical history from Mrs Alabi and then examined Carleen's wrist which was noticeably swollen, discoloured and painful on movement. I sent her for an X-ray.

On her return she asked to speak with the social worker and myself on her own. She was not willing to talk about her wrist at all. She said she was very unhappy at home. She said that Mr Jones touched her in her 'private places' when her mother is out. She said this had been going on for over a year and began when her mother was in hospital having Dwayne.

She described how Mr Jones sometimes came into her bed at night and fondled her. She referred to him as Frank. It last happened two weeks ago. She said she tried to escape a year ago but couldn't manage to tell the social worker why she wanted to leave. She thought her mother suspected something but they had never spoken about it. When things got bad last week she went to her Dad's and took the money from Delphine's purse so that she could run away but she went to a friend's house.

I explained to Carleen that we would need to speak with her mother and talk to a police colleague. Carleen just wanted the abuse to stop but was worried about her sister Lindy remaining safe.

I would not consider an examination for child sexual abuse at this stage as there was insufficient evidence to suggest that this was necessary. Such an examination would be intrusive and I would always be cautious in making such a decision and would discuss it fully with my colleagues. Carleen's wrist was not broken but was a sprain and I advised Mrs Alabi to use a support bandage on it and give pain relief.

Social worker

The police officer and I spoke with Mrs Alabi and explained what Carleen had said to the paediatrician and myself. Carleen had agreed for me to do this. Mrs Alabi was shocked but said some of the account made sense to her. I contacted my team manager and outlined the disclosure and Carleen's concerns about what might happen to Lindy if she left the home. She also said that she had told Ady and that was why he stayed out so much. He was very angry with Frank Jones. She said Frank had not threatened her but somehow she knew she shouldn't tell. She thought no one would believe her. I explained that although Mrs Alabi was shocked she wanted to support her daughter. We agreed to further discuss the case with our police colleagues and to ask Frank Jones to move out of the household whilst we investigated and to organise a strategy meeting for 11.30 a.m. tomorrow.

I went home with Mrs Alabi and without giving Mr Jones any details of the disclosure I asked him to move out during the investigation. Initially he was angry and resistant but he was made aware of the legal position and as he had nowhere to stay I arranged bed and breakfast accommodation for him. My colleagues in housing made sure the accommodation did not currently have children staying there. I returned to the office and telephoned all the agencies involved with the family to invite them to the strategy meeting.

STOP

Key points for the trainer to discuss and clarify

- **The prompt for a child's disclosure may well be concern for a sibling**

- **Gender issues in interviewing Carleen**

- **What would happen if Frank had refused to move out?** Legal safeguards may be needed, e.g. Emergency Protection Order (EPO) with exclusion order attached, Police Power of Protection.

- **What are the options if Mrs Alabi refused to cooperate with the investigation?**

- **Children's services have responsibility to house an alleged perpetrator during an investigation rather than moving the child**

- **The child may think that the non abusive carer or parent knew what was happening:** Often the family are also victims of the abuse and they may be duped by the cunning of the perpetrator or experience harm themselves. There is, however, always the possibility that they were collusive in the abuse.

- **Importance of evaluating the need to interview the child without the parent or carer present**

- **Carleen speaks of 'private places' and 'coming into her bed and fondling her':** At this stage the meaning of these phrases is unclear and unknown which does not prove sexual abuse. The child's account must be gained through an Achieving Best Evidence interview and assessed for validity when collated with all other available information. Consideration should be given to a forensic medical examination based on what Carleen says in the interview. It is important to discuss implications of such an examination i.e. the who, what, when, where and how such an examination should take place.

  As a result of what Carleen says there may be a need to collect forensic evidence from the location of where the abuse took place such as clothing and bedding. The timescales for such forensic retrieval are:

  o semen 7 days in the vagina
  o semen 72 hours in the mouth or anus
  o on other items such as bedding, clothing and furniture there is no time limit even after washing.

Handout 6b – Case Study Continued – Tracking a Child Protection Referral

The following day

A strategy meeting is chaired by the team manager in children's services.

Team manager

I explained the purpose of the meeting. I asked individuals to introduce themselves and the agency they represented. I also took apologies. I then checked the family details and said how I would manage the meeting. The social worker would briefly outline the history and events leading to the meeting and then we would discuss each child individually.

Social worker

I outlined children's services previous involvement with the family. A year ago the school made a referral as Carleen had requested to go into care. An initial assessment was completed and Carleen was interviewed on her own. She had said she disliked Frank and that her mother gave all the attention to Dwayne but she didn't want any help. Support services were offered but the family declined. The Education Social Worker had made contact with children's services because Ady was roaming the streets and he and his friends were sniffing glue. Advice was given about local resources.

On Monday this week I had received the referral from the school about possible physical abuse and during the medical examination Carleen had disclosed possible sexual abuse. Mrs Alabi had cooperated with the investigation.

The paediatrician was unable to attend the meeting but had reported to me that the injury to Carleen's wrist was consistent with her account of what had happened and she also provided information about the disclosure.

Police officer CAIT

I have completed police checks and there were various records of Mr Alabi's violence towards Mrs Alabi in the past when they were married and lived in a different authority. The reports showed that the children had twice witnessed the violence. Mrs Alabi had moved into a women's refuge and was later re-housed in this authority.

There is some information about Mr Frank Jones. Thirteen years ago a bus conductor called the police when a fifteen year old girl reported that Mr Frank Jones had indecently assaulted her. When the police visited him they found pornographic magazines on the living room table and at that time he lived on his own. He denied the allegation and there was insufficient evidence to charge him.

I spoke to Mrs Alabi this morning and she has discussed the disclosure with Carleen and they wish to pursue criminal proceedings. Mrs Alabi had not been aware of the earlier investigation concerning Mr Jones.

Education social worker

Ady's school attendance has deteriorated significantly over the last year. He is having some problems at school and turns to his friends for support and sometimes abuses substances with them. Ady is critical of his father's violence towards his mother and remembers going into the refuge. He does however, value his relationship with his father and enjoys his contact at alternate weekends. He does not like Frank and felt pushed out when his mother had the other children. He has tried to support Carleen when times have been bad.

Head teacher

Carleen attends school regularly. She feels much the same as Ady that her mother lost interest when the other children came along. Over the past year she has struggled academically and has had some difficulties with peer relationships. She is not disruptive in class and has a good relationship with the Head of Year who she approached last year about coming into care.

    She visits her birth father once a fortnight. They usually get on well and enjoy various activities. She also gets on well with Delphine most of the time, although she knows Delphine is relieved when she goes back home.

Nursery teacher

Lindy attends nursery on a regular basis. I have referred her to the child psychiatrist as we had concerns about her speech, she still wets the bed and has temper tantrums. She also lacks concentration.

Health visitor

I have concerns for Dwayne. Mrs Alabi recently took him to the clinic and it was noted how much time he spent strapped in his buggy. He looked tired and lethargic and I did not hear him talk. His weight has dropped from the tenth percentile to the third. I have referred him to the paediatrician for further assessment.

Narrator

Members of the Strategy Meeting had to consider the information available to them and then decide whether or not the threshold for a Section 47 investigation had been met. Further action must be agreed where relevant and whether or not an Initial Child Protection Conference is indicated.

Decisions of the Strategy Meeting

Action	Person responsible	Timescale
Section 47 agreed	police and social worker	immediately
Carleen to be video interviewed	police and social worker	within 2 days
Paediatric examination to be considered	paediatrician/police/social worker	within 2 days
Ady to be video interviewed as possible witness	police and social worker	within a week
Core assessment	social worker	35 days
Strategy meeting to reconvene	team manager	depends on progress
No Initial Child Protection Conference at this stage	team manager	

STOP

Key points for the trainer to discuss and clarify

- **The importance of collating and evaluating prior information**

- **The importance of obtaining the sibling's view**

- **Decision-making at a Strategy Meeting:** This must include details of who is responsible for taking the action and within which timescale. In the Victoria Climbié case there were two strategy meetings that made a total of 34 decisions but there was no record of who was responsible for the actions or by when these should be completed. The consequence was that many of the decisions were not implemented leading to tragic consequences.

- **The relevance of percentile charts and of ensuring specialist health interpretation of them**

- **The decision *not* to convene a child protection conference:** This is a senior management decision. In the Victoria Climbié case a box had been ticked at a strategy meeting indicating the need for a conference. The team manager decided that the case was not child protection and the social worker did not therefore convene a conference. In fact this decision should have been made at a more senior level and in consultation with the agencies which had been party to making the original decision.

Handout 6b: Case Study Continued – Tracking a Child Protection Referral

Narrator

Carleen was interviewed at the child interview suite by the social worker and police officer. Mrs Alabi waited in a separate room. Carleen repeated the allegations against Mr Jones about sexual abuse. She gave a clear and detailed account. Ady who had agreed to be interviewed said nothing had happened to him but that he had witnessed offences by Mr Jones against Carleen. He was a very good corroborative witness. Carleen also was examined by the paediatrician and some evidence was found to support the allegations.

Mr Jones was arrested at the Bed and Breakfast accommodation and admitted nothing at the interview. He was bailed to return after six weeks and the case was presented to the Crown Prosecution service for a decision about prosecution.

The strategy meeting was reconvened and each professional gave information about the assigned tasks and there was discussion about the need for a child protection conference. As Mr Jones worked as a driver for learning disabled children a separate strategy meeting was held to consider his employment situation and to ensure other children were safeguarded. It was agreed that Mrs Alabi had cooperated throughout.

Carleen no longer had any contact with Mr Jones and the professionals considered that Mrs Alabi could protect her from harm.

The police spoke to Delphine and she admitted hurting Carleen and was remorseful. She said she had been preoccupied with her work and her own children and that she found the older two children hard work. She said she now realised the importance of contact for Ady and Carleen with their father. Delphine was given a 'warning' by the police. It was believed that this incident was unlikely to happen again.

Dwayne had begun to gain weight and it was agreed that a Child in Need plan (Section 17) could be put in place to monitor the welfare of all the children as they were no longer at risk from harm by Mr Jones.

Child in Need Plan

This is a multi-agency meeting with parents present, chaired by a senior social work practitioner and reviewed after three months.

Decisions

- The social worker would be the lead worker.
- A referral would be made immediately to the Child and Adolescent Mental Health team by the social worker for an assessment of each child's individual needs and to make recommendations for therapeutic work.
- There was a particular request for play therapy for Lindy to see if it could be established whether or not she had been sexually abused.

- The community paediatrician and health visitor would monitor, on a monthly basis, Dwayne's weight and general health.
- There would be no contact between Mr Jones with the children in view of the criminal proceedings and Mrs Alabi was advised to consider an injunction should it be necessary.
- The social worker would visit three weekly to monitor and support the family.
- Children's services would consider the use of a family support worker to assist Mrs Alabi to set boundaries and establish routines within three weeks.
- School staff would continue to monitor and support the children.
- The Education Social Worker would support Ady in returning to school full time.
- Mr Alabi agreed to have the children every weekend and Mrs Alabi welcomed this.
- A core assessment to be continued by the social worker within the timescale of 35 days.
- The Child in Need Plan would be reviewed in three months time.

Child in Need Review

This meeting was chaired by a senior practitioner from children's services. Those attending were the social worker, child psychiatrist, family support worker, nursery teacher, health visitor, head teacher and Mr and Mrs Alabi.

The purpose of the meeting was to review the Child in Need Plan. Each agency reported on their involvement and on the progress that had been made. The reports were positive and a decision was made for the social worker to withdraw from the family. The play therapist did think that Lindy may have been inappropriately touched by Mr Jones but nothing could be proven.

Police officer CAIT

The Crown Prosecution Service decided that there was sufficient evidence to pursue a criminal prosecution. During the trial Mr Jones agreed to plead guilty to two counts of indecency with a child and he received a two year prison sentence. Carleen was supported in making a claim to the Criminal Injuries Compensation Board and then we concluded our involvement.

The risk must be re-examined when the perpetrator is released from prison.

STOP

Key points for the trainer to discuss and clarify

- **The role of the Crown Prosecution Service and criteria for their decisions:** The Code of Practice is available on the following link:http://www.cps.gov.uk/ publications/ docs/code2004english.pdf

- **Section 17 (CA 1989) Child in Need protocols:** To promote the welfare of children in need.

    Duty of local authority to safeguard and promote the welfare of children in need through the provision of services if children are unlikely to achieve or maintain a reasonable standard of health and development or if health and development is likely to be significantly impaired without such services. To promote the welfare of children with disabilities.

- **Role of the lead worker**

- **Role of the family support worker**

- **The importance of supporting young people's claims to the Criminal Injuries**

- **Compensation Board. Details available on website: www.cica.gov.uk**

- **The role of the Child and Adolescent Mental Health Service in direct work but also in the provision of consultation**

The case study moves from the scenario two years ago to the present day

Handout 6b: Case Study Continued – Tracking a Child Protection Referral

Probation officer

Mr Jones is due to be released on licence. I contacted children's services to arrange a meeting about licence conditions. Mr Jones has been in contact with Mrs Alabi and said he found prison depressing and difficult. He wants to resume his relationship with her and wants to be a Dad to his children Lindy and Dwayne.

Multi-agency professional planning meeting

This meeting was chaired by the Probation Officer. Those attending were the social worker, housing officer, school and police officer from the Public Protection Unit. There were apologies from the nursery and from the Child and Adolescent Mental Health service.

The meeting was to reach agreement on any conditions deemed necessary to ensure Carleen, Ady, Lindy and Dwayne are safe and to assess any risk to the public from Mr Jones.

Probation officer

Whilst in prison Mr Jones has not fully engaged in any sex offender programme. He has stated to other prisoners that he had only admitted the offence in order to ensure a reduced sentence and has not taken responsibility for the sexual abuse. Using probation's standard format Mr Jones was assessed as at low to medium risk of future offending.

Following discussion the following decisions were made:

- The housing officer to support Mr Jones in finding appropriate housing on release from prison.
- Mr Jones to sign on the Sex Offenders Register on release from prison.
- Mr Jones to be monitored by the Public Protection Unit, Probation and the Multi-Agency Public Protection Arrangements (MAPPA).
- The social worker to ensure that children's services assess the current situation and any contact between the children and Mr Jones has to be agreed by children's services.
- Mr Jones must not have contact with Carleen or Ady.
- Mr Jones must not live in a household with a child under the age of 16 years.
- CAMHS to continue to work with the children therapeutically.

Social worker

I undertook an initial assessment and Mrs Alabi felt that she could no longer trust Mr Jones. The children missed him when he first moved out but she now felt confident in caring for the children as a single carer and did not want contact to resume. She was advised to see a solicitor. Mr Jones was also advised to seek legal advice and he did not pursue the issue of contact. As a result the case was closed to children's services.

Mr Jones was monitored by the Public Protection Unit and through the MAPPA. Towards the end of his licence period the police became aware that Mr Jones was in a relationship with a woman Ms Olu who has two children Sade aged 12 years and Carlos aged 10 years. Mr Jones has said that he planned to move in with the family when his licence expired in two weeks time.

I visited Ms Olu who although she was reluctant to meet me did accept the appointment. Mr Jones had told her about his offence but she believed that he had 'learnt his lesson' and that 'God had forgiven him'. She was convinced that he would not harm her children and she is currently four months pregnant.

I explained that children's services have concerns and that a strategy meeting will be convened. I said that I would recommend an initial child protection conference. Ms Olu was unhappy and asked me to leave the house. I completed an initial assessment and invited relevant professionals to the strategy meeting.

Narrator

Strategy meeting

This was chaired by the team manager and attended by the social worker, police officer (PPU), and head teacher. There were apologies from the school nurse, the GP, probation officer and the CAIT. CAIT no longer had a role in this case as there was no allegation of crime.

The strategy meeting followed the same format as before beginning with the reason for the meeting and to then consider the needs of each child individually. The school had no concerns about either child and their attendance was good. They achieve academically to a high standard. There were concerns about Mr Jones joining the household and it was agreed to proceed to an initial child protection conference.

STOP

Key points for the trainer to discuss and clarify

- **The role of the MAPPA and probation service** (DfES, 2006: 12.12)

Handout 6b: Case Study Continued – Tracking a Child Protection Referral

Narrator

Initial Child Protection Conference

This conference was chaired by an Independent Reviewing Officer. Attending the conference were the social worker, police officer (PPU) team manager, police officer CAIT, head teacher, school nurse, probation officer, Ms Olu and Mr Jones. Apologies were received from the GP who sent a report.

The social worker had written a core assessment and shared it with the family prior to the conference which had to be held within 15 days of the decision made at the strategy meeting.

Both carers met with the chairperson prior to the meeting and were advised about who would be attending and how the conference would be organised. They were also told about expected behaviour and the complaints procedure.

Whilst the chairperson met with the carers, the other professionals read the core assessment and after introductions the social worker summarised the report. Professionals and the carers were able to ask questions and seek clarification. Both the police officers and the probation officer outlined their involvement in the case. The meeting then focused on each child with contributions from health and education. Each agency had to submit a written report.

The chairperson summarised the information received and asked the professionals to reach a decision about whether or not the children should be the subject of child protection plans and if so under which categories of abuse.

Decisions

- Sade was to be the subject of a child protection plan under the category of sexual abuse as it was agreed that she was likely to suffer sexual abuse.
- Carlos did not require a child protection plan as there was no evidence to suggest that he would be at risk of sexual abuse.
- It was not recommended that the unborn baby would need to have a child protection plan at birth. Such a decision could be made at a later date.
- An outline protection plan was agreed.
- The duty social worker would remain the key worker until the case transferred to a long term team.
- The core group would meet within 10 days and would include the carers, social worker, head teacher, school nurse and police officer (PPU).
- The decisions were framed under the headings of the five outcomes as defined in *Every Child Matters* (DfES, 2003) and shown below.

Being Healthy. The school nurse would undertake health checks with mother's consent every three months.

Staying Safe

- The social worker would visit announced and unannounced at least every two weeks.
- The social worker would undertake work with both children about keeping safe. This should begin immediately.
- Mr Jones was to be risk assessed by a specialist Sex Offender Unit which would report to the next review.
- Ms Olu's ability to protect the children would be assessed by the Sex Offender Unit which would report to the next review.
- The PPU would continue to monitor Mr Jones and report to the MAPPA monthly.

Enjoying and Achieving. The school staff to monitor the children and alert the social worker immediately of any concerns

Making a positive contribution. Not applicable

Achieving economic wellbeing. Not applicable

Three months later Child Protection Review Conference

The review was chaired by an Independent Reviewing Officer. Attending the review were the social worker, team manager, Police officer (PPU), Police liaison officer (CAIT), head teacher, school nurse, probation officer from the Sex Offender Unit and Ms Olu. Mr Jones sent his apologies.

Social worker

I have written a review conference report. Ms Olu has been resistant and angry about the decision for Sade to need a child protection plan and feels that children's services have victimised Mr Jones for the one mistake he has made in his life. It has been difficult to engage with Sade and Carlos as they feel that by speaking to a social worker they are being disloyal to their mother. Mr Jones thinks that I am placing undue pressure on him. He says that he has made one mistake and has been to prison for it. He says he is not like other child sex abusers. Mr Jones and Ms Olu have however accepted the referral to the specialist Sex Offender Unit.

Police officer PPU

I have continued to monitor Mr Jones who thinks that I victimise him. He has been unclear as to his current employment but on the most recent visit he agreed to provide me with the details.

Police officer CAIT

Nothing to report.

Head teacher

Sade continues to attend on a regular basis and academically is making good progress. She has been quiet lately and fell out with her best friend although they have become friends again. Carlos attends well and is also making good academic progress but he is beginning to veer towards children with difficult behaviour.

School nurse

I met with Sade and her weight is of a little concern. She tells me she does eat well and did agree to meet with me again. Ms Olu agreed to monitor her at home. There are no concerns about Carlos.

Probation officer: Sex Offender Unit

I have not begun my assessment but the referral has been accepted and appointments have been arranged for Ms Olu and Mr Jones. We realise that Ms Olu is heavily pregnant and we will make sure the assessment is completed within six weeks.

Narrator

Ms Olu was not pleased with the social worker's report and did comment on all the agency reports. The chairperson summarised the information and asked each professional for a view about whether Sade still needed to be the subject of a child protection plan.

The key worker was to remain the allocated social worker. The core group consisted of Ms Olu, Mr Jones, social worker, school nurse and the police officer PPU. This group would meet every two months prior to the next conference in six months time.

Again using the headings of the five outcomes as defined in *Every Child Matters* the decisions were:

> **Being healthy.** Sade's weight to be monitored monthly by the school nurse.
> **Staying safe.**
>
> - Social worker to visit every two weeks.
> - Social worker to ensure appropriate plans are in place whilst Ms Olu gives birth to ensure Sade and Carlos are not in the sole care of Mr Jones. The outcome of the risk assessment of Mr Jones and Ms Olu's ability to protect to be shared with the social worker as soon as possible. This risk assessment to include whether or not Mr Jones poses a risk to Carlos.
> - A strategy meeting to be convened with regard to the unborn baby.
> - Mr Jones to provide details of his employment to the Police Officer (PPU) within two days.

© Liz Davies and Debbie Townsend. *Joint Investigation in Child Protection.* www.russellhouse.co.uk

- Mr Jones and Ms Olu were informed that young people must not visit the address without prior agreement from the social worker.
- The carers were informed that if they failed to comply with the protection plan then legal advice would be sought immediately.
- The named midwife for safeguarding to be informed by the social worker of concerns about Mr Jones so that safeguards may be put in place when the baby is born.

Enjoying and achieving. School staff to continue to monitor and alert the social worker to any concerns.

Sade and Carlos to be offered the school counselling service.

Making a positive contribution. Not applicable

Achieving economic wellbeing. Not applicable

During the six months, Ms Olu gave birth to a daughter Fola. The specialist assessment concluded that Mr Jones was medium to high risk of re-offending and Ms Olu was not able to offer adequate protection to her children. It was not thought that Carlos was at risk of sexual abuse from Mr Jones. Ms Olu was advised that Mr Jones would need to leave the household or the Local Authority would initiate care proceedings in order to remove all three children from her care. She was very distressed but did agree that he should leave the household.

An agreement was drawn up between Ms Olu and Mr Jones about supervised contact with Fola. A strategy meeting was held concerning Fola and it was agreed that an initial child protection conference would be convened to consider whether or not she needed to be the subject of a child protection plan and under which category.

Six months later Review Child Protection Conference

This conference was chaired by an Independent Reviewing Officer and in attendance were the social worker, team manager, police officer (PPU), head teacher, school nurse and Ms Olu. Apologies were received from the GP, police officer (CAIT) and probation officer (SOU).

Social worker

I have completed my review report and all agencies have received a copy. I summarised the information.

Police officer PPU

Mr Jones has now moved to a single bedroom flat and continues to feel victimised. He is resistant to joining the treatment programme recommended by the specialist assessment and he believes that as Fola is his baby he should be given unsupervised contact with her.

Head teacher

There are no concerns about Sade. She seems more confident now since Mr Jones moved out of the house. Carlos's behaviour has continued to deteriorate and he is still drawn towards young people who have difficulties. He is also becoming defiant towards his mother.

School nurse

I have no concerns about Carlos and Sade has begun to gain weight.

The decision was made that Sade and Fola still needed child protection plans and the plans for both were similar. Both the police officers from PPU and CAIT will make unannounced visits to the home address to ensure that Mr Jones has not returned. If this did happen then children's services would convene a legal planning meeting to consider legal action to protect the children from harm.

STOP

Key points for the trainer to discuss and clarify

- **Assessing risk posed by a child sex abuser**
- **Assessing the non abusive parent's capacity to be a proactive protector**
- **Strategies to protect the children**
- **The Child Protection Conference – purpose and protocol and review process** (DfES, 2006: 5.80–5.132)
- **Legal Planning Meetings**

NOTE

At this stage participants usually focus on the perpetrator and the children become forgotten. The trainer must refocus the debate back onto the key point about whether or not the children in this scenario have gained safety from significant harm.

Child Protection, Assessment, Investigation and Intervention Continued

Presentation 6: The Child Protection Conference

The purpose of a child protection conference is:

- To bring together and analyse in an inter-agency setting the information which has been obtained about the child's health, development and functioning, and the parent's or carer's capacity to ensure the child's safety and promote the child's health and development.
- To make judgements about the likelihood of a child suffering significant harm in future.
- To decide that future action is needed to safeguard the child and promote his or her welfare, how that action will be taken forward and with what intended outcomes.

(DfES, 2006: 5.80)

Making the decision as to whether the child needs to be the subject of a child protection plan

Is the child at continuing risk of harm?

- The child can be shown to have suffered ill-treatment or impairment of health or development as a result of physical, emotional or sexual abuse or neglect and professional judgement is that future ill-treatment or impairment is likely.
- Professional judgement substantiated by the findings of enquiries in this individual case or research evidence is that the child is likely to suffer ill-treatment or the impairment of health or development as a result of physical, emotional, or sexual abuse or neglect.

(DfES, 2006: 5.94)

The objectives of the child protection plan are to:

- Identify risks of significant harm to the child and ways in which the child can be protected through an inter-agency plan based on assessment findings.
- Establish short and long term aims and objectives that are clearly linked to reducing the risk of harm to the child and promoting the child's welfare.

- Be clear about who will have responsibility for what actions – including action by family members – within what specified timescales.
- Outline ways of monitoring and evaluating the progress of the plan.

(DfES, 2006:5.100)

The core group

- All members are jointly responsible for the formulation and implementation of the child protection plan as a detailed working tool refining the plan as needed and monitoring progress against specified objectives as defined at the initial child protection conference.
- Membership:
  - key worker – takes the lead
  - child – and if appropriate, the family
  - professionals and foster carers with direct contact with the family
- First meeting within 10 days of the conference.
- Record of meeting to include record of agreed action.

(DfES, 2006: 5.110–5.113)

The key worker

- Is responsible for making sure that the outline protection plan is developed into a more detailed inter-agency plan.
- Should complete the core assessment of the child and family securing contributions from the core group members and others as necessary.
- Is also responsible for acting as the lead worker for the inter-agency work with the child and family.
- Should co-ordinate the contribution of family members and other agencies to planning the actions which need to be taken, putting the child protection plan into effect and reviewing progress against the objectives set out in the plan.

(DfES, 2006: 5.107–5.109)

Activity 9a: Child Protection Conference – Role Play

Aim: For participants to gain an understanding of the complexities of decision making at a child protection conference and to gain an awareness of the pitfalls that may distract from the task of providing the child with protection.

Delivery: Participants are handed roles and labels and given a few minutes to sit at a central table and read quietly. The social worker and lawyer should sit next to the chairperson and the parents and their friend the other side of the chairperson. The health visitor and nurse manager should sit together as should the head teacher and the nursery teacher. Each is given a copy of the social work report and it is explained that this is not as full as such a report would normally be because this is a training exercise. They are also informed of the process. Participants are informed that they can act their part but should not alter the facts which are designed to fit together for the purpose of learning.

Observers must sit outside the conference. Two observers are asked to consider the views of children, Amy and Caroline. At the end they feedback whether or not they thought the children's best interests were served by the conference and how they experienced the process through the eyes of the child. The trainers let the conference take its course and do not interject. Participants will learn from their mistakes.

It makes good sense to appoint someone as a chairperson who has some experience of the conference process. Trainers can write notes to the chairperson to assist the process if necessary. The conference progresses until decisions are made about the children's need for a protection plan and under which abuse category. Participants will need to refer to the categories of abuse outlined in *Working Together* (DfES, 2006: 1.30–1.33). The conference does not continue into devising the protection plan. The outcome of this conference should be to provide child protection planning for Amy but not necessarily for Caroline as this will depend on the outcome of the discussion during the role play.

The trainers explain that if the role play summaries have sentences in italics these are advisory notes. It is important that participants do not just read out the summary but base their presentations on the content.

Trainers prepare in advance:

- A photograph of a thriving four-year-old girl in a ballet dress which is given to the mother to show to the conference as 'proof' of her daughter's wellbeing.
- A simple child's drawing of a child sitting on the swings crying under a rain cloud whilst her school friends play happily in the sunshine is given to the nursery teacher. She will present this as evidence of Amy's unhappiness.
- Percentile charts to be presented by the health visitor.

Trainers brief the paediatric rheumatologist that they must state the medical jargon as printed. At the end of the role play each person is asked to state their first name and to say that they are not the person who they were playing in role. Participants should then leave the conference table and return to their seats as before, where discussion and feedback will take place. Please note that Mr Prior's previous family history has not been added to the genogram because this is information presented during the conference and it is important to note how participants assess the relevance of this information.

List of roles for allocation: Those asterisked are essential. If the numbers are too small some professionals could present the other's reports:

Independent Reviewing Officer/ Chairperson*	Christine Okubenego
Minute taker	Evelyn Lloyd
Social worker*	Gillian Beck
Paediatric rheumatologist*	Dr Joan Atkinson
General practitioner*	Dr Gupta
Mother*	Marilyn Linden
Stepfather*	Larry Prior
Nursery teacher*	Mrs Matthews
Head teacher*	Mrs Clarke
Health visitor*	Fumi Chung
Police CAIT*	Lucy James
Family friend*	Vanessa Creighton
Team manager	James Firth
Housing manager*	Neville McKay
Solicitor	Neena Patel
Child psychiatrist*	Dr Katherine Michaels
Probation officer*	Martin Donaghue
Named safeguarding nurse	Wendy Richards
Child: Amy	Observer role
Child: Caroline	Observer role

Conference process

- Introduction by Chair.
- Introductions – name and role.
- Presentation of social work report.
- Sharing of information related to referral.
- Chair summarises facts and key points.
- Discussion and decision about whether children need to be the subject of a child protection plan and under which abuse categories.

Handout 7: Child Protection Conference

Social Work Report

By Gillian Beck social worker in the Referral and Assessment Team

Family Composition

Mrs Marilyn Linden	mother	age 34yrs	White UK
Mr Larry Prior	stepfather	age 40yrs	White UK
Caroline Linden	daughter	age 12yrs	Dual heritage White UK/Irish
Amy Linden	daughter	age 4yrs	Dual heritage White UK/Irish
Gwen Prior	mother of Mr Prior	age 76yrs	White UK

Schools

Caroline: Secondary School
Amy: Primary School

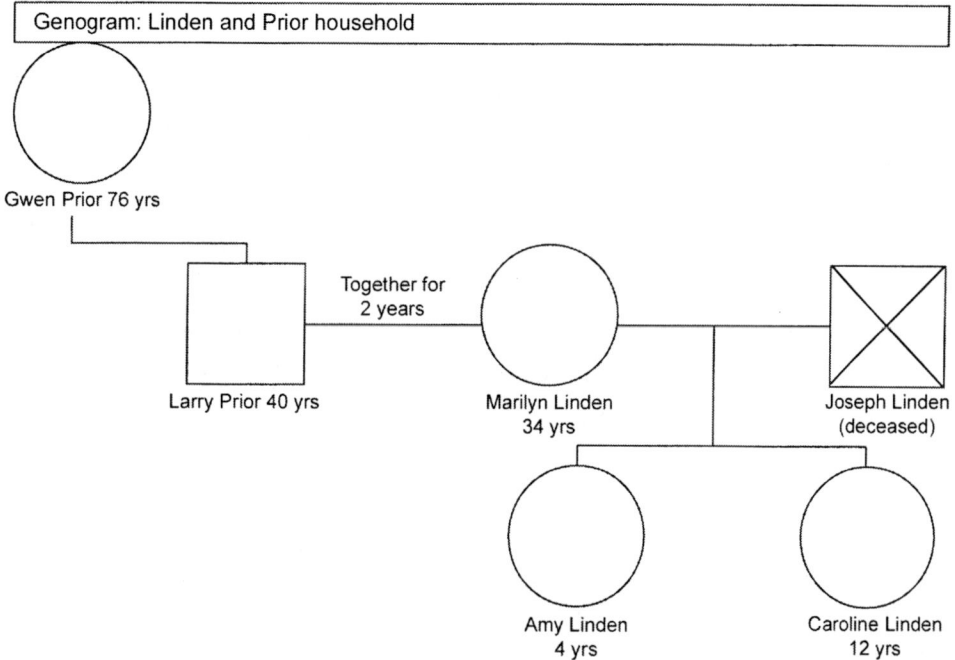

Genogram: Linden and Prior household

Last week Mrs Clarke, Head teacher of the Primary School, rang children's services to report that Amy was in severe pain. She has juvenile rheumatoid arthritis and Mrs Clarke had noticed that she seemed worse. Her parents seem to insist on alternative remedies for the condition against medical advice.

An initial assessment was completed and the mother, stepfather and both children were interviewed individually. The relevant checks were made and agencies contacted.

James Firth, team manager, decided that it was important to convene a child protection conference to ensure full sharing of information across agencies.

Children's services recommend that the child should be the subject of a child protection plan under the category of neglect because the family are not complying with medical advice and not administering the required medication, therefore the child is suffering significant harm.

Roles

Independent Reviewing Officer and Chairperson: Christine Okubenego

You are the chairperson of this conference. You are independently appointed and do not line-manage anyone at the conference.

You begin as follows:

> *This is a child protection conference concerning Amy Linden aged 4 years and Caroline Linden aged 12 years convened under the Local Safeguarding Children Board Child Protection Procedures to consider whether or not Amy and Caroline need to be the subject of a child protection plan.*
>
> *Everything we discuss here is confidential and must not go outside this conference unless to other members of your own agency and even then, on a strictly 'need to know' basis.*
>
> *I also ask you to be aware of the Equal Opportunities Policy and the importance of showing respect for each other.*
>
> *We will begin with introductions. Please say your full name, your role and the reason why you are here today. Then we will take information about the recent referral from the social worker's report.*
>
> *I am Christine Okubenego and I will be chairing this conference.*

Indicate to the next person to begin the introductions.

You then proceed. You begin with the social worker presenting her report. You then need to continue with each person who has information about the reason for the conference. You continue with information from people who have historical knowledge of the family. The mother and stepfather's views must be obtained throughout. The friend should not be allowed to interrupt too much.

After collecting the facts and views you will summarise the key aspects for the benefit of the conference.

There will then be a discussion about the decision to make the children the subject of a child protection plan.

The decision is NOT a vote. You make the final decision after allowing full debate and gaining everyone's views.

Minute taker: Evelyn Lloyd

You make a record of this conference asking for clarification should you need it.

You do not need to write down every word that is said but make a record that will be useful for all the participants.

It is particularly important that you record clearly the decisions about categories and the need for a child protection plan. You do not participate in the discussion.

Social worker: Gillian Beck

You are a social worker with just one year of experience in this post. You speak to your report.

You add that the family belong to a spiritual healing group and are very committed to their views on alternative healing. You have found talking to them about this quite inspiring. Mrs Linden does take Amy regularly to the naturopath Dr Malachy who seems to be very good with Amy.

You found Mrs Linden very open with you and welcoming of your visit. She gave you Dr Malachy's number and you have spoken to him. He is willing to be helpful to the conference. You have asked him for a report. He had much praise for Mrs Linden's care of Amy. Her percentiles are 25 per cent weight and 15 per cent height.

You know Mrs Linden has strong views about the hospital doctors but after all it is your view that everyone has a right to some freedom of choice in treatment issues.

You interviewed Mr Prior and he seemed very supportive to Mrs Linden. His mother also lives with the family and he spoke warmly of her.

You observed Amy at school and saw that she has mobility difficulties. You think she needs more help and you have asked the occupational therapist to advise. Amy didn't want to speak with you even though you did try. The teacher showed you some drawings she had been worried about. Amy was well dressed, clean and looked about the right weight for her age. You think the school may be exaggerating the problems.

The home was beautifully kept and there was evidence of many toys and play things and a lovely garden full of slides and swings.

You spoke to Caroline at home. She was a bit loud and stroppy which you thought typical of a 12 year old. Caroline has a favourite band and she was hooked up to her walkman most of the time. You asked her about Amy and she said, 'Mum sees to **her**' You asked if she helped her Mum and she said, 'No, **she** won't let me do anything. I wouldn't want to anyway she is such a winge.'

Caroline's teacher said she had referred her to the Child and Adolescent Mental Health Service (CAMHS) for an assessment because of learning problems. It was thought she wasn't achieving her potential.

Paediatric rheumatologist: Dr Joan Atkinson

You present the following information to the conference:

You have known Amy since she was two when this condition came to light.

As soon as she was walking stiffness was observed and Mrs Linden has always been alert to the problems. You say that they will all know that Amy has pauciartucular (*pronounced PAW see are tick you lar*) juvenile rheumatoid arthritis. This affects mainly girls and shows swelling and inflammation in the knees and other joints. She has an anti-nuclear antibody in her blood called ANA. It is an autoimmune disorder and can lead to the eye disease uveitis. Her joints are growing at different rates leading to instability and mobility difficulties. She requires growth hormones to rectify this.

She needs blood tests regularly to test for erythrocyte sedimentation rate (ESR). In JRA cases this can be an elevated rate which shows that the body is inflamed.

She needs X-rays to examine the cartilage damage.

Your aim is to reduce swelling of the joints to improve quality of life. You want to do this by non-steroidal anti-inflammatory drugs such as Ibuprofen but also her condition requires DMARDS, disease modifying anti-rheumatoid drugs. You want to prescribe Methotrexate as a matter of urgency. If this is not applied then she could be blind within five years. Methotrexate will slow down the progression of the disease and mitigate against the blindness possibility.

You also know that Amy attends hospital regularly for physiotherapy and hydrotherapy. The reports have been given to you for this conference.

The physiotherapist says she can't continue treating Amy because of the high level of pain she is experiencing without the Ibuprofen being administered.

The hydrotherapist says that Amy is brought every week without fail but she has noticed a deterioration in her condition and that she now presents as an unhappy child.

You sum up that you think it is in Amy's best interests to:

- have Ibuprofen prescribed and Methotrexate
- have regular blood and X-ray monitoring
- have physio and hydrotherapy
- have growth hormones

Your attitude to the mother is rather dismissive during the conference. You are actually quite angry that she is not listening to your expertise about what you believe is harming the child. You want legal action to impose the medical regime.

You wait to be asked for clarification of these complex terms.

Uveitis = inflammation of the inner eye. The condition continues into adulthood.

ESR = how quickly blood cells fall to the bottom of a test tube.

You can also add in discussion that you have consulted widely with other paediatric specialists e.g. at Great Ormond Street who support your proposals.

After the police speak about Mr Malachy you can add that you have also heard that he may be disreputable. There has been some debate in the journal *Complementary Medicine*.

General practitioner: Dr Gupta

You have known the family for five years and have all the previous notes. You have admiration for the family in this case. You obviously respect Dr Atkinson's specialist view but the family cannot be criticised for their level of care. There is no way that this constitutes neglect. It is your view that these are intelligent parents who believe in alternative treatments. Marilyn's whole life focuses on the care of Amy. She is totally devoted. Sometimes you worry more about Caroline who has to take a back seat, but that can't be helped of course. Marilyn had a terrible time when her husband died very suddenly in a car crash. You supported her at this time.

You have prescribed the occasional anti-inflammatories for Amy but you cannot say whether they have been given to her. You have been worried of late at the acceleration of her illness. You asked for a second paediatric opinion from Dr Marriot at Edinburgh University Hospital. He reviewed all the paperwork only a month ago and came to the same conclusions as Dr Atkinson, who after all is recognised as at the top of her specialism.

The physiotherapist recommended you provide some splints for Amy, which you have done, but you are not sure they are often used.

You have asked a Home Start voluntary worker to visit to give Mrs Linden some support in the home. You thought that might take some pressure off the family. You believe she visited for the first time two weeks ago but you haven't had any feedback as yet.

Mother: Mrs Marilyn Linden

You have studied everything about this condition; you were a dental nurse after all! Amy does have flare-ups and remissions and currently she is in a little flare-up. This is bound to happen. But these flare-ups are few and far between and it doesn't mean she is getting worse. You are quite diligent in applying the physical therapies. You know they maintain muscle tone and preserve joint movement. She follows a daily exercise programme. You go into school every day, morning and afternoon, to do this. You are following all the physiotherapists instructions.

As the social worker said, you also take her to the naturopath who is Dr Malachy. He has told you of the severe side effects of the medical drugs. Liver damage is well recorded as a side effect from Methotrexate. You ask the meeting:

'Would you want your daughter to get that side effect?'

'Oh no the doctor doesn't tell you about the side effects!'

'These big pharmaceutical companies rely on doctors, like her, pushing their harmful products on the innocent.'

Dr Malachy advises a non-dairy diet with lots of ginger, pineapple and tumeric.

Amy also takes Omega 3 and fatty acids through eating lots of nuts and seeds.

You advise this conference to look at some of the websites and learn for themselves that what you are saying is true. You say that the doctor hasn't explained that this autoimmune condition leads us to attack our own synovium (*only explain if asked i.e. material which lines the joints*). The symptoms are worse in the morning when you give her your best attention and run a warm bath full of aromatic oils. The doctor also hasn't mentioned that Amy gets fevers which come and go and you nurse her through all this and much more!!

You can add:

You see a change in her spiritual demeanour. You say that what matters is her holistic care. Amy isn't more unhappy. The day the hydrotherapist saw her she had a tummy ache. She gets ordinary things, good and bad days like any other child. She sometimes dances to ballet music which she loves. You have a photo of her which was taken only last week. You pass the photograph of Amy in her ballet dress around the room.

Stepfather: Larry Prior

You really don't see why the school had to report this to children's services. You reprimand the nursery nurse for being so foolish.

You say that you and Marilyn have been together two years and you've seen the family photos showing that Amy is getting better than when she was first diagnosed.

Marilyn is the most caring mother anyone could find. She works day and night for this child. How can anyone suggest she neglects her? Your mother had very bad arthritis. She lives with you. She followed the alternative route and was completely cured. Your friend Vanessa here can speak about that. You have seen the flare-ups but they don't last long. You help all you can. You spend time also with Caroline and try and help her with her homework and things her mum hasn't time for like shopping for clothes. You have also made sure the family get all the disability benefits.

You do take Amy swimming as she loves to splash around. You take Caroline too. It gives Mum a break. You are a medical librarian so you have looked up all the facts on this. Marilyn is doing everything she can and more.

You were the subject of a Community Service Order for a minor drug offence some years ago and saw a probation officer.

You also had a previous family and have two children who are now teenagers.

Nursery teacher: Mrs Matthews

Amy is a lovely girl. But now she is looking frail. She can't participate much in lessons as her joints are so stiff. She seems much less mobile than usual. Also one of her little friends said she saw her crying in the toilets. It is obvious she wants to do so much as she is a very bright child, but her body won't let her.

She did a drawing the other day – here it is . . . (you pass round the drawing of Amy on the swings crying, separate from her friends).

Her mother does come in every day to do the exercises but they cause Amy such pain she cries.

The other children in the class find it distressing hearing Amy cry.

You then begin to be a bit tearful and say, 'sorry but this really upsets me . . .'

Head teacher: Mrs Clarke

You have made a point of checking up on this with Mrs Matthews as this case has been bothering you. These are the reasons why you referred the case to children's services:

- Amy is obviously in pain and the parents won't give her the required medication.
- Amy is an intelligent little girl not fulfilling her educational potential and children's services are colluding with that if they let this carry on.
- The case must go to court if the mother won't agree to the doctor's orders.
- You see her every day in school and you know what she suffers. You won't let this carry on. You have spoken to your own lawyers who said the Children Act can be used. You want it used immediately.

You can tell everyone that Amy would be close to the top of the class if she had proper treatment. It breaks your heart to see her not able to go on the school outing or join in many of the games classes. This isn't an isolated flare-up as Mrs Linden would have you believe. You and the school staff see it all the time.

The school nurse has sent a brief report which you present verbally (Amy is still under the care of the health visitor). It says that Amy is small for her age and shows slow growth. She does eat well and the nurse sees her every two weeks. She thinks Amy needs more equipment in school and wants the Occupational Therapist to reassess.

You think children's services are being too considerate to the mother's needs and not understanding the daughter's situation.

Health visitor: Fumi Chung

You work at Dr Gupta's surgery and have known the family since Amy's birth.

You have obtained all the files. Amy was a wanted child but her birth followed the terrible tragedy of Mr Linden's sudden death in a car crash. Marilyn was devastated.

She was quite depressed after the birth but tried to pull through. She was on anti-depressants for some time. It took her a long time to reduce her dependency on them. To her credit, with the doctor's help, she did manage this. She wasn't able to breastfeed as she was still in trauma. It was a double blow when Amy was diagnosed with JRA. Mrs Linden does get depressed sometimes but wouldn't anyone who has to be on the go all the time to care for Amy? Amy was born by Caesarian section as there were some complications at the birth. The midwives noticed that Mrs Linden was initially reluctant to hold the baby.

You have visited Marilyn every month, since Amy was diagnosed, to offer support. You are worried about Marilyn because, although she seems very settled with Larry, they never get a break and you have tried to organise some respite care but they will never accept this. The only help that was acceptable was when you organised a play scheme for Caroline. Marilyn is so independent and is getting a lot of help from Dr Malachy so you don't think you can do much more. You keep a record of all the appointments Marilyn takes Amy to and you also keep an eye on the outcomes reported by the other therapists at the hospital. You are quite thorough as a worker but glad to let Marilyn do things her own way and let you become less involved.

Police Child Abuse Investigation Team officer: PC Lucy James

You wonder what is known about Dr Malachy.

You have obtained a newspaper report stating that he was struck off from the Register of Osteopaths and Chiropractors. There also seems to have been some questioning of his new age methods. He seems to charge a lot of money for his services. He may mean well but you think some clarification of his authenticity is needed.

You take a strong line on this as you are worried about the exploitation of the family by this man who you think might well be unqualified for the work he is doing. You intend to find out more about his activities. You have done the usual police checks on both carers and nothing relevant has emerged. However, there was one report of a domestic incident two months ago. Police were called by neighbours after hearing the older girl shouting that no one listened to her and she ran down the street saying she was leaving home.

Mr Prior did have a caution for a drug offence but you don't think this needs to be shared today.

Family friend: Vanessa Creighton

You have a tendency to interrupt.

You live next door. You have known Marilyn and Larry since you moved in, two years ago. It is hard having a disabled child, which you know a lot about because your sister is disabled. You say that Marilyn and Larry do everything they can. Amy isn't an easy child. She can be very moany and would drive anyone mad! She is also heavy to lift when she can't get up the stairs. You say that quite often you are called in to help.

Caroline can be a handful too. She can be very demanding and shouts a lot.

Still they are a lovely family. You get together with them with your little boy to watch television sometimes.

You are a trainee lawyer and you tell the conference that the social worker can't take Amy away without firm evidence of abuse and you consider they haven't got any evidence.

You know Mrs Prior who you say is the living proof that the alternative methods work.

Team manager children's services: James Firth

You are concerned because the named doctor for safeguarding rang you to say that Mrs Linden is negatively influencing other parents at the hospital clinics. She gives out leaflets for Dr Malachy's clinic and tells them to take their children off the medication because she says it damages their health. One parent has apparently already taken her child off the hospital books. You may need a separate professionals meeting to consider the wider implications of this.

You think this case is primarily a health matter and you require clarity from the medical professionals present as to the exact nature of the risk to Amy.

You can't see what effect a legal order would have at the moment. It would only antagonise the parents who you want to work with in a positive way. You would like time to gain their full cooperation.

Housing manager: Neville McKay

You have been asked by Mr Prior to re-house his mother because Marilyn is finding it too stressful having her in the house. Mr Prior hadn't told Marilyn about making this request but you feel that you should report it to the meeting.

The family have quite a lot of housing points because of Amy's disability and you quite probably could re-house Mrs Prior within six months. You have spoken to her and she has told you that she is worried about Caroline and she even asked if Caroline could be moved out with her which, in your opinion, seemed very peculiar.

Mrs Prior is a lively lady with her own circle of friends and an active life. She sometimes takes Caroline to the theatre or to local poetry and music group meetings.

Solicitor: Neena Patel

You provide legal advice to the conference. This means being aware of the criteria for making decisions about children being the subject of a child protection plan as outlined in *Working Together* (DfES, 2006: 5.94). You will need to read out the criteria and the categories being considered (as relevant) (DfES, 2006: 1.30–3).

You do not take part in the discussion about registration other than to advise on the above.

Child psychiatrist: Dr Katherine Michaels

You think that Caroline is at risk. Her school has referred her to your Child and Adolescent Mental Health Service for an assessment. Her behaviour at school has been showing lack of concentration and you think she may be being emotionally abused. From what you have heard you offer your expert opinion. Caroline has experienced the death of her father and must have her own needs. She also has a disabled sibling. Who is there to listen to Caroline and how she is feeling? You ask Mrs Linden about Caroline's schooling and if she attends open evenings and school plays. You happen to know that no-one came to see Caroline when she was playing in the orchestra. Mrs Prior has got her interested in music of all kinds.

The school says Caroline is fond of Mrs Prior and she plays for her the latest tracks and likes hearing Mrs Prior's classical collection.

You ask Mr Prior if Caroline talks to him about how she feels.

You recommend the whole family attend your clinic for family therapy and that Caroline and Amy be seen individually. This will allow a thorough specialist assessment to be completed.

You offer a professional opinion about Amy. You think her emotional state needs closely monitoring and recording over time to compare with the mother's view.

You suggest that this systematic collection of data is the only way to establish what is really happening. You ask Dr Atkinson to do the same with the physical symptoms. You want the joint swelling to be closely measured regularly to give professionals the facts about flare-ups or remission patterns. It is your opinion that there has been way too much speculation in this conference! The paediatrician should coordinate weekly reports from all professionals involved.

Probation officer: Martin Donaghue

Mr Prior was once given a short Community Service Order for a drugs offence. He co-operated well with the requirements of the order. He then had a previous family and his wife left him because she said he had a serious drug habit though this was never proven. As far as your records show his wife has two children who would be now aged

14 and 16 years. When the Order finished it was your understanding that he remained on the counselling scheme. You do not think he has told his new partner anything about this. The family lived in another authority then and as far as you know that local authority children's services have all the information. You didn't know him well as you were not the supervising officer at the time.

(Only if asked, you elaborate that this community service order was for cannabis possession.)

Named safeguarding nurse: Wendy Richards

You manage the health visitor and liaise with the other health professionals. You made sure that all relevant information was available to this meeting from the community health service. You know that Amy and Caroline did not have any vaccinations because of the mother's beliefs. You offer comment on what you have heard and you think your health visitor should be being more proactive and you are a bit fed up that Fumi Chung places so much trust in Dr Malachy. Now your suspicions are confirmed as information is revealed throughout the conference about him. You have heard from another parent that he is trying out some new remedies on her children.

Amy

You will listen carefully throughout the conference and consider what you as a child might think about it. Have the group properly represented your views and your best interests?

You will make notes and prepare to address the conference at the very end speaking in the first person as the child.

Caroline

You will listen carefully throughout the conference and consider what you as a child might think about it. Have the group properly represented your views and your best interests?

You will make notes and prepare to address the conference at the very end speaking in the first person as the child.

Feedback

First the two observers as Amy and Caroline need to feedback. Trainers then ask participants to identify information about actual or likely significant harm covering the keypoints as follows:

Amy

- She is in constant pain and she may go blind within five years (reports from head teacher, hydrotherapist, physiotherapist, paediatrician and nurse).
- She suffers flare-ups (report from paediatrician and other specialists).

- She does not use the splints or anti-inflammatories or recommended medication (reports by GP and paediatrician).
- She has poor educational development (reports from school and child psychiatrist).
- She has slow growth patterns (reports from health visitor and nurse).
- There is a history of loss and bereavement in the family aligned with Amy's birth and there may be delayed grief reactions (reports from health visitor and GP).
- There is a lack of take-up of services (reports from GP and health visitor).
- The stepfather may misuse drugs (reports from probation officer and police officer).
- The risk of parental non-compliance with a protection plan is high (report from paediatrician and GP).
- The timescales for Amy's needs are immediate. She cannot wait for the parental attitude to shift.
- The mother and stepfather acknowledge the flare-ups and severity of the condition but are not effectively responding in particular to Amy's immediate need for pain relief.

Caroline

- She has emotional problems and this affects educational attainment (report from school via child psychiatrist).
- There is a lack of parental involvement in the school.
- The step-grandmother related her concern to housing.
- She has experienced both the death of her father and her sister's disability.
- The mother says little about Caroline.
- The timescales for intervention to protect may possibly be longer for Caroline.
- Mother suffers depression and stepfather may misuse drugs.

Trainers obtain feedback to identify who has communicated with the children

Amy

- The nursery teacher brings Amy's drawing.
- Amy would not speak with the social worker.
- Apart from the family, those closest to Amy are the teacher, hydrotherapist, physiotherapist and paediatrician.

Caroline

- She was interviewed by the social worker.
- She spoke to her teacher who spoke to the child psychiatrist who brought the child's voice to the conference.
- The stepgrandmother communicated the child's views to the housing department.

Trainers ask: was the decision making process effective? What interfered with the process and prevented Amy and Caroline gaining effective protection?

Key points to be debated

- The conference discussion tends to divide the participants. The debate normally fixes on differing views about conventional and alternative medicine. The child may get lost in this debate. The child psychiatrist suggested one way of evaluating the facts by taking regular measurements of Amy's joint swelling and assessing whether or not she does go into remission. This view represented a negotiation process between the professionals and the family and avoided a conflict.

- There must be a consideration of what might assist such a negotiation. The alternative practitioner could be asked to provide reports. This might engage him in the debate rather than add to his power over the parents by keeping him outside of the process. The head teacher might be encouraged to shift away from the threat of legal action in order to allow the parents to give way a little on the medication issue and allow Amy to have pain killers which would enable her to tolerate the hydro and physiotherapies. Family therapy might also enable some shifts in parental thinking to take place in order to support Amy and Caroline's best interests.

- The parents quote the paternal grandmother's cure by the alternative therapies but without clarification this is confusing the facts. Adult and juvenile rheumatoid arthritis are different illnesses. The grandmother's cure is of no relevance.

- Participants will need to reflect on their own comfort zones and whether they favoured one form of medical intervention over and above another. How did their personal views impact on their decision making?

- There is extensive use of jargon which should have been challenged during the conference and participants should have made sure that they understood the issues. (Pauciarticular ,ANA, ESR, DMARDS, Uveitis, Synovium, Percentiles, Methotrexate).

- What were the implications of the treatment plan suggested by the paediatrician? The doctor predicts that without medication Amy may be blind within five years. This fact is only mentioned once and may get lost. The concept of 'respectful uncertainty' is relevant to this case study, i.e. the ability to challenge even professionals of high status in a respectful way.

- Whether the child had vaccinations is not a child protection issue. Parents have a right to choose whether or not to vaccinate their children. It is their human right. Lack of immunisations may be a factor in neglect cases but only as an indicator of not accessing health resources in general terms.

- The professionals tend to split and take sides. It is helpful to write on a flip chart who took which side.

- The conference should have considered the needs of both children.

- Both parents are middle class and exceptionally caring. They do not fit a stereotype of neglectful parents. They are very capable of researching the medical issues. The children's needs may be lost as professionals over-identify with the parents.

- The balance of power in the conference should be analysed. The nursery teacher is close to Amy. She is emotional in her presentation. This may lead to her being unheard when in fact she carries the child's voice. She brings the only communication from Amy which is her drawing.

- The parents should be given the opportunity to address the conference separately should they wish to do so or should the chair advise. There may be power differentials between the parents which hinder one or both of them participating to the full.
- There should have been attention to detail and checking of facts. Names should be checked for pronunciation.
- There should be emphasis on absent information. Home Start had been into the home and yet were not represented.
- The detail of the stepfather's previous family history is unknown. This could have included vital information for safe decision making at this conference. Checks would have to be made about this history. This would include telephone calls, reports faxed through or the conference reconvened when the information has been received. The child psychiatrist asked for an end to speculation.
- Sharing confidential information needs to be discussed. The police officer may or may not share the fact that Mr Prior has a conviction for drug misuse. Was this relevant information to share or not? Consider what options the police officer had, for instance, she could have presented the information to the chairperson for a decision about relevance.

Activity 9b: Alternative Child Protection Conference – Role Play

Aim: To provide an opportunity for participants to role play a conference scenario which is less complex than the scenario in Activity 9a and to enable a focus mainly on process. Participants to gain an understanding of the complexities of decision making at a child protection conference and to gain in awareness of the pitfalls that may distract from the task of providing the child with protection.

Delivery: Participants are allocated roles, given labels and have a few minutes to sit at a central table and read quietly. The social worker and lawyer should sit next to the chairperson on one side and the parents and their friend on the other side. The head teacher should be next to the nursery teacher and the nurse manager next to the health visitor. Each is given a copy of the social work report and it is explained that this is not as full as such a report would normally be because this is a training exercise. They are also informed of the process.

Participants are informed that they can act their part but should not alter the facts which are designed to fit together for the purpose of learning.

Observers must sit outside the conference. Two observers are asked to consider the views of Susan and Gemma. At the end they feedback whether or not they thought the childrens' best interests were served by the conference and how they experienced the process through the eyes of the child. The trainers let the conference take its course and do not interject. Participants will learn from their mistakes.

It makes good sense to appoint someone as a chairperson who has some experience of the conference process. Trainers can write notes to the chairperson to assist the process if necessary. The conference progresses until decisions are made about the children's need for a protection plan and under which abuse category. Participants will need to refer to the categories of abuse outlined in *Working Together* (DfES, 2006: 1.30–3). The conference role play does not continue into devising the protection plan.

The trainers may prepare percentile charts for the health visitor to present to the conference and a photograph of a happy child for the parent to show to the conference as 'proof' of Susan's wellbeing.

Please note: Mark age nine years has not been included in the genogram or family composition as his existence is presented as new information to the conference. It is important to see if participants notice the existence of this child and whether they include him in their protection planning. There is no absolute right or wrong outcome to this conference. It will depend on what emerges during the role play.

At the end of the role play each person is asked to state their first name and to say that they are not the person who they were playing in role. Participants should then leave the conference table and return to their seats as before for the feedback. At the very end of the feedback Susan's statement is read out.

List of roles for allocation. Those asterisked are essential. If the numbers are too small some professionals could present the other's reports:

Independent Reviewing Officer and Chairperson*	Christine Okubenego
Nursery teacher*	Meryl Matthews
Nurse manager	Angela Daniels
LA safeguarding manager	Ruth Millar
Team manager children's services*	James Firth
Head teacher*	Mrs Clarke
General practitioner	Dr Gupta
Paediatrician*	Joan Atkinson
Minute taker	Evelyn Short
Social worker*	Gillian Beck
Health visitor*	Fumi Chung
Mother*	Carmen Shore
Father*	Graham Shore
Police officer*	PC Lucy James
Probation officer*	Neena Patel
Friend*	Vanessa Creighton
Solicitor	Gavin Michaels
Child	Susan
Baby	Gemma

Conference process

- Introduction by Chair.
- Introductions – name and role.
- Presentation of social work report.
- Sharing of information related to referral.
- Chair summarises facts and key points.
- Discussion and decision about whether children need to be the subject of a child protection plan and under which abuse categories.

Handout 8: Alternative Child Protection Conference

Social Work Report

Last week Mrs Clarke, head teacher, called children's services to report that Susan Shore had a bruise on her face and multiple bruises on her arm. Later that day the social worker visited Mrs Shore with PC James. Mrs Shore admitted hitting Susan.

A paediatric assessment took place at hospital and subsequently Susan returned home with her parents.

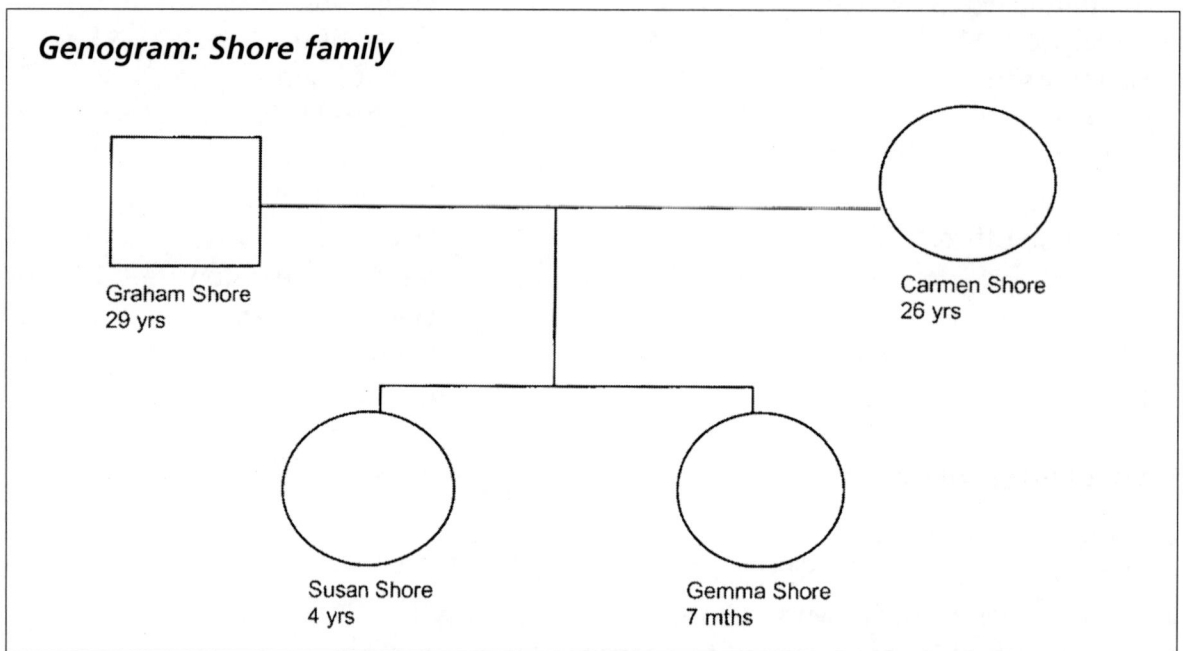

Genogram: Shore family

Graham Shore
29 yrs

Carmen Shore
26 yrs

Susan Shore
4 yrs

Gemma Shore
7 mths

Family composition

Mr Graham Shore	father	29 years
Mrs Carmen Shore	mother	26 yrs
Susan Shore		4 years
Gemma Shore		7 mths

Ethnic origin: White UK

Roles

Independent Reviewing Officer and Chairperson: Mrs Christine Okubenego

You are the chairperson of this conference. You are independent and do not line-manage anyone at the conference.

You open the conference by stating its purpose as follows:

> *This is a child protection conference convened under the Local Safeguarding Children Board Procedures to consider whether Susan or Gemma Shore need to be the subject of a child protection plan.*
>
> *Everything discussed here is confidential and must not go outside this conference unless to other members of your own agency and, even then, only on a strictly 'need to know' basis.*
>
> *The conference will be conducted in the context of the Department's Equal Opportunity Policy and I expect you to all pay due respect to each other's opinions and views. We will begin with introductions. Please say your full name, your role and the reason why you are here today. Then we will take information about the recent referral from the social worker's report.*
>
> *I am Christine Okubenego and I will be chairing this conference.*

Indicate to the next person to begin the introductions.

After the introductions, you then proceed. You begin with the social worker presenting her report. You then need to continue with each person who has information about the reason for the conference. You continue with information from people who have historical knowledge of the family. The mother and stepfather's views must be obtained throughout. The friend should not be allowed to interrupt too much.

After collecting the facts and views you will summarise the key aspects for the benefit of the conference.

There will then be a discussion about the decision to make the children the subject of a child protection plan.

The decision is NOT a vote. You make the final decision after allowing full debate and gaining everyone's views.

Minute taker: Evelyn Short

You have been trained to take minutes.

For the purpose of this role play you do not need to write down a record of the meeting but you may note key points. You are not required to participate in the discussion.

Paediatrician: Dr Joan Atkinson

You were contacted by Gillian Beck, social worker last week because Susan Shore had been seen by her teacher to have bruises on her face and arm. You later saw Susan with

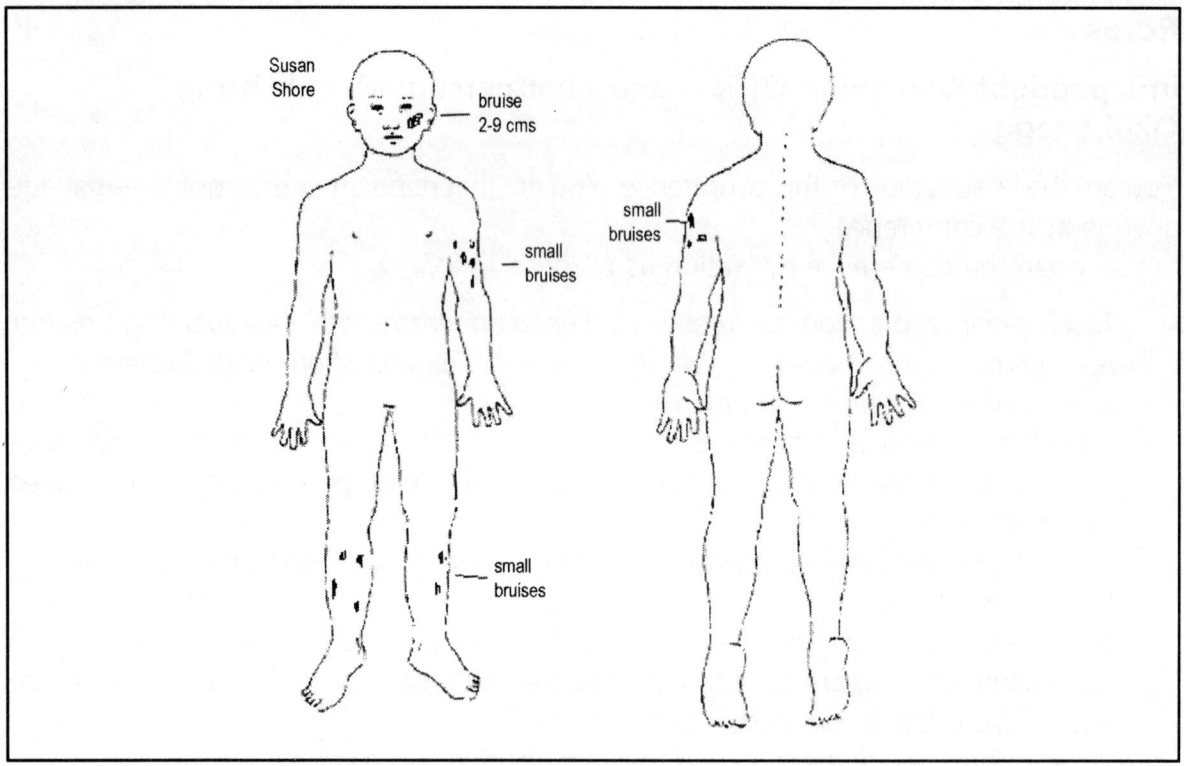

her mother, baby sister Gemma and Gillian the social worker. You examined Susan in the presence of PC Lucy James from the Police Child Abuse Investigation Team.

Mrs Shore said she had lost her temper last Saturday, but now she regretted what had happened. She had told Susan to say she had fallen off her bike as she was scared that children's services might take Susan away.

Susan was a little apprehensive but appeared to relate well to her mother. On examination you found a bruise across the left cheek measuring approximately 3 × 2 cms. It was fading.

On the top of Susan's left arm were bruises which fitted the impressions left by finger pressure. Susan's shins also had small fading bruises. You completed a diagram to show to the conference.

Later on you contacted the General Practitioner, Dr Gupta, to discuss the case. He told you that he felt the general care of the children was open to question. However, he did wonder if Mrs Shore would deliberately hurt them as he knew from the family history that Mrs Shore was herself physically abused as a child.

You inform Gillian Beck of the outcome of the examination.

Local authority safeguarding manager: Mrs Ruth Millar

You are very experienced in child protection work.

Your role in the conference is to ask relevant questions to clarify points raised and to offer advice as to whether the children should be the subjects of a child protection plan. You must be prepared to make a statement of your professional opinion.

Head teacher: Mrs Clarke

You have been a head teacher for seven years.

Mrs Matthews, teacher of the nursery class came to you one morning last week to say that she was concerned about bruises on Susan Shore. She had taken the child's story of falling from her bike at face value earlier in the day but had since discovered marks on Susan's arm which had the appearance of finger marks.

You remember Mrs Shore coming to school to register Susan for the nursery because both she and the two children looked unkempt and you had talked to her about school uniform and how she could get some items of the uniform second hand.

You told Mrs Matthews that you would contact children's services and you spoke to Gillian Beck, social worker.

Father: Mr Graham Shore

You were a car mechanic until you were made redundant a year ago. You feel bad because you can't support Carmen financially and you sometimes get drunk as a means of escape.

You and Carmen got married when Carmen was pregnant with Susan. You know Carmen has been depressed lately and have seen her hit Susan sometimes. Susan is a handful and you didn't see any harm in a bit of discipline. Carmen doesn't hit Gemma but shouts at her and loses patience because once she starts crying she never seems to stop.

You don't like the idea of children's services getting involved but you won't complain if Carmen gets help with the kids.

You are cross with the nursery staff who contacted children's services and can't understand why they didn't tell you first.

You tell the conference that you have another child, Mark age nine years from a previous relationship. Mark visits alternate weekends.

Last year you had a conviction for driving whilst under the influence of alcohol and had a community service order for four months. You are known to the probation service.

Named safeguarding nurse: Angela Daniels

You have a responsibility to advise the conference on health matters and support the health visitor, Fumi Chung. You are experienced in child protection and feel confident to express a view based on your experience. Ms Chung has already discussed this case with you.

You might like to sit next to the health visitor.

Mother: Mrs Carmen Shore

Things have not been going well for your family lately. Your husband was made redundant a year ago and you now have financial problems. Your gas is about to be disconnected. The children can get you down. Susan still wets the bed and she can be very demanding, anyway a smack or two didn't do you any harm.

You had a termination of pregnancy a month ago and your GP helped you but you didn't tell your husband. You did not want to upset your husband because he gets drunk and that is distressing for you and the children.

You feel relief at having admitted to hitting Susan and although you don't like the idea of the involvement of children's services you hope you might get some help with your problems.

You do feel ashamed that you are at an all time low. If you could get back to your part-time job at the supermarket you might feel better.

You were cross that the nursery staff spoke to children's services without telling you first.

You have brought a photograph of Susan looking very happy to show to the conference. You have a conviction for shoplifting from some years ago.

Team manager: Mr James Firth

Your department is very understaffed.

Gillian Beck spoke to you after she was contacted by a local school about Susan Shore, aged four.

Following discussion with Gillian you decided to convene a child protection conference. You have not as yet had the opportunity to update yourself as to what has happened since then. You will be thinking whether or not this case can be 'child in need' rather than 'child protection' as you are worried about the high numbers of children who are currently the subject of child protection plans.

Nursery teacher: Meryl Matthews

You have worked at the school for three years. Susan began in September.

You remember her coming with her mother as Mrs Shore had shouted at Susan over a minor matter. You noticed at the time that Susan smelt of urine and have noticed this a few times since.

Last week Susan came to school with a fading bruise across her left cheek. She had missed school the previous day. When you asked her what happened she said she had fallen off her bicycle. Later in the morning she said her arm hurt and when you looked you noticed numerous bruises.

You informed your head teacher, Mrs Clarke, who referred the case to children's services. You are anxious that Mrs Shore will be angry with you for not telling her first.

This is the first child protection conference you have attended. You get a bit emotional when describing Susan as a rather quiet little girl who loves drawing but doesn't make friends easily. You show the conference a drawing of Susan's where she shows herself looking very sad.

General practitioner: Dr Gupta

You knew Mrs Shore as a little girl, as the family have lived in your area a long time.

Her parents believed in physical punishment –sometimes using a ruler or belt – and you feel that Mrs Shore probably uses similar methods with Susan.

Mrs Shore has presented at surgery a number of times recently with episodes of depression following a termination of pregnancy which Mr Shore did not know about. She has confided in you about her husband's drinking problem.

You received a phone call from Dr Atkinson last week concerning Susan. You told her you had not seen the family for over a month.

You have agreed to attend this conference because you know the background knowledge you have will be useful, but you are unsure whether it is necessary for you to share all the information you have in front of the parents.

Health visitor: Fumi Chung

You have known Mr and Mrs Shore for three years. About a year ago Mr Shore was made redundant and this put considerable strain on the family. Mrs Shore was expecting Gemma at the time.

When you first met the family, Susan was a lively toddler who had a disruptive sleep pattern. Her growth and development have been normal but she is not yet dry at night. Her immunisations are up to date. You applied for a nursery place to help Susan have more stimulation and to give the parents a break.

Gemma was premature and has been brought to clinic a few times. She will shortly be due for an assessment. This had been your next planned visit following a home visit when Gemma was six months. You didn't see Mr Shore at that visit but you thought Mrs Shore was tense. She said she was fed up with Susan wetting the bed and you talked to her about this.

You think that the standard of hygiene could be improved. You have had to talk with Mrs Shore about feeding bottles which are left lying about. You always feel that Mrs Shore is trying her best for the children and they do have a good relationship with her. However, it seems that the last year has been particularly trying.

You were notified about the conference and told the named safeguarding nurse, Angela Daniels.

You called to see the family two days ago but they were not in.

You present both percentile charts to the conference.

Police Child Abuse Investigation team: PC Lucy James

You have been a member of the team for some time and work closely with children's services.

You visited Mrs Shore, Gemma and Susan with Gillian Beck last week.

Mrs Shore answered the door holding Gemma in her arms. Susan was sitting at the bottom of the stairs sucking her thumb. At first Mrs Shore said Susan had fallen off her bike but eventually she told you that her husband had been made redundant and that the baby wouldn't stop crying. She was at breaking point.

She described how at the weekend Susan had been naughty and Mrs Shore had caught her by the arm and lashed out hitting her round the face. You noticed the house looked chaotic.

You went with Mrs Shore, Gemma, Susan and Ms Beck to the hospital and you were present during the examination by Dr Atkinson.

Ms Beck told you about the decision to call a conference and you checked police information on the family.

Mr Shore has one conviction for driving whilst under the influence of alcohol last year and had been threatening to the police officer. Mrs Shore has one conviction for shoplifting four years ago.

Social worker: Ms Gillian Beck

You are recently qualified.

Last week you received a call from Mrs Clarke, head teacher.

She was concerned about Susan Shore age four years who had a bruise on her face and multiple bruises on her arm. Mrs Shore had already collected Susan.

You spoke to your team manager James Firth and telephoned PC James to discuss the case. You arranged a paediatric assessment.

You went with PC James to visit Mrs Shore.

She answered the door holding Gemma in her arms. Susan was sitting on the bottom of the stairs sucking her thumb. At first Mrs Shore was abusive and reluctant to talk saying that Susan had fallen off her bike.

Eventually she told you that her husband had been redundant for a year and that the baby wouldn't stop crying. She was at breaking point.

Mrs Shore said that Susan had been naughty at the weekend and so she had caught her firmly by the arm and lashed out at her hitting her face. She said she was very sorry and that she didn't usually beat her kids. She agreed to take Susan to see the paediatrician.

Dr Atkinson saw Susan with PC James and it was agreed that Susan should go home with her mother. You took them home and explained about the conference.

Probation officer: Neena Patel

You worked with Mr Shore last year after his conviction for driving whilst under the influence of alcohol. He received a Community Service Order for four months which you supervised.

You advised him to have counselling from the Alcohol Counselling Service but he wouldn't attend the sessions. He was a binge drinker and about every three weeks would become very drunk indeed which was worrying. When he was made redundant he got depressed and drank heavily. You are concerned because his previous relationship was difficult because of his heavy drinking and his first wife has custody of their child Mark.

You will advise that he seeks some counselling although you feel sure he would not hurt the children whom he obviously loves very much.

Solicitor: Mr Gavin Michaels

You are the local authority legal advisor to the conference. You advise on whether or not the criteria for the children being the subject of child protection plans has been met and on any other matters which may arise. You may refer to *Working Together* (DfES, 2006: 1.30–3 and 5.94).

Friend: Vanessa Creighton

You have come to the conference to support your neighbours. You have a little boy Thomas, the same age as Susan. Sometimes you look after Gemma to give Carmen a break because you have noticed that she is stressed and shouts a lot at the children. You think there are too many people at the conference and that it is a very intimidating process for the parents. You feel very sorry for them and at times during the conference you try to explain to them what the professionals are meaning.

You are a teacher yourself but have stopped work at the moment because of caring for Thomas as you are a single parent.

Feedback

Trainers obtain feedback about actual or likely significant harm identified to include:

- Patterns of bruising on Susan which are indicative of fingertip bruising (report from paediatrician).
- Bruise on left cheek on Susan (report from paediatrician).
- Mrs Shore said she lost her temper (report from paediatrician).
- Mrs Shore told police officer she 'lashed out' at Susan because she had been 'naughty' (report from police officer).
- Mrs Shore depressed and shouts at children (report from Mr Shore).
- Susan unkempt (report from teacher).
- Mrs Shore shouts at children (report from friend).
- Mr Shore previous history of a drink/drive conviction and previous wife gained the custody of son Mark – history unknown (report from probation officer).
- Mr Shore made redundant – financial difficulties (report from social worker).
- Hygiene problems (report from health visitor).
- Mrs Shore fed up with Susan wetting the bed (report from health visitor).
- Mrs Shore was hit with a ruler and belt – might do the same to her children (report from GP).
- Susan said her arm hurt (report from teacher).
- Susan smells of urine (report from nursery teacher).
- Mr Shore gets very drunk (report from Mrs Shore).
- 'A smack or two does you no harm' (report from Mrs Shore).
- Gemma unkempt (report from teacher).
- Gemma cries a lot (report from Mr Shore).
- Mark visits at weekends – facts unknown (report from Mr Shore).

Trainers obtain feedback about who has communicated with the child

The paediatrician, social worker and police officer all saw Susan but there is no report of them speaking with her. Other professionals such as the health visitor and GP have also seen Susan but do not report speaking with her. The nursery teacher is the key source of information about Susan's perspective. She said that Susan told her that her arm was hurting and when asked about what had happened, Susan told her that she had fallen off her bike. There is very little information directly from Susan.

Trainers ask: Was the decision making process effective? What interfered with the process and prevented Gemma and Susan gaining effective protection?

Key points for debate

1. Information provided by the probation officer and Mr Shore himself raises questions about the past history of his previous relationship and the fact that he did not gain custody of his son Mark. It would be dangerous practice to reach conclusions on this case without having access to the past case history. This conference may have to be reconvened or paused pending the obtaining of this information from another local authority.

2. Mark visits alternate weekends and there will be a need to liaise with the authority where he lives in order to share information and assess risk.

3. The team manager wishes to keep this case as 'child in need'. Although the facts in this case are not very complex, there is usually a wide range of opinion as to whether or not the children need a child protection plan at this moment given the mother's admission and Mr Shore's willingness to access advice and support. However, his cooperation needs testing as previously he had refused to access counselling for his alcohol problem.

4. The mother's admission of hitting Susan may lead to participants over-identifying with the mother and placing too little emphasis on the needs of the children. The impact on decision-making of the way the parents present in the conference role play will need to be analysed.

5. Mr and Mrs Shore may need to present information separately to the conference if both their views are to be heard in full.

6. Mrs Shore's termination of pregnancy is known to the GP and may or may not be shared during the role play. It is important to discuss how relevant sharing this information was or would have been. The GP might have shared it with the chairperson beforehand or Mrs Shore might have been seen separately to enable this aspect to be discussed if relevant. (It is not unusual in the role plays for the GP to disclose this information to the entire conference and for Mr Shore to appear very shocked as he had not known about it before).

7. Police information about previous convictions may or may not have been shared in the role play. The parents should have been made aware prior to the conference of what information was to be shared and why. The drink/drive conviction was relevant

in this case and should have been shared but Mrs Shore's conviction for shoplifting may not have been deemed relevant. Again the chairperson will make a decision about the importance of sharing particular information.

8. The needs of all three children must be debated. Participants tend to focus on the risk to Susan. Decisions about the need for child protection plans must be made for Gemma and Susan and a recommendation to another authority in the case of Mark.

9. Debate should take place about the category in this case. There is evidence of physical harm but is there also evidence of neglect to a degree that would lead to use of this category of registration? How are words like 'unkempt' actually defined and how should such judgements be evaluated?

10. In making decisions about physical harm in this case it is clear that there are medically verified injuries consistent with the parental explanation. However, was the significance of the bruising really debated? Small bruises on the front of Susan's shins may be common to children of that age. The bruises may have been caused at different times which may indicate a repeated pattern of physical harm. Were there gaps in knowledge about the injuries or does the paediatrician explain clearly and understandably what has happened? For the purposes of deciding on whether a child protection plan is needed, there must be a view that the harm is likely to continue. How might this judgement be reached?

11. There are power imbalances in this conference. The nursery worker, who has little status, knows Susan better than other professionals and participants should reflect on whether her voice was heard.

12. The impact on the family of Mr Shore's misuse of alcohol must be evaluated.

13. Because Mrs Shore has a known history of physical harm when she was a child does not necessarily mean that she will harm her own children. Her attitudes towards physical punishment need to be explored. She has already said that smacking didn't do her any harm and the general practitioner who knows the family well does think that patterns may be being repeated. However, this is an aspect of risk which needs further exploration.

14. Did the participants feel confident to question the paediatrician's findings and to seek clarification?

A trainer then reads aloud the following perspective from Susan who gave this letter to her teacher:

> *Mummy says Daddy drinks all the food money. Mummy cries when Daddy hits her and then she hits me and I hit Gemma. That makes Gemma cry. I really like my teacher – I told her I fell off my bike because Mummy didn't want me to get her into trouble. I talk to my doll Emily all the time and she cuddles me when I'm hungry. I wish Mrs Matthews would be my Mummy.*

Presentation 7: Professional Dangerousness

In child protection work professionals may unwittingly collude with, or maintain the dangerous dynamics of abusive families – these pitfalls in practice are a dynamic known as professional dangerousness.

Twelve lost opportunities to protect Victoria were identified in the Victoria Climbié Inquiry. Each one is an example of professional dangerousness and confirmed the dynamics which have been already well defined by many previous child abuse inquiries. There is substantial knowledge about how to keep children safe and these lost opportunities primarily demonstrate lack of compliance with the existing sound legislation, policy and procedures.

Some of the dangerousness factors are organisational.

Participants are asked to guess which Inquiry the following quotation comes from:

> *. . . a story unfolds, in the report of small carelessnesses, pressures of other work, difficulties of staffing and human procrastinations and failures to cooperate, by which few workers, if they are honest, have not at times been tempted from their standards, but which collectively resulted in individual tragedy and public scandal.*

> (DHSS: 1982: 1)

It relates to an inquiry about the death of Dennis O'Neill, a child who died in 'care' in 1945. It could so easily have been the Victoria Climbié Inquiry.

It has often been said that in 30 years of many fatal child abuse inquiries the performance of child protection systems has not been transformed.

Reder and Duncan with reference to the Climbié case comment that:

> *We would like to propose that no further public inquiries are commissioned before all training and resource deficiencies identified over the last 30 years have been remedied.*

> (Reder and Duncan, 2004: 112) (see also Munro, 1995 and Munro, 1996)

Repeatedly child death tragedies demonstrate that staff:

- Are inexperienced.
- Lack training and resources.
- Are over worked, with poor management and supervision.

Keeping within a safe working environment is absolutely essential to being an effective protector.

> *At a general level every professional requires a secure setting in order to undertake the demanding work of child protection. Many factors contribute to a secure setting, including adequate training, regular supervision and support, clear procedural guidelines, adequate funding and staffing, low staff turnover, an optimal caseload,*

continuity in management, a stable organisational structure, good secretarial back-up and so on . . .

(Reder et al., 1993: 69)

It is significant that almost every child death from abuse, where the child is known to children's services, has taken place when a service is under reorganisation and systems are in chaos.

Much reference is made to Child Abuse Inquiries but it is known that the dynamics of child abuse are the same whether or not a child dies or is seriously injured from the abuse. Learning from inquiries about child tragedies teaches essential lessons about child abuse in every situation. Batty (2003) provides a useful summary of child abuse inquiries.

The Inquiry into the case of Victoria Climbié identified twelve 'lost opportunities' when it would have been possible to recognise Victoria as a child in need of protection and therefore to act to save her life. Neil Garnham QC set out these 'lost opportunities' in his opening statement to the Inquiry. This is available online at http://www.victoria-climbie-inquiry.org.uk/Evidence/Archive/Sept01/260901latestp4.htm/

Activity 10: Understanding Professional Dangerousness. Victoria Climbié: the Lost Opportunities

Aim: To provide participants with an opportunity to learn the key pitfalls in practice due to professional dangerousness and to assess the impact of these in the case of Victoria Climbié.

Delivery: Participants work in small mixed groups to discuss which of the 14 listed aspects of professional dangerousness apply to each of the 12 lost opportunities in the Victoria Climbié case. Each group is provided with the list and with one or two of the lost opportunities. They should explore which of the aspects of dangerousness apply to their particular summaries. Each group then feeds back their findings. Trainers should make comparison with the feedback provided to enable the whole group to learn from all the examples.

Handout 9: Professional Dangerousness

Key examples of professional dangerousness

1. **Rule of optimism:** Professionals tend to want to believe that all is well for the child. Even when the indicators of abuse are visible there is a tendency to explain them away and be convinced that the child is safe. This is a form of denial and probably the most common form of dangerous practice. In one case the social worker saw the child looking sick but afterwards saw her with the family on an outing. He allowed himself to believe the latter to be proof of the child's safety and thought his original concerns to be unfounded.

2. **The Stockholm syndrome:** This theory is based on hostage situations where the people taken hostage begin to identify with the cause of the terrorists. It is a survival mechanism common in child abuse cases. Sometimes a parent or abuser is powerful and intimidating, perhaps critical of professionals and the worker will begin to see the adult's point of view rather than the child's. It is one way that the worker feels safe at the expense of the vulnerable child.

3. **Professional accommodation syndrome:** The worker may mirror the child's retraction of abuse, deny the reality of the abuse and be keen to be persuaded that any allegation by the child must be suppressed. Any other possible reason for the abuse will tend to become accepted in preference to considering the possibility that abuse has occurred.

4. **Exaggeration of hierarchy:** Adults of low status who report abuse may not be heard or taken seriously even though they may be close to the child e.g. neighbours, friends or a nursery worker. A psychiatrist, lawyer or paediatrician will probably get their important opinions heard more readily by other professionals. In one child abuse scandal the cook in the children's home had a wealth of information about the child abuse taking place but was not interviewed by the inquiry.

5. **Concrete solutions:** Professionals respond swiftly to abuse situations with practical solutions such as housing, washing machines, or money rather than by investigating and attempting to verify the alleged abuse.

6. **Assessment paralysis:** Sometimes professionals feel helpless and incapacitated. It might be thought that change is hard to achieve because the family have always lived in an abusive way and it is just their way of life. Chronic neglect and inter-generational sexual abuse are often ignored because of this attitude.

7. **Stereotyping:** Professionals may make assumptions about how families bring up their children. These may include cultural stereotypes. In one case the stereotype of the black grandmother being able to cope with every situation falsely portrayed her as a protector of the child against a powerful and abusive adult within the family.

8. **False compliance:** Parents may be able to convince professionals that they are cooperating to protect the child but in fact a skilled practitioner who can analyse parental behaviour will be open to considering the possibility of them being abusive.

Professionals may become enmeshed with the family and be so collusive with the carers that they do not see the needs of the child.

9. **Omnipotence:** Professionals believe that they know the best interests of the child and will not revisit their perceptions in the light of new evidence.

10. **Closure:** Families may shut out professionals. Calls go unanswered, appointments are missed, curtains are closed and doors locked. Child deaths from abuse are often preceded by closure. This dynamic may be mirrored by professionals avoiding contact with the family.

11. **Role confusion:** Professionals may be unclear about tasks and assume that someone else is responsible for protecting the child. In child protection everyone has prime responsibility for the safety of the child. Clarity of decisions is essential. In one case a health visitor said she would see the baby and the social worker assumed that the health visitor was visiting the home. Instead, she was seeing the baby at the clinic and no-one saw the appalling conditions in the home.

12. **Children unheard or parent and carers unheard**: Every child abuse inquiry highlights the central importance of listening to the child. Although children do find it hard to speak of abuse it has been shown that prior to a child's tragic death they have often forewarned someone in authority about the risk. Similarly prior to fatally harming a child, carers often raise the alarm by telling a professional that they are afraid of hurting the child or they cannot cope.

13. **Information which is emotional, recent and vivid takes precedence over the old:** Inquiries inevitably demonstrate that there was, among agencies, a great deal of knowledge and understanding about actual or potential harm to the child. New information must be examined in the context of prior facts. The importance of chronologies to allow analysis cannot be over emphasised. This information must be transferred as a family moves between authorities. This is sometimes referred to as The Start Again Syndrome which prevents practitioners from having a clear understanding of a case based on past information (Brandon et al., 2008: 11).

14. **Non-compliance with statutory procedures:** Inquiries commonly report that legislation, policy and practice are sound but that professionals did not comply with their implementation. When child protection procedures are in place such as conferences and strategy meetings, children generally become safe. Formal procedures allow for collation and analysis of all available information.

The twelve lost opportunities

One: Ealing Social Services, spring 1999

Victoria Climbié first became known to social services when she arrived with her aunt Marie-Therese Kouao, in the London Borough of Ealing. Between 26th April and 7th July Marie-Therese Kouao visited social workers fourteen times in her pursuit of housing support and subsistence money so that she could stay in England. Victoria was with her on seven visits.

Staff who saw Victoria had two concerns:

- Some noticed that the relationship between Marie-Therese Kouao and Victoria was not one of mother and daughter.
- One member of staff, described Victoria's dishevelled appearance which was in contrast to that of her carer.

Pamela Fortune, social worker, saw Kouao on 17th June for an assessment interview but found this difficult to complete as a decision had already been made to stop payments and offer her tickets to return to France. Staff who saw the pair may have concluded that Victoria's appearance was part of an attempt to persuade the authorities to hand out money or that their observations were not important enough to refer.

Two: Warnings from a relative

Ealing eventually found Marie-Therese Kouao and Victoria somewhere to live in neighbouring Brent.

In June 1999, Ester Ackah, a distant relative by marriage of Marie-Therese Kouao, anonymously telephoned social workers in Brent and warned them that Victoria was in danger. She reported cuts and bruises on Victoria and this information was faxed to Brent children's services on 18th June.

What happened to the information is unclear. Senior social worker Edward Armstrong denied that his team received details of a potentially serious child protection case. He said he had not received the fax but had a telephone call, which included concerns about Victoria wetting herself, but nothing about cuts and bruises. He said his team were told of a case where a child was not in school. Two unannounced visits to the accommodation were arranged but there was no record of these.

Two social workers tried unsuccessfully to see Marie-Therese Kouao on 14th July, almost a month after the warning. They assumed the family had moved without making checks with the landlord. No further action was taken by the authority.

There was failure to ensure Victoria got proper schooling.

Three: First hospital admission

The first time that doctors saw Victoria Climbié was when she was admitted to the Central Middlesex Hospital on 14th July 1999. Some weeks before, Marie-Therese Kouao had moved in with Carl Manning with whom she had started to have an affair.

Victoria was placed under police powers of protection by Brent police child abuse investigation team which intended to investigate the following day. However, this protection was withdrawn following the doctor's advice to the police that the issue was not child protection but rather housing and finance. The social worker and police officer did not speak to Victoria.

Victoria was taken to hospital when Avril Cameron, the daughter of her childminder, believed that Victoria had been scratched and cut. Recorded injuries were; burn on face, old injuries on side of face, bloodshot eyes, loose skin hanging from eyelid, fingers oozing pus and face swollen. Dr Ekundayo Ajaye-Obe told the inquiry that he did not accept the explanation from Marie-Therese Kouao that Victoria had caused the injuries by scratching scabies sores.

He referred to the hospital's consultant paediatrician, Dr Ruby Schwartz, who overruled Dr Ajaye-Obe's diagnosis and agreed that the wounds were the result of scratching at scabies sores. Marie-Therese Kouao took Victoria home. The hospital arranged no follow up even though it was clear that Victoria was being cared for over long periods by an unregistered childminder. The childminder was not visited by social services.

At the inquiry, Dr Schwartz said that while she did not suspect physical abuse, she did have other concerns. She claimed she had contacted children's services on the discharge day, but the inquiry questioned this.

Confusingly, a letter to social services, written by yet another doctor, arrived with Lisa Arthurworrey, Haringey social worker, on 2nd August. It stated, 'no child protection concerns' and 'marks due to scabies'.

Neil Garnham QC, counsel to the inquiry, described the failure of others to question the apparent differences of opinion at the hospital as 'disturbing'. 'It was as if the critical faculties of all other professionals were simply suspended', he told the inquiry (Garnham, 2003).

Four: Visits to Ealing social services

Marie-Therese Kouao visited Ealing social services the day after Victoria had been discharged from hospital. Reception staff noted that Marie-Therese Kouao left Victoria for an hour on her own and Victoria appeared to be sick.

Staff at the office said that the case, which they considered to be a housing issue, was closed. Social worker Pamela Fortune said that Kouao had a part-time job, could provide financially for Victoria and that she seemed to be a loving mother. Concerns about Victoria having been left alone in Ealing's reception were not passed to Brent.

Neil Garnham QC told the inquiry that this visit represented a missed opportunity to intervene because staff at Ealing should have been aware of the case history to date.

Five: Second hospital admission

On 24th July, Victoria was admitted to North Middlesex hospital suffering scalding to her head and face. She also had multiple marks on her body, including some that looked like belt buckle marks on her shoulder. A skeletal survey was made and photographs were taken. A dermatologist was consulted.

Staff noted that she had few clothes and was not brought any treats or food. She stood to attention in front of Marie-Therese Kouao. The hospital record stated, 'wets herself in front of mother'. Victoria was brought to hospital five and a half hours after the scald. There were inconsistent explanations for the injury, said at different times to have been caused by water from the tap, the kettle and a cup.

Social services did not ask Victoria what had happened until she had been in hospital for two weeks, despite initial concerns about non-accidental injury, by which point she was being discharged to the care of Marie-Therese Kouao. There were no arrangements for her to be monitored.

The Enfield hospital social worker discussed Victoria with staff but did not interview her. She said that she had no clear suspicion of child abuse from the first referral. There was no investigation of her injuries.

With Marie-Therese Kouao and Victoria now living with Carl Manning, the case was in Haringey council's hands.

A strategy meeting held in Haringey was chaired by Rose Kozinos who had not read the referral prior to the meeting. Decisions were made but poorly recorded without timescales or clearly allocated roles.

The designated social worker, Lisa Arthurworrey, had not handled such a complicated case in her career. She had never conducted a Section 47 investigation, held a large caseload and spoke of minimum supervision. When she rang the nurse and doctor they focused on neglect and not physical harm and did not mention belt buckle marks. Some marks were explained as due to infection through scratching scabies and two thumb marks were unexplained. Nurses' concerns about child abuse had not been recorded sufficiently to allow the information to be communicated effectively to the police and social worker.

The inquiry heard that there was little exchange of information between the hospital and social services.

Counsel Neil Garnham QC said this led to a 'battle of conflicting assumptions' (Garnham, 2003) where each body believed that the other was fully aware of the suspicions.

Doctors believed that Victoria had been abused, but did not realise that neither social services nor the police were aware of the evidence.

PC Karen Jones, the police officer assigned to the case, did not visit Marie-Therese Kouao or Manning prior to Victoria's discharge because she feared that she could have caught scabies.

Six: Tottenham child and family centre

Barry Almeida, a senior Haringey social worker, referred Victoria Climbié's case to the NSPCC Tottenham Child and Family Centre on 5th August 1999.

However, the centre was confused as to why it was being handed the file. The notes suggested that it would not be their kind of case.

Sylvia Henry from the Centre says she spoke to Mr Almeida to clarify matters and was told that the family were no longer in the authority so that the case had actually been closed. At the inquiry, Mr Almeida said that he had no recollection of this conversation.

Seven: Health visitor follow-up

This issue proved to be one of the most contested points in the inquiry with two completely conflicting versions of events.

Rachel Crowe, of North Middlesex Hospital, said that she referred the Victoria Climbié case to a community health visitor, Ms Brown. Ms Brown said that she did not receive any instructions or papers to follow up the case.

Eight: Visit to Carl Manning's flat

Social worker, Lisa Arthurworrey, eventually made two visits to Manning's flat after Victoria had been discharged, the first being on 16th August 1999.

The second took place days after Manning began forcing Victoria to sleep in the bath. Ms Arthurworrey told the inquiry that she saw no evidence of child abuse on either occasion. Her focus was on the carer not the child. But Ms Arthurworrey noted that Marie-Therese Kouao reverted to French when child protection matters were raised. An interpreter was present. Arthurworrey considered Victoria's deferential behaviour to Kouao as possibly related to cultural norms of respect.

Neil Garnham QC argued that Ms Arthurworrey did not see through an act put on by Marie-Therese Kouao and Manning.

> *It may be thought that the fact that they succeeded so conspicuously in fooling the social worker is attributable, in part, to Ms Arthurworrey's willingness to accept what she saw and heard at face value.*
>
> (Garnham, 2003)

He told the inquiry:

> *She never troubled to speak to Victoria during those two visits. She never sought to discover how Victoria spent her days, she never sought to take any active steps to address the fact that Victoria was not receiving education.*
>
> (Garnham, 2003)

The team manager, Carole Baptiste, did not read the strategy meeting notes during supervision with Ms Authurworrey and decided that the case was one of family support.

Nine: Letter to Petra Kitchman

On 13th August, Mary Rossiter, consultant paediatrician at North Middlesex Hospital, wrote to Petra Kitchman, Haringey's child protection advisor. 'I have enormous concerns about this child who is now lost to follow-up somewhere in Haringey' she wrote, 'what are you going to do?' Ms Kitchman said the letter did not arrive for another seven days. What happened next remains unclear. Ms Kitchman said that she relayed these concerns to Lisa Arthurworrey but Ms Arthurworrey says she did not do so at the time, but only on 4th October in a rush. Earlier perceptions of the case as family support, might at this stage have been reviewed as child protection. There was no face to face discussion between Ms Kitchman and Dr Rossiter. Kitchman said that she had not read Victoria's file or she would have known that no section 47 had been completed.

Ten: Second letter to Petra Kitchman

Dr Rossiter's second letter to Ms Kitchman, on 2nd September 1999, containing details of the evidence of abuse recorded at the hospital, arrived while the social worker was on leave. This letter referred to evidence of looped wire marks.

Ms Kitchman said that on her return she raised this with Ms Arthurworrey, something that the case worker denied. In her evidence, Ms Arthurworrey said that had she been sent the letter or the medical details she would have 'run to her manager'. Kitchman admitted that she had failed to provide Arthurworrey with any proper advice in relation to the case.

There was a further visit to Manning's flat by Lisa Arthurworrey on 28th October and the focus was still on the housing situation.

Eleven: Sexual abuse allegations

Marie-Therese Kouao telephoned Haringey social services on 1st November 1999 and alleged that Carl Manning had sexually abused Victoria. Victoria told Lisa Arthurworrey, 'I'm not lying, I must tell you more, it is true'. Allegations included digital penetration. Arthurworrey arranged for Kouao and Victoria to stay with friends but did not check on the adequacy of the arrangement.

Neil Garnham QC said that the allegation was probably untrue but had given both police and social services an opportunity to investigate. If they had investigated at this stage, they would have discovered that Victoria was suffering serious and continual abuse at the hands of Carl Manning and Marie-Therese Kouao.

Marie-Therese Kouao withdrew the allegations the next day but social workers decided to hold a strategy meeting to discuss the case of Victoria. Rose Kozinos chaired the strategy meeting and admitted she did not read the case file prior to the meeting. The team made 15 decisions that largely focused on making contact with Victoria, Carl Manning and Marie-Therese Kouao. No review meeting was planned and there were no timescales or clear allocation of roles.

Arthurworrey had no training in child sexual abuse investigation and said she could not take the strategy meeting decisions further because she was unable to gain contact with the family. A letter from the police officer, Karen Jones, to Kouao was delayed for weeks because of waiting to translate it into French. This letter asked for a reason for the withdrawal of the allegations.

Twelve: Final visits to Manning's flat

Lisa Arthurworrey told the inquiry she attempted to contact Marie-Therese Kouao in person with three visits to Manning's flat between December 1999 and January 2000. On all three occasions she received no answer.

She told her supervisors that it was possible that Kouao and Manning had returned to France with Victoria. Despite no evidence to support this theory, case notes from 23rd December, written by Ms Arthurworrey's supervisor, concluded that Marie-Therese Kouao and Victoria had left the area. Supervision for Arthurworrey by two different managers, during this stage of the case, was minimal.

On 18th February the social workers again wrote to Marie-Therese Kouao saying that the case, still regarded as a housing matter, would be closed if she did not contact the department.

The police wrote a report stating that the allegation could not be substantiated after hearing that social services had closed the file.

Haringey closed the case on the 25th February 2000. At 3.30 p.m. the same afternoon, Victoria was declared dead at St Mary's Hospital Paddington.

Feedback: many other examples may be added to this list

First lost opportunity

- 1. Rule of optimism
    - It was assumed that Victoria's appearance was a ruse to obtain money. Abuse was not considered.
- 4. Exaggeration of hierarchy
    - Reception staff of low status made important observations which went unheard.
- 7. Stereotyping and cultural assumptions
    - Assumptions were made about the family background in France. In fact the French authorities already had concerns about the care of Victoria.
- 13. Priority given to recent, emotional and vivid information
    - Information about the history of the family was not collated.
- 14. Non-compliance with statutory procedures
    - Victoria was neither assessed as a child in need (CA 1989, Section 17) nor as a child in need of protection (CA 1989, Section 47).

Second lost opportunity

- 1. Rule of optimism
    - An anonymous call received little attention.
- 4. Exaggeration of hierarchy
    - A relative was unheard.

- 10. Closure
  - ○ Access to the family was difficult. Instead of raising professional anxiety this led to less action.
- 13. Priority given to recent, emotional, vivid information
  - ○ Checks were not made about the housing situation.
- 14. Non-compliance with statutory procedures
  - ○ Victoria's need for education as a child in need was ignored.

Third lost opportunity

- 1, 3 and 4. Rule of optimism, professional accommodation syndrome and exaggeration of hierarchy
  - ○ The police and social workers were persuaded by the opinion of the paediatrician.

- 1. Rule of optimism
  - ○ The childminder was not interviewed and neither was the person assumed to be Victoria's mother.
- 4. Exaggeration of hierarchy
  - ○ The childminder was unheard.
- 11. Role confusion
  - ○ Conflict between professionals is a common cause of professional failure to protect children.
  - ○ Formal protocols allow for debate and resolution of conflictual views however any unresolved conflict must be referred to the Local Safeguarding Children Board.
- 12 and 14. Children unheard and non-compliance with statutory procedures
  - ○ The police officer and social worker did not comply with the Home Office guidance concerning the interviewing of child witnesses. Victoria should have been spoken to by them to enable a decision about the need for a formal video interview conducted under the 'Achieving Best Evidence' Guidance (CJS, 2007).
  - ○ There was no strategy meeting or Section 47 investigation which would have allowed full professional debate of the known facts and decisions to have been made about the protection needs of Victoria. In the absence of multi-agency discussion and decision making, the paediatric view was accepted by default and the complexities of Victoria's injuries were not investigated. This would have involved the medical view being considered in the context of interviews of the carer and child, as well as of the referrer. The history of the family would also have been obtained. Lord Laming spoke of the need for 'respectful uncertainty' which is the ability to politely challenge another professional view.
  - ○ The medical fax sent to Lisa Arthurworrey required interpretation by a medical professional. If there had been a child protection conference a health

professional would have been allocated to the case and would have clarified to social services any child abuse issues in the document.

- ○ The doctor who said there were 'no child protection concerns' was not in a position to make this comment as there had been no multi-agency investigation.

Fourth lost opportunity

- 1. Rule of optimism
  - ○ Social worker believed Kouao was a loving mother.
- 4. Exaggeration of hierarchy
  - ○ Reception staff went unheard when they made important observations of child neglect.
- 5. Concrete solutions
  - ○ A focus on housing need obscured Victoria's need for protection.
- 13. Priority given to recent, emotional, vivid information
  - ○ There was a lack of collation of historical context.

Fifth lost opportunity

- 1. Rule of optimism
  - ○ The nurses described Victoria as a 'little ray of sunshine' and this was the key phrase retained by the social worker involved.
- 8. False compliance
  - ○ Marie-Therese Kouao seemed to be compliant with the authorities and her inconsistent explanations for the scald went unchallenged, as did the delay in her arrival at the hospital. She said she had taken a taxi but no checks were made with the taxi company.
- 10. Closure
  - ○ The police officer was avoiding contact with the family. Whether or not the needs of the officer were valid, the important point is that the child was not seen at home.
- 11. Role confusion
  - ○ The paediatricians assumed that police and social workers knew the facts and were acting to protect. The lack of formal procedures allowed for confusion and for no formal exchange of information or plans to protect. The Enfield social worker was involved because Haringey did not have a social work service at the hospital. Because of this resource issue, the child was not interviewed by a hospital social worker and the case was not co-ordinated or led by the hospital team. A conference held at the hospital would have ensured that relevant medical staff attended and that information was fully shared.
- 13. Priority given to recent, emotional and vivid information
  - ○ As the case progressed the results of the skeletal survey and the photographs were never accessed by other professionals. This important evidence was lost.

© Liz Davies and Debbie Townsend. *Joint Investigation in Child Protection.* www.russellhouse.co.uk

- o Also important early facts such as thumb marks and apparent belt buckle marks were lost as the case progressed and were never the subject of Section 47 investigation.
- 14. Non-compliance with statutory procedures
  - o Victoria was interviewed at the hospital but had not been made safe. It was unreasonable to expect her to speak to professionals about her situation when she knew she could be removed by her carers at any time from the safety of the hospital.

Sixth lost opportunity

- Closure
  - o There was collusion with the family's attempt to exclude professionals.
- Role confusion
  - o There was confusion between agencies as to their role.

Seventh lost opportunity

- 14. Non-compliance with statutory procedures
  - o If there had been formal procedures it would have been clarified which health professional held responsibility for the protection of Victoria and gaps would have been identified.

Eighth lost opportunity

- 1 and 12. Rule of optimism and child unheard
  - o Victoria's voice went unheard. This visit was a lost opportunity in speaking with her alone. This omission was mainly because the social worker was not in an investigative mindset. She was not conducting a Section 47 jointly with police. She had the view that she was visiting a refugee family who needed help with housing. When Marie-Therese Kouao told her that she had already found a school for Victoria there was no reason to disbelieve her. She had been defined as a co-operative and vulnerable carer and she was not questioned rigorously about the abuse allegations.
- 6. Assessment paralysis and 9. Omnipotence
  - o Haringey managers had already decided that Victoria was a child in need and not a child in need of protection. They did not shift from this view throughout the 10 months that Lisa Arthurworrey held the case.
- 7. Stereotyping and cultural assumptions
  - o Lisa Arthurworrey did fail to question abuse within the family, but she was correct to consider the impact of culture on a child's behaviour. In fact, it was the inquiry which stereotyped Arthurworrey's response, as they assumed that she was of African Caribbean origin and applying her knowledge of this culture to an African child. In fact, Arthurworrey is of dual heritage – African

(Nigerian) and African-Caribbean. The key issue is the importance of considering cultural explanations for behaviour, whilst being open to also considering the behaviour as an indicator of child abuse.

- 8. False compliance
  - o The carers were apparently compliant and when the social worker told her supervisor of her concerns about Marie-Therese Kouao reverting to French, when questioned about Victoria's safety, the manager did not reinforce the social workers concern and retained a child in need approach uncritical of the carers.

Ninth lost opportunity

- 14. Non-compliance with statutory procedures
  - o Child protection advisors are an important safety net to address problems when they arise. Petra Kitchman should have noted the lack of formal child protection procedures in this case. It was her responsibility to re-examine the progress of the case once concerns had been raised.

Tenth lost opportunity

- 5. Concrete solutions
  - o A continued focus on housing for the family diverted the focus away from Victoria's needs.
- 11. Role confusion
  - o Poor communication led to confused expectations about what was happening in the case and by whom. If formal procedures had been in place this would have clarified roles, responsibilities, and tasks.

Eleventh lost opportunity

- 3. Professional accommodation syndrome
  - o Because the professionals denied that there had been abuse Victoria remained unprotected.
- 7. Stereotyping
  - o It was assumed that Marie-Therese Kouao was making the allegations in order to obtain housing. As a carer she had been stereotyped as manipulative without proper investigation of the allegation of sexual abuse.
- 11 and 14. Role confusion and non-compliance with statutory procedures
  - o Decisions at the strategy meeting did not include details of who should complete each task and there were no timescales for action. The result was confusion and inaction to protect.
- 12. Child unheard
  - o Victoria's voice went unheard. This brief statement by Victoria is of great significance and yet was not taken seriously. Lisa Arthurworrey was untrained

in the formal interviewing of children and held back from speaking to her further. She should not have been in this situation, as once a referral was received from Marie-Therese Kouao, there should have been a joint interview of Victoria by police and social services. Given the situation she found herself in, Lisa Arthurworrey could have asked a few open questions of Victoria as she was wanting to speak at that time. Marie-Therese Kouao later retracted the allegation and it was Marie-Therese Kouao who was heard by the professionals, but this should not have prevented the case being fully investigated including a formal interview of Victoria.

- 14. Non-compliance with statutory procedures
    - ○ The allegations included a statement that Victoria had been sexually abused by digital penetration. This always indicates the need for a paediatric assessment as there may be infection or harm caused by such abuse. The first pathologists report found evidence of sexual abuse but this was discounted by the second pathologist.

Twelfth lost opportunity

- 5. Concrete solutions
    - ○ The focus still remained on housing.
- 7 and 10. Stereotyping and Closure
    - ○ Lisa Arthurworrey continued to visit. She tried to contact the family despite having been told three times by managers to close the case. However, finally both social services and the police ceased to pursue the case. The family did visit France twice later on in the year, but the assumption was made that they had moved there permanently.

Presentation 8: Contribution From Survivors of Child Abuse

The trainers should involve a survivor from a local survivor's group. Useful contacts might be made through the following groups:

- National Association of People Abused in Childhood (NAPAC) www.napac.org.uk
- CIS'ters, Child Incest Survivors Support Group; 02380 338080
- Teresa Cooper's website; www.No2abuse.com
- Care Leaver's Association; www.careleavers.com
- A National Voice; www.anationalvoice.org
- Understanding child sexual abuse and male rape; www.SurvivorsUk.org
- The Survivor's Trust; www.thesurvivorstrust.org

A very useful video to show is that of Fred Fever, author of *Who Cares?* (1994). The Department of Health training pack *Towards Safer Care* (2000) includes a five minute presentation of his personal testimony about his history of child abuse within the care system. He was, 'twenty years in care for a crime he didn't commit' (1994: 201).

The presentation should be no longer than two hours. The survivor and the participants will need preparation before the session and an opportunity to debrief afterwards. The survivor should be asked how they would like the session to be organised. They may wish to speak unprompted or prefer to respond to agreed questions. It should be clarified that the survivor may choose not to respond to particular questions. Asking participants to present their questions, in writing in advance, can be of help but there will inevitably be fresh questions following the presentation.

It is very important that the contributor is paid for their time and provided with expenses or an agreed contribution made to their organisation. Attention must also be paid to their travel arrangements and to be sensitive to their practical needs such as for breaks, refreshments and any materials they may need. They also need to receive the feedback about their contribution.

Survivors who have worked with the authors and contributed to joint investigation courses were asked for their perspectives for this book.

Phil Frampton is the author of *Golly in the Cupboard* (Frampton, 2003) and co-founder of the Care Leaver's Association. His book is his account of his childhood in the care of Barnardo's during the 1960s. He has made an immensely valuable contribution to many courses reading extracts from his book. He contrasts throughout his own perspectives on events with those of the professionals as recorded in his files. He also examines current policy issues relating to child protection and children in care:

> *Prejudices born of ignorance are the scourge of society, and sadly this also applies to the caring professions. These prejudices can so warp professional judgments that they lead to great damage being inflicted on the vulnerable brought about by ignoring the voice of those society has deemed in need of protection.*

My childhood friends in care suffered terribly because of the Things We Never Said and Words They Never Heard. From listening to young people in care and care leavers, I know that terrible harm continues to be done today out of ignorance of the complex experiences and opinions of service users.

Most people in the caring professions have never suffered going through the care system, so it beats me how they can think that they know how best to meet the needs of children in care – unless they encourage young people and survivors to speak out and unless they give sufficient weight to the service users words; a weight well beyond those who may produce worthy texts without any comprehension of the real complexities facing those in care. Listen and you will learn.

Peter Saunders is Chief Executive of the National Association of People Abused in Childhood. He has also contributed to many courses and described his own experience of child abuse in the context of professional responses to him as a vulnerable child. In his presentation he also explains the work of NAPAC as an organisation supporting adult survivors of child abuse. He sometimes is accompanied by other survivors from the organisation who also value the opportunity to contribute to professional learning:

Two key groups of people that NAPAC is occasionally asked to speak to are social workers and police officers. For any professional body involved in child protection I think it essential they are given the opportunity to listen to survivors of abuse talk about their experiences. Abuse is such a secret, shameful and isolating crime that only those who have suffered can really understand the true impact and therefore pass on an invaluable insight. That insight, which none of us as survivors wished we had, is I believe, useful to those working to protect children. It is a crying shame that survivors of abuse are not given a greater voice given how many of us have suffered and how our Government, some so-called child protection charities and society generally bang on about protecting our most vulnerable citizens.

Demetrious Panton was abused in care. In 1978 he was abused by a man called Bernie Bain, the head of a children's home in the London Borough of Islington. But it was 17 years before a police investigation uncovered the true extent of the abuse. Detective Superintendent John Sweeney led the inquiry. In 1995 police found out that Bain was living in Morocco. He was still abusing children many years after Demetrious had first reported the abuse. When alerted to an investigation of Demetrious's case by the Today programme, Margaret Hodge, then Minister for Children, wrote to the Chairman of the BBC and called Demetrious 'an extremely disturbed person'. He took legal action and she made a public apology:

I have taught on these courses many times and described my experiences of abuse within the Islington Care System from when I was just 10 years old. I am still amazed at the lack of awareness within the social work and police professions regarding child abuse and how perpetrators are able to access the most vulnerable. Of course social work has come along way from when I first reported being sexually abused whilst in care. Then the idea that children in care could be sexually abused, let alone by 'respected' care workers, was simply unimaginable. Yet, as in my case, social workers were suspicious about my abusers. They knew there wasn't something 'right' about their behaviour. But in some cases they didn't have the skills to confront the abuser or to provide me with the mechanism whereby I could confirm their suspicions. Police and social workers on the courses know the theory but it's a whole different thing to meet a survivor who can present the child's perspective. I always tell the police and social workers that the most important quality for them is to have humanity.

Teresa Cooper has written about her experiences of neglect, psychological, physical and sexual abuse within the care system in her book *Trust No One* (2008). When she lectures to police and social workers she vividly describes her experience of being kept in solitary confinement and forced to take large quantities of psychiatric drugs on a regular basis. Teresa also explains how she has survived to research and challenge the systems that oppressed her and introduces participants to her website www.No2abuse.com

That trainee social workers and police must desire to succeed and to work so hard to deal with child abuse is paramount – not only to their time as future workers but also to how they treat and deal with a child in their care and with child abuse. Child abuse is ugly and needs the right care to understand and deal with it. I have to say I'm impressed with training methods that include survivors because of the impact it has on those working in child care that inevitably reflects on the child in a vulnerable position and for those working with them as individuals.

Taking part in the training of social workers and those involved in child care is so positive and should be protocol as it brings about an understanding of social care on a new level. I know how hard trainee professionals are working to correct past mistakes and to turn child care into a rewarding and caring profession – which can be achieved. Making a difference comes not only from hard work but from compassion and positive changes must come from within the person. Investigating historic abuse can only help because we have to start at the beginning in order to see and understand where it went wrong.

Listening to a child is paramount to their care and well being. Giving trainees the ability to see within the survivor's mind and experiences can only help towards changes and how they provide care for children. There is a lot to be learnt from historic abuse and those changes need to be made from the heart of the social care system where a child will rely on the discretion of the social worker, how the social worker sees the child they are caring for and the trust that the child can have in the carer. A child in care will also rely on their social worker and the relationship they develop – relationships are ever important to a child's development. There is also a need for change in the social branding of children in care and to treat them as individuals and understand their needs.

I applaud survivors being introduced into teaching about the welfare of children who have suffered abuse because they have first hand experience and ability to show where positive changes can be made and learnt from. This benefits not only the social worker and police officer, but also the child in their care. Social workers act as parents and the child needs to have trust and faith in their decisions. Listening to a child is the simplest and most important form of care and yet it is the one side of care that is rarely used. These are the key points I make when I teach them.

Communicating with Children, Corroborating a Child's Statement and Child Sexual Abuse

Presentation 9: Listening to Children

Children and young people are rarely heard. Children who have been abused and neglected are heard even less. It is as if they are further abused and neglected by society in general, as well as by the abusive adults. The reality may be that we do not want to hear what they say because their words are too painful (Goddard, 2003: 33).

A NSPCC study concluded that 72 per cent of sexually abused children stated that they were too frightened to tell anyone at the time of the abuse and 31 per cent still had not told anyone by early adulthood (Cawson et al., 2000). ChildLine, in a survey of calls concerning child sexual abuse, concluded that 'on average children contact ChildLine much sooner after the abuse begins than they used to' (ChildLine, 2007: 1). To speak about abuse is a deeply painful task for a child or adult survivor. The abusers insistence on secrecy with direct or indirect threats is a powerful influence on the child. The abuser utilises a state of fear in the victim to obtain compliance.

Disclosure typically occurs later in life when the survivor wishes to prevent other young people suffering the same abuse. It is often said that children tell about four adults before being listened to. Children will tell in any way that occurs to them. This may be messages conveyed through their behaviour such as self harm, drug/alcohol misuse, running away, aggression or attempted suicide. They may test the water by telling a small part of what happened in order to see if the listening adult is willing to hear. Children need to be safe before they can speak about abusive experiences. When Victoria Climbié was interviewed in hospital about the burn she said little, but this was not surprising as she had not been assured of her safety. Madge Bray illustrates this in her story of 'Tracey' a young child who could not speak about how she was sexually abused until her request for a large uniformed police officer to be in the room had been met (Bray, 1997: 50).

Reasons why a child might not tell about child abuse

A child may:

- Be threatened by the abuser – threats may be implicit given abuse of power.
- Be threatened by peers also involved in the abuse.
- Think they are to blame and fear punishment.
- Fear loss of family or school.

- Be emotionally dependent on the abuser.
- Think no-one will believe that s/he is being abused.
- Have a low sense of self esteem making disclosure difficult.
- Think the abuse is normal behaviour.
- Not wish to betray the abuser.
- Fear public exposure.
- Have ambivalence about taking part in the abuse.
- Lack faith in the justice system.
- Lack language/communication skills to disclose abuse.

Activity 11a: Communicating With Children – Carousel

Aim: For participants to develop skills in responding to the child's statements.

Delivery: The participants form two circles. The outside circle faces inwards and the inside circle faces outwards to form a carousel. The participants on the outside play the part of children asking questions and are given cards each with one question on it. They ask the question of the person opposite them in the inner circle who plays the part of an adult to provide a clear, sensible and age appropriate response to the question. After a short while, the trainer tells the participants to move round and the outside circle move once to the left to ask the same question of the next adult. The people in the inner circle remain stationary throughout. The trainer should allow about one minute for each question. It is useful to have a bell or whistle to signify the need to move round.

Once the participants have completed a whole rotation they reverse places in the carousel. Those that played children become the adults and those that played adults become the children. Another rotation is completed.

First read out the following excerpt from Madge Bray (cited in Milner and Carolin, 1999: xi).

> *There are many children for whom the slow, gnawing, jagged woundedness of verbal, physical and sexual assaults on minds and bodies perniciously tears at the fabric of their wellbeing and is fearful beyond telling.*
>
> *Common to all suffering is fear. And fear lives in all of us. Its positive short-term purpose helps us to deal with danger, but in a concentrated form its effects can be lifelong. It paralyses our thinking. It changes the way our bodies behave. It alters our capacity to trust the world. It causes us to lose trust in ourselves. Its cumulative legacy prevents us from loving fully and from being all that we are.*
>
> *To be heard and understood without judgment, to have another human being bear witness to both our suffering and our joy is a basic human need. To share time with a person who, with wisdom and compassion, can see through the smokescreen of our defensiveness and truly hear what is often beyond words – this is the very stuff of healing.*

Handout 10: Communicating with Children

I'm seven: What is child abuse?

I'm four: What do little girls have where their willies should be?

I'm eleven: Why don't children have sex?

I'm thirteen: John says he wanks, that's disgusting isn't it?

I'm five: How did the baby get into Mummy's tummy?

I'm six: What do kidnappers do to children when they get them in the woods?

I'm seven: How can Aunt Jane be having a baby when she isn't married?

I'm fourteen: If you want a baby and stop using condoms, do you catch anything?

I'm nine: What is a condom?

I'm five: Are all strangers kidnappers?

I'm twelve: Why do gays get AIDS?

I'm fifteen: Mike says I can't love him if I won't have sex, what do you think?

I'm eight: Why can't children play sex?

I'm two: How will the baby get out of Mummy's tummy?

I'm fourteen: That man buggered me didn't he? Does that mean I'm gay?

I'm four: Shall I show you my Mary-Ann?

I'm six: What does masturbation mean?

I'm seven: What is child sexual abuse?

I'm ten: I mostly like what Uncle Jim did to me. Does that mean I'm bad?

I'm six: If you have twins, do you need two Daddies to make them?

I'm seven: Lisa says all grown ups do Frenchies. Do you do Frenchies?

I'm eight: What's oral sex?

Feedback: The participants playing the adults need to reflect on how the activity makes them feel. If they are reluctant to read or use some of these words they need to consider how they may not be able to respond to a child who is calling out to them for help. If they admonish the child for use of such foul language or tell them that they are too young to know such things, they may be closing down an opportunity for a child to tell them that they are being harmed. Such responses reflect the adult's need not to be exposed to the horror of abuse which interferes with the child's need to be heard.

Some participants may assume that they had to explain complex issues to the child. However, does a young child need to know what masturbation is? It could be that they have merely overheard the word in the playground or from an older brother or sister. It is important not to corrupt the innocence of the child by introducing concepts to them inappropriate to their age. Yet the child may be testing the worker to see if they can hear their statement of abuse. An adult may be using the child to masturbate them or be masturbating the child. The worker should not close the door to a possible disclosure of abuse. It is best for the worker to begin by asking the child where they heard the word and state that it is a very long word for a child of six years to know. They then take their cue from the child and continue from there.

False assumptions are commonly made. Did they assume 'Mary-Ann' was a word the child was using for her vagina? It might of course be her doll or something else altogether. Again the starting point is to ask the child to say what she means by her Mary Ann. Similarly with the 'Frenchies' question where the child may be referring to 'french-kissing' but also may mean something quite different. Children will have many terms for sexual activity or parts of their body. Some may be the accepted terms used in their family and some may be words an abuser has used to divert attention away from the abuse should a child begin to speak about it. For instance, a child may be told to call the abuser Batman so that when disclosing abuse by Batman the adults think it is a fictional cartoon character.

Children may be expressing serious worries that they have. Children are exposed to the media and may well hear stories about adults kidnapping children. A response to this question might be to explore where they heard about it and to ask if this is worrying them. One response might be to explain the importance of children keeping safe in relation to strangers. It is always important to acknowledge the child's feelings by saying, 'I'm sorry this is worrying you'. The child will then know that they are being heard.

False reassurance should not be given such as 'of course you haven't caught anything'. If the child is really worried about having infections then it is important to acknowledge the anxiety and offer to assist them to speak to a specialist doctor. It is important not to dismiss a child's feelings by saying, 'of course you aren't bad'. It needs to be acknowledged that some children do gain pleasurable experiences from sexual abuse but emphasise that the abuse was wrong because they are an innocent and powerless child. Whatever they felt it was not their fault. Professionals will probably feel strongly that the child is not bad, dirty or abnormal but the child has been contaminated by the abuse and may well feel all these things and more. It is not unusual for a child who has suffered abuse to wash very frequently and some survivors have even drunk bleach to try and clean their insides of the horror. These feelings must not be dismissed but acknowledged so that healing can take place.

Children who have suffered abuse will tell adults in any way they can – sometimes they test a particular professional by these kinds of questions. But equally such questions could be completely innocent. This is not an easy task. Professionals need to learn to respond carefully to the needs of the child, not jump in quickly with adult agendas, and yet be open to the possibility of abuse.

Activity 11b: Responding to Complex Questions – Carousel

Aim: To provide an opportunity for participants to practice responses to complex questions linked to disclosure.

Delivery: The participants form two circles. The outside circle faces inwards and the inside circle faces outwards to form a carousel. The participants on the outside play the part of children asking questions and are given cards each with one question on it. They ask the question of the person opposite them in the inner circle who plays the part of an adult to provide a clear, sensible and age appropriate response to the question. After a short while, the trainer tells the participants to move round and the outside circle move once to the left to ask the same question of the next adult. The people in the inner circle remain stationary throughout. The trainer should allow about one minute for each question. It is useful to have a bell or whistle to signify the need to move round.

Once the participants have completed a whole rotation they reverse places in the carousel. Those that played children become the adults and those that played adults become the children. Another rotation is completed.

Alternatively the statements may be discussed in small groups taking one question after another and practising responses with trainers advising throughout.

Handout 11: Responding to Complex Questions

- Will Mum and Dad go to prison?
- I can't tell you. My Mum will kill me for telling.
- What will happen to me now I've told you?
- I don't want my brother going into care.
- She's my dad's girlfriend and he loves her lots. If I tell you my Dad won't believe me.
- Why did this happen to me?
- Will you tell my parents what I told you? I'm too frightened.
- My friends will want to know why I'm talking to you. What should I say?
- Do you think my Mum will believe me?
- Why must you tell anyone else? You can stop it can't you?
- No one will believe me now because I lied at the beginning when I said nothing happened.
- She was the teacher how could I tell her to stop?
- I will tell you, but don't tell anyone else.
- I hate my family I don't want to go home.
- My Mum doesn't love me. So she will be cross I told you she hit me.
- I think I'll be in trouble because I've done something too. I touched my willy as well.
- Do you think I should keep a secret when I don't want to?
- I don't want him to go to prison, he is the only one who loves me.
- Why did he have sex with me I didn't like it?
- Do you think my Mum will mind me talking to you like this?
- I can't say the words – can I write it down?
- If I tell you will I go into care?
- I don't like your face.
- I feel so guilty because I liked what he did, it made me feel good. That's wrong isn't it?
- He really spoils me and my brother, if I tell he won't buy us sweets ever again.
- I can't tell you want happened it's so rude.
- I was told not to say. That said if I did they'd kill me and my family.
- Now that I've told you, you won't tell my parents will you? They'll get angry.
- Did anything bad happen to you when you were younger?
- Can I come and live with you?
- Now I've told you do you still like me?
- I feel so bad and dirty I want to kill myself.
- What do you think I should have done when he tried to have sex with me?
- You are a grown up so you can just go and tell him to stop hitting me can't you?
- Why did he have sex with me?
- Yes I feel unhappy. I can't tell you, you won't understand.
- He said if I told you he would say I liked it and I took money from him.
- I had sex, so what I liked it? Older men make better lovers. What is it to you?

- Why did this happen to me?
- Will all my friends at school know about Mr Brown touching my breasts?
- Will you tell the policeman I made it all up?
- Am I going to be safe?
- Can I still get married?
- Do you think I'm normal?
- I'm really dirty aren't I?
- Mum says I have to go into care if dad gets put away because of me.
- What will happen to my sister now?

Feedback: Trainers feedback that it is important;

- Not to provide the child with false reassurance. If there are further decisions to be made, and the answers are not known at the time, it is important to tell the child that a meeting will be taking place to discuss what has been said but they will be fully informed about any decisions or actions. The child needs to know that their safety is an adult responsibility and that they will be finding the best way forward for them.
- To provide the child with acknowledgement of their feelings and not be dismissive. If they say they feel dirty then that is what they feel. It is not appropriate to tell them they are not dirty but rather say, 'I can understand that after everything you have been through that you do feel dirty. How can I help you to feel better about yourself?'
- Neither the social worker nor police officer are judge and jury, and cannot tell the child they believe them, as all the evidence is not collated at this stage. It can be said that they take the child's statement very seriously indeed, are listening very carefully and will do everything they possibly can to make sure they are safe.
- If a child says they don't like a particular worker it may be for many different reasons but it could be that the worker reminds them of the abuser. It is important to explore the feelings rather than take personal offence.
- Some children who have suffered sexual abuse will be worried that in their culture they may be unmarriagable. It is important for cultural advice to be sought and specialist services to be provided.
- Children may feel more able to write down an account of what happened or part of the account than say the words out loud. Once in written form they may then be able to speak about the difficult issues.
- Children cannot be offered inducements, even if these seem quite usual, as it could be said that the child was bribed into making an account.
- It is not appropriate for the worker to share personal abusive experiences with the child. The response might be, 'like most people I've had ups and downs in my life, but today is about you and I'm here to listen'.

Useful resources to assist children in speaking about what is happening to them but which do not make assumptions are:

Bruzzone, C. (1996) *All About Me*. Surrey: Small Publishing.
NSPCC (1997) *Turning Points. A Resource Pack for Communicating with Children*. London: NSPCC.
Peake, A. and Rouf, K. (1989) *My Body My Book*. London: The Children's Society.
Striker, S. and Kimmel, E. (2004) *The Anti-Colouring Book*. New York: Scholastic.

Activity 12: Adult Agendas

Aim: To enable participants to empathise with the difficulty children have when trying to speak to a professional about child sexual abuse.

Delivery: This is a whole group activity.

Content: The trainer asks the participants to make groups of two, then to stand facing each other and close their eyes. The trainer asks that they think about the last time they had a positive, enjoyable sexual experience. The trainer leaves them for a minute to think of this. They are then told that when the trainer tells them to open their eyes they are to relate to the person opposite their memory of their positive sexual experience. The trainer waits a few moments and then asks them to open their eyes and turn to their neighbour. Immediately the trainer then **stops the activity** and tells them to go back to their seats **as this is as far as the exercise goes**. They are asked to take a few moments to reflect on how they felt about disclosing such personal information to someone in the group.

Feedback: The trainers explore feelings of exposure, embarrassment, fear and nervousness and discuss how they might have felt if the experience remembered had not been positive and if they were being asked to relate the detail to a complete stranger. The trainers refer back to what is expected by police and social workers when interviewing children and if the participants found the activity difficult they should reflect on what a child might feel when being interviewed about child abuse.

Hear Us See Us (Nelson, 2008) is based on research with young people who have been sexually abused and tells of their experience of professional responses.

Activity 13: Corroboration of a Child's Statement

Aim: To provide participants with an opportunity to collate forensic and other information to allow for analysis of a child's statement about abuse. For participants to gain an understanding of the importance of evidence gathering and forensic retrieval in an investigation.

Delivery: Participants are split into groups of four. Each group is given a copy of the scenario and asked to imagine that they are conducting this investigation. Participants are told to study the information and produce a list of everything they feel is evidentially valuable and could be corroborated by one means or another.

Handout 12: Child's Statement

James is 10 years old. Whilst changing for a PE lesson today his teacher, Mr Wallace, noticed that he seemed to be in pain and moving very slowly. Mr Wallace approached James and asked him if he was alright. James became very upset and told him that he couldn't move fast because his back was hurting.

Mr Wallace asked him what he had done to his back and James told him that it happened last night at home. Mr Wallace asked him how he hurt his back and James told him that his dad did it. James said, 'my dad got really angry with me and hit me lots of times, with his belt, on my back'. Mr Wallace asked James if anyone had looked at his back since it happened, he said nobody had seen it and without being asked, he lifted up his shirt up to show Mr Wallace his back. Mr Wallace saw several red welt marks, in a crisscross pattern, across his back and told James that he would get some medical attention for him.

James went on to say that, last night, just before East Enders started, his mum and dad were arguing with each other again. He said they were shouting really loud and his dad got so angry with his mum that he punched a hole in the kitchen door with his fist. James said then his dad started shouting at him for not being in bed and chased him upstairs. When they got to his bedroom his dad took his belt off and whipped him across his back and bottom with it.

James said that his brother David, aged eight years, had tried to stop his dad by jumping on his back but it didn't work. His dad just threw him off and he ended up in the corner crying because he bumped his head on the cupboard. James said he could hear the baby next door crying and he thought that it was his screaming that had woken the baby up because once his dad stopped hitting him and left the bedroom he couldn't hear the baby crying any more.

Feedback: Trainers take feedback from each group referring back to the scenario given at the beginning of the task. Trainers are to draw out, from the groups, all possible pieces of corroborative evidence which could add to the validity of the child's account. The discussion should include the following:

- victims evidence – James' account
- medical evidence – welt marks
- other witnesses – mum, neighbour, David
- material evidence – photographs, clothing, belt, hole in the door
- sensory responses – what was heard, felt, seen etc.
- timing – television programme.

Presentation 10: The Paediatric Perspective

Trainers should invite the named paediatrician, or a forensic medical examiner, to give a presentation about *Working Together* from a health perspective. Participants should have an opportunity to ask questions about local practice issues. The presentation should include some understanding of forensic medical processes and dilemmas (DfES, 2006: 2.27–2.96).

Activity 14: Un-Trivial Pursuit: Child Sexual Abuse Quiz

Aim: To provide participants with a knowledge base of research and information about child sexual abuse.

Delivery: The trainer provides sets of cards numbered 1–40. Each card has a question on one side and the answer on the other. In mixed groups of no more than eight participants the cards are discussed. Each participant in turn takes the pack of cards and reads the question from the top card. The group debate the answer to the question before the participant turns over the card and reads the answer. The pack is then passed to the next person in the group to ask the next question. Trainers circulate and encourage debate.

Handout 13: Child Sexual Abuse Quiz

Questions
1. How many sexual offences against children result in a criminal conviction?
2. How effective is police action to stop the production and distribution of abusive images of children?
3. How many children, who are sexually abused, tell someone?
4. What do you do if you come across a website containing abusive images of children?
5. How many children know the person who abuses them?
6. Why do people sexually abuse children?
7. What is the extent of abusive images of children on the internet?
8. What is the incidence of child sexual abuse?
9. What is the impact of child sexual abuse on male survivors?
10. At what age does sexual abuse of a child commonly begin?
11. How long are children sexually abused for?
12. What percentage of rape victims are children?
13. How many registered child sex offenders are there in the UK?
14. How many crimes against children go unreported?
15. What is the recent increase in offences of making, taking or possessing abusive images of children?
16. Where do most sexual crimes against children take place?
17. Does a history of child sexual abuse lead on to sexual offending behaviour in adulthood?
18. What do you know about the organised sexual abuse of children in the Isle of Lewis inquiry?
19. Of children who run away, how many children are thought to have been the victims of sexual assault?
20. How many children are subject to a child protection plan under the category of sexual abuse? Is this an increase or decrease since 2000?
21. What is the incidence of sexual abuse of disabled children?
22. What is the child sex abuser re-offending rate?
23. How extensive is sex tourism?
24. What are the key characteristics of a child targeted by a child sex abuser?
25. Child sexual abusers are all 'dirty old men'.
26. Is it wrong to take photos of a baby or toddler lying naked on a rug or in the bath or pool?
27. Of children who go missing, how many are under the age of 11 years?
28. What were the main learning points from the case of Fred and Rose West in 1995?
29. What is known about the institutional abuse of children?
30. Is it true that generally, in organised abuse cases, the perpetrators are convicted because of the serious and wide scale of the abuse and because there are multiple victims?

31. Some artists argue that their contentious artistic work does not contain abusive images of children.
32. Professionals can notify the local community about the presence of a known child sex abuser in the locality.
33. If a child tells you that they have been sexually abused by another child, must you inform the police?
34. What percentage of survivors consider themselves damaged by having been sexually abused as a child?
35. Children are most likely to discuss an allegation of sexual abuse immediately after an incident.
36. Of children who run away how many are forced to leave home by their carers?
37. What effect does the search of a child sex abuser's address have?
38. How many adolescents die every year as a result of child abuse?
39. Are child witnesses believed through the court process?
40. What information should social workers keep about known and suspected child sex abusers?

Answers

1. How many sexual offences against children result in a criminal conviction?
Only 1 in 50 sex offences against children result in a conviction (Stuart and Baines, 2004).

Recorded offences of gross indecency towards children doubled between 1995 and 2001 but the conviction rate dropped from 42 per cent to 19 per cent.

> *It is clear from the extremely low rate of convictions for child sexual abuse that there has been no progress on bringing perpetrators to justice.*
> (Utting, W. (2005) *Progress on Safeguards for Children Living Away from Home.* 140–1

One in three children reporting abuse are under the age of 8. Of four authorities studied only between 0 and 5% of cases involving children under the age of 8 reached court.

During the Waterhouse Inquiry into abuse in children's homes in Wales police interviewed 2,500 people leading to the investigation of 500 complaints of physical or sexual abuse and only eight people were prosecuted and six convicted.

The most vulnerable children are almost totally failed by the criminal justice system.

Utting, W. (1997) *People Like Us. The Report of The Review of The Safeguards For Children Living Away From Home.* London: HMSO.

2. How effective is police action to stop the production and distribution of abusive images of children? 7,200 men in the UK identified by Operation Ore accessed a gateway to abusive images of children. A total of 13,000 pictures led to only 25 children being identified (*Sunday Herald*, 2008). Operation Cathedral targeted an internet site called Wonderland and police seized 750,000 abusive images of children. Over 1,200 children were identified in these images but only 18 were discovered of whom three were found in the UK.

The Child Exploitation and Online Protection Centre (CEOP) encourages reporting of such images and informs the public about the issue. Every adult identified through such seized material should lead to a Section 47 (Children Act 1989) strategy meeting to consider the risk to children. This rarely happens as the images are so seldom identified.

(Downey, R. (2002) Victims of Wonderland. *Community Care* 7–13th March).

3. How many children, who are sexually abused, tell someone? Only a quarter. Most tell a family member or friend. Very few tell police or social workers. www.stopitnow.org

Fifteen per cent of a national sample of 998 children aged 8–11 years said they would not talk to anyone if they had a problem.

Seventy-two per cent of sexually abused children did not tell anyone about the abuse at the time. Twenty-seven per cent told later. Thirty-one per cent still had not told anybody by early adulthood.

Cawson et al. (2000) *Child Maltreatment in the UK. A Study of the Prevalence of Child Abuse and Neglect*. London. NSPCC

Ghate, D. and Daniels, A. (1997) *Talking About My Generation: A Survey of 8–15 Year Olds Growing up in the 1990s.* London: NSPCC.

4. What do you do if you come across a website containing abusive images of children? A report should be made to the Internet Watch Foundation. www.iwf.org.uk

5. How many children know the person who abuses them? More than 8 out of 10 children know their abuser as they are family, friends, neighbours and babysitters. Many hold responsible positions in society and about a third are from professional backgrounds.

- One per cent of children experienced sexual abuse by a parent or carer and three per cent by another relative in childhood.
- Eleven per cent experienced sexual abuse during childhood by people known but unrelated to them.
- Five per cent experienced sexual abuse by an adult stranger or someone they had just met.

Cawson et al. (2000) *Child Maltreatment in the UK. A Study of the Prevalence of Child Abuse and Neglect*. London: NSPCC.

6. Why do people sexually abuse children? The reasons are not known. Some abusers recognise it is wrong, others in their distorted thinking, consider the behaviour to be normal and that it is their way of showing love to children. Some have been abused themselves but not all and some come from violent or unhappy backgrounds.

www.stopitnow.org

7. What is the extent of abusive images of children on the internet? Over 100,000 websites contain abusive images of children (www.ceop.gov.uk).

8. What is the incidence of child sexual abuse? Cawson et al. (2000) reported in their study that 18 per cent of children had experienced sexual abuse. Kelly et al. (1991) found that 21 per cent of young women and 7 per cent of young men had experienced sexual abuse involving physical contact before the age of 18 years.

www.survivorsswindon.com/stats/

9. What is the impact of child sexual abuse on male survivors? Research conducted with 2,500 men who had a history of child sexual abuse found that they were twice as likely than non-abused men to report depression and self-harm and four times more likely to kill themselves.

King, M. (2002) Sexual Molestation of Males: Associations with Psychological Disturbance. *British Journal of Psychiatry*, 181: 153–7, cited on the website www.survivorsswindon.com/

10. At what age does sexual abuse of a child commonly begin? In 67 per cent of cases, abuse began before the age of 11 years.

NSPCC (1997) *Childhood Matters. National Commission of Inquiry into the Prevention of Child Abuse*. London, NSPCC.

11. How long are children sexually abused for? In 50 per cent of cases the sexual abuse lasted between 2 and 18 years.

NSPCC (1997) *Childhood Matters. National Commission of Inquiry into the Prevention of Child Abuse*. London: NSPCC.

12. What percentage of rape victims are children? Over a quarter. 27 per cent of all crimes of rapes recorded by the police were committed against children under the age of 16. 4 per cent were committed against children between the ages of 0–9 years and 23 per cent against children between the ages of 10–15 years. Two thirds of male victims of buggery and indecent assault were under the age of 16 years, 27 per cent of these were under the age of 10 years and 43 per cent between ages 10 and 15 years.

A half of female victims of indecent assault and buggery were under the age of 16 years. 17 per cent were under the age of 10 years and 34 per cent between ages 10 and 15 years.

Harris and Grace (1999) *A Question of Evidence? Investigating and Prosecuting Rape in the 1990s*. London: Home Office research study 196.

13. How many registered child sex offenders are there in the UK? About 29,000 individuals were registered as sex offenders in England and Wales in 2006. This figure includes offences against both adults and children. There are no separate statistics for children. The Sex Offenders Register came into force in 1997 and includes all sexual crime. People convicted before 1997 are not required to register. Failure to register is an offence which carries a term of imprisonment. In 2007 the Violent and Sex Offender Register (ViSOR) was developed as a pilot to extend the work of MAPPA to both violent and sex offenders.

Batty, D. (2006) *Q & A: The Sex Offenders Register. The Guardian*, 18.01.2006
http://education.guardian.co.uk/schools/story/0,1689261,00.html

14. How many crimes against children go unreported? There is concern that as much as 95 per cent of sexual crime against children is unreported.

NCIS (2003) *UK Threat Assessment of Serious and Organised Crime. Sex Offences against Children including Online Abuse.*
www.ncis.co.uk

15. What is the recent increase in offences of making, taking or possessing abusive images of children? In 2006 the Internet Watch Foundation's annual report stated that the severity of online child abuse content was increasing with a four fold rise in images depicting the most severe abuse. 80 per cent of the children in the images were female and 91 per cent under 12 years. 90 per cent of commercial sites were hosted in Russia or the US. The total of reports was 31,776 in 2006. In 2006 the Foundation gave 11 evidential statements to UK police.

http://www.iwf.org.uk/media/news.196.htm

16. Where do most sexual crimes against children take place? Eighty per cent of sexual assaults against children take place in the home of either the victim or the offender.

Grubin, D. (1998) *Sex Offending Against Children: Understanding the Risk.* Police Research Series Paper 99. London: Home Office.

17. Does a history of child sexual abuse lead on to sexual offending behaviour in adulthood? In the majority of cases people who have survived child sexual abuse do not go on to become abusers.

A study at Great Ormond Street Hospital in London found that 12 per cent of male victims of child sexual abuse subsequently abused children themselves.

Grubin, D. (1998) *Sex Offending Against Children: Understanding The Risk.* Police Research Series Paper 99. London: Home Office.
Salter et al. (2003) Development of Sexually Abusive Behaviour in Sexually Victimised Males: A Longitudinal Study. *The Lancet,* 361 (February).

18. What do you know about the organised sexual abuse of children described in the Isle of Lewis inquiry? In 2003, nine people were arrested on charges including the rape of children. In 2004, all cases were dropped although the chief constable said it was his view that he had sufficient evidence to charge all the people involved. In a recent inquiry considering the interests of three of the child victims, author Alexis Jay expressed a belief that all three children were repeatedly sexually abused with over 200 indicators of child abuse including sexual, physical, neglect and emotional abuse.

Social Work Inspection Agency, (2005) *An Inspection into the Care and Protection of Children in Eilean Siar.* Edinburgh. Scottish Executive. www.swia.org.uk/

19. Of children who run away, how many children are thought to have been the victims of sexual assault? One in nine young people were sexually assaulted during the time when they had run away.

One in twelve runaways said they had been hurt or harmed on the most recent occasion they ran away.

Biehal, N. et al. (2003) *Lost from View: Missing Persons in the UK.* Bristol: Policy Press.

Rees, G. and Lee, J. (2005*) Still Running II: Findings From The Second National Survey of Young Runaways.* London: The Children's Society.

20. How many children are subject to a child protection plan under the category of sexual abuse? Is this an increase or decrease since 2000? In 2007 there were 2,500 children's names on the child protection register or subject of a child protection plan, under the category of sexual abuse. This was a reduction since 2000 when there were 5,100.

DCSF (2007) National Statistics. Referrals, Assessments and Child Protection and Young People who are the Subject of a Child Protection Plan or are on Child Protection Registers, England, ending 31st March 2007.
http://dcsf.gov.uk/rsgateway/DB/SFR/s000742/index.shtml

21. What is the incidence of sexual abuse of disabled children? Disabled children are 3.1 times more likely to be sexually abused than non-disabled children.

Sullivan, P. and Knutson, J. (2000) Maltreatment and Disabilities: A Population Based Epidemiological Study. *Child Abuse and Neglect*, 24, 10: 1257–73.

22. What is the child sex abuser re-offending rate? One in four child sex abusers who had abused children outside the family were reconvicted within six years.
Hood, R. et al. (2002) *Reconviction Rates of Serious Sex Offenders and Assessments of Their Risk. Findings 164.* London: Research, Development and Statistics Directorate, Home Office. p.4

23. How extensive is sex tourism? Child sex tourism is the commercial sexual exploitation of children by men or women who travel from one place to another, usually from a richer country to one that is less developed and then engage in sexual acts with children, defined as anyone aged under 18 years. British child sex offenders travel mainly to Eastern Europe (particularly the Czech republic and Romania), South East Asia (particularly Thailand, Cambodia, the Phillipines and Vietnam), India (Goa), Brazil and Cuba. Spain and Greece are also popular as they have a lower age of consent than the UK. Sixty per cent of all tourism to Thailand, and fifty per cent of all tourism to Kenya, Phillipines and South Korea is sex tourism. The Sexual Offences Act 2003 states that British citizens and residents who commit offences against children overseas can now be prosecuted in the UK. All registered sex offenders have to notify police if they leave the UK for three or more days.

www.ecpat.org.uk/

24. What are the key characteristics of a child targeted by a child sex abuser?
Abusers target vulnerable children and in particular those who are often alone or desirous of attention.

25. Child sexual abusers are all 'dirty old men'. Masson and Erooga (1999) estimated between 25 per cent and 33 per cent of all alleged sexual abuse involves young, mainly adolescent, perpetrators. Abel (1985) found that as many as half of convicted child sex abusers began offending during adolescence. Corby highlights research stating that many young child sex abusers have been themselves sexually abused (Corby, 2006: 130).

The statistics for child sexual abuse by women vary considerably from between 5 and 25 per cent of the total. ChildLine figures for 2004–5 revealed that 11 per cent of callers about sexual abuse were about abuse by female abusers. Out of 6000 girls calling about sexual abuse, 3 per cent were calls about female abusers and 2 per cent about their mothers. Of over 2,000 boys calling about sexual abuse 35 per cent were referring to a female abuser and 17 per cent were calling about their mothers (Ford, 2006: 10).

Abel, G. et al. (1985) Sexual Offenders: Results of Assessment and Recommendations for Treatment. In Ben-Aron, H. et al. (Eds.) *Clinical Criminology*. Toronto. M M Graphics.
Corby, B. (2006) *Child Abuse Towards a Knowledge Base*. Berkshire: Open University Press.
Ford, H. (2006) *Women Who Sexually Abuse*. London: Wiley.
Masson, H. and Erooga, M. (1999) Children and Young People who Sexually Abuse Others: Incidence, Characteristics, Causation. In Erooga, M. and Masson, H. (Eds.) *Children and Young People who Sexually Abuse Others. Challenges and Responses.* London: Routledge.

26. Is it wrong to take photos of a baby or toddler lying naked on a rug or in the bath or pool? Such photos are not defined as abusive, but such material could, if available, be of interest to a child sex abuser.

27. Of children who go missing, how many are under the age of 11 years? Over a quarter had run away before the age of 13 years and one in ten before the age of 11 years.

Rees, G. and Lee, J. (2005*) Still Running 2: Findings from the Second National Survey of Young Runaways*. London: The Children's Society.

28. What were the main learning points from the case of Fred and Rose West in 1995? The key questions raised were why:

- The community did not report the most serious criminal matters of child abuse.
- The West's previous history of sexual offending and their known involvement in pornography were not taken into account in assessments.
- There was no collation of evidence of children missing from care establishments.

Bridge Child Care Consultancy (1996) *Heather and Charmaine West Serious Case (Part 8) Review*. Gloucester: ACPC.

29. What is known about the institutional abuse of children? A study of 16 NSPCC projects concerning investigations into institutional abuse found 76 allegations of abuse by 67 children against 50 alleged abusers. Thirty-three related to physical abuse, 24 to sexual abuse, 16 to inappropriate restraint and a minority to inappropriate care.

Between 1997 and 2000 the Crown Prosecution service rejected 79 per cent of cases of institutional abuse referred by police. For more recent information about institutional abuse see the website of Jersey Senator Stuart Syvret on http://stuartsyvret.blogspot.com/

Barter, C. (1998) *Investigating Institutional Abuse of Children: An Exploration of the NSPCC Experience.* London. NSPCC.
http://www.nspcc.org.uk/Inform/research/Findings/investigatinginstitutionalabuse_wda48234.html
Utting, W. (2005) *Progress on Safeguards for Children Living Away from Home.* York: Joseph Rowntree Trust. 141.

30. Is it true that generally, in organised abuse cases, the perpetrators are convicted because of the serious and wide scale of the abuse and because there are multiple victims? Manchester University research found that the criminal justice system is unable to deal with complex cases of organised abuse and only a minority of suspected perpetrators are convicted.

Gallagher, B. (1998) *Grappling with Smoke. Investigating and Managing Organised Child Sexual Abuse. A Good Practice Guide.* London. NSPCC

31. Some artists argue that their contentious artistic work does not contain abusive images of children. Art is no defence against a charge concerning abusive images of children under any legislation. This does not prevent much current debate about contentious art exhibits.

32. Professionals can notify the local community about the presence of a known child sex abuser in the locality. If there is clear child protection justification then professionals can inform the local community about a local child sex abuser. 'Megans Law' (community notification), now widely implemented in the US, has not been implemented in the UK despite Sarah's Law campaign following the murder of Sarah Payne. Community notification when it is professionally agreed, is the responsibility of the local Multi-Agency Protection Arrangements (MAPPA).

Further information is available from the following:

Home Office (2007) *Keeping Children Safe From Sex Offenders. How Sex Offenders Are Managed.* London: Home Office. http://www.homeoffice.gov.uk/documents/child-safe/
Fitch, K. (2007) *Sex Offender Management.* London: NSPCC. http://www.nspcc.org.uk/Inform/policyandpublicaffairs/sexoffendermanagement_wdf50066.pdf
Nelson, S. (2004) *Neighbourhood Mapping for Children's Safety.* Edinburgh: Womanzone.

In 2008 the Home Secretary announced plans to run a pilot scheme that enables parents to be informed if anyone who has regular unsupervised access to their children poses a risk.

33. If a child tells you that they have been sexually abused by another child, must you inform the police? You must report to the local authority children's services and they will contact the police Child Abuse Investigation Team to convene a strategy meeting.

34. What percentage of survivors consider themselves damaged by having been sexually abused as a child? Fifty-four per cent reported a damaging effect on their lives, sixty-seven per cent when abuse interfamilial and seventy-five per cent if the abuser was a parent. The greatest reported damage was if abuse took place before the age of 10 and if it was repeated. However, even if the child was too young to remember the abuse or their relationship to the abuser was distant, these factors did not alter the implications for intervention.

Sarah Nelson (2001) writes about the physical impact of child sexual abuse and the link between unexplained physical conditions and survivors accounts of physical pain.

Baker, A. and Duncan, S. (1985) Child Sexual Abuse: A Study of Prevalence in Great Britain. *Child Abuse and Neglect.* 9: 457–67.

35. Children are most likely to discuss an allegation of sexual abuse immediately after an incident. In a study of 10 young adults sexually exploited as children through abusive images, none had told freely of the events in 28 years. This provides a very different view to the idea that children make false allegations (Svedin, 1996).

A NSPCC study concluded that 72 per cent of sexually abused children said they were too frightened to tell anyone at the time of the abuse and 31 per cent still had not told anyone by early adulthood.

Svedin, C. and Bach, K. (1996) *Children who Don't Speak Out about Children being used in Child Pornography.* Sweden: Radda Barnen.
Cawson, P. et al. (2000) *Child Maltreatment in the UK* .London: NSPCC.

36. Of children who run away how many are forced to leave home by their carers? Twenty-six per cent of young runaways felt that they were forced to leave home. Over two thirds (68 per cent) said their parents or carers did not report them missing to the police on the most recent occasion that they were away.

Rees, G. and Lee, J. (2005) *Still Running 2. Findings from the Second National Survey of Young Runaways.* London: The Children's Society.

37. What effect does the search of a child sex abuser's address have? To search a premises for abusive images of children is one of the most effective ways of gaining evidence about the sexual abuse of children. Photographic or video evidence may minimise the need for child witnesses to appear in court, provide corroborative evidence and assist in identifying other perpetrators.

38. How many adolescents die every year as a result of child abuse? There are no statistics. Deaths of young people from overdoses, suicide or other causes such as hypothermia are not recorded as deaths from abuse even though these young people may well have suffered child abuse both earlier in their childhoods and also through organised crime networks.

39. Are child witnesses believed through the court process? Out of 50 children interviewed, 23 were clear that the defence representative had accused them of lying, and sometimes the accusation was made more than once.

Plotnikoff, J. and Woolfson, R. (2004) *In Their Own Words. The Experiences of 50 Young Witnesses in Criminal Proceedings.* London. NSPCC and Victim Support.

40. What information should social workers keep about known and suspected child sex abusers? It is important for social workers and other professionals to report suspected and known child sex abusers to the Multi-Agency Public Protection Arrangements through their agency representative on this committee.

Activity 15: The Dynamics of Child Sexual Abuse: Learning from the Case of Mary Bell

Aim: To provide participants with an in depth understanding of the dynamics of child sexual abuse and learning from a survivor's account.

Delivery: The trainer introduces the material and then reads out the story. The trainer pauses at the breaks to make comment on the dynamics illustrated by the account. The trainer warns the participants about the distressing nature of the account.

Content: Introduction: Mary Bell in 1968, at the age of eleven was tried and convicted of manslaughter after the death of two small boys in Newcastle-upon-Tyne. Author, Gitta Sereny attended the trial and wrote a book at the time about the trial of this small child in an adult court. Mary Bell spent 12 years in prison. In later years on release from prison and following her mother's death, Mary began to talk about her childhood experiences of abuse. Gitta Sereny, with the help of Mary Bell, wrote another book *Cries Unheard* from which this extract is taken. There was public outrage when it became known that Mary Bell had received some payment for her contribution to the book. The media declared that no child murderer should gain payment for writing about their experiences. The public did not wish to hear that the child they had demonised had suffered so much as a child victim of adult abuse. Yet many books are accepted by the public as written by criminals, gangsters and murderers and become best sellers. The response to the publication of *Cries Unheard* sadly led to the press locating Mary Bell. She had to seek protection for herself and her daughter.

Mary is now in her 40s. Her mother has died. Only at this stage of her life is she able to speak of the abuse by her mother. This is not uncommon. Children rarely speak of abuse as children. Many will wait until they are adults and often until when the abuser is dead.

Mary Bell's account of her experience

Excerpt from Sereny, G. (1999) *Cries Unheard. The Story of Mary Bell*. London: Macmillan. 334–6:

> *The story sounds as if it was all one memory, told in one breath, but it wasn't like that at all. I was, I must admit, at first so sceptical about the details that she remembered, and so concerned at the horrific nature of them, that I made her tell me three times. The first time was two weeks after we began to talk, in July 1996. The last time was at the beginning of December. In July it took her four days to get it out, sometimes in a monotonous voice but more often in deep distress, her face growing paler and paler, breaking into a sweat and finally, she would speak through desperate sobs, reverting at times, as she had done before under extreme emotional pressure, to the present tense.*

Comment

Survivors when speaking about childhood abuse may well revert to the present tense as they relive the experience. An older woman may speak in a childish voice and act in a childlike manner when describing abuse at a young age. To speak about the abuse is to re-experience the horror of it.

Account continued

She couldn't remember how old she was, but she thought four or five. 'I wasn't yet in school,' she said. She remembered being made to sit in the living room and that there was a man on the bed with her mother. 'What I remember, this man's penis is all white, that's what I remember, really white and when he . . . er . . . you know, stuff comes, I just couldn't understand it, where it came from, you know, or what it was.' She moved her nose as if she was smelling something nasty. 'There was this smell, horrible, nasty like . . . But it was horrible, and then I was on the bed, and then . . . they turned on me.'

Comment

Professionals expect children to remember details such as times and places but children are more likely to retain memories associated with important life events such as family celebrations or religious festivals. Mary makes the link with the abuse being at a time before she began school which was a significant life event. Children's memories will be accessed more easily if connected to sensory experiences such as taste, touch, hearing or smell. Mary Bell refers to the nasty smell which has remained in her memory for all the years. It is an important factor in validating a child's statement if they can describe a related sensory experience which is not something they would learn from watching a video. Children have described how an adult smelt of alcohol or cigarettes or the sounds the adult made during the assault.

Account continued

As she answered my questions, one memory went into another. 'I had these little white socks on and just a little top and um, a nappy, a nappy type thing . . . and my mother,' she sighed deeply, 'my mother would hold me one hand pulling my head back, by my hair, the other holding my arms back of me, my neck back like and . . . and . . . they'd put their penis in my mouth and when . . . when, you know, they . . . ejaculated, I'd vomit.'

Comment

Her memory of small white socks and a nappy are memories which identify for her that she was vulnerable as a small child. As she builds on her memories she is able to describe the actual acts of abuse. In interviewing children it can help to slowly build on the details they can recall, perhaps the less painful peripheral details, and then work towards an account of what happened. Children will frequently describe the colour of the wallpaper in the room or the back of the chair as they gently allow themselves to get closer to remembering and describing the pain of the abusive acts.

Account continued

Sometimes she would blindfold me – she called it 'playing blind-man's buff'. And she would tie a stocking around my eyes and lift me up and twirl me around, laughing. And then she'd put a thing . . . a silky thing around my face to . . . to keep my mouth open and it was so dreadful, with the rosaries, you know, bumping into me you know, I felt so bad, so bad.

Comment

Abusers will sometimes frame their abusive acts within childish games or nursery rhymes. Sometimes they describe themselves as a cartoon character so that, if the child discloses, their account will confuse the adults who will think the child is in a make-believe world and the identity of the abuser remains secret.

In the Orkneys case the children described a 'spin the bottle' game and stated how they had to be hooked into the centre to be abused. In another case, one boy could only constantly repeat the 'goosy, goosy gander' nursery rhyme. This was the important clue to the fact that he was abused by his foster carer. She had sung to him the rhyme 'where shall I wander, upstairs and downstairs in my ladies chamber' during the abuse. He was so traumatised by the abuse that he could only repeat the rhyme.

Account continued

'You told me that when your dad was around, you always felt safe', I said. 'So why didn't you tell him then? Why didn't you ask him for help?'

'I was so frightened because before it, or later she says if I ever told anything I would be taken away and locked up. You know I told you about the sentry box on the Tyne Bridge? That's where she said I would go. And she said nobody would believe me. And anyway, I think I must have thought it was my fault. I had done wrong and was being punished. I . . . I . . .' She cried and cried. It was one of the very worst moments of our time together . . . 'I felt so . . . so dirty.'

Comment

This paragraph describes many of the reasons why children may not tell about the abuse. Mary was directly threatened and thought no-one would believe her account. She blamed herself for the abuse. The abuser had made sure that she had internalised the cause of the abuse because she was 'naughty'. She also felt contaminated. Some survivors speak of drinking bleach to try and clean the abuse away. Others take many showers every day or obsessively wash their hands.

Account continued

'How often did this happen?' I asked.
   'I don't know. Not that often perhaps, or maybe quite a few times. I don't know.'

Comment

Mary really does not remember exactly how often the abuse happened. If abuse is a regular occurrence then one abusive incident will merge into another and the account may well be confused. To obtain a clear account focusing on the first or last time it happened may assist the memory.

Account continued

I knew that a medical examination before she went to Red Bank had shown her to be intact. 'Did the men touch you below?' I asked. It was very, very difficult for her to find the words for the answer.
   'Yes, but . . . and I don't mean . . . Not, you know. I don't think it was there with their penis . . . I mean I was held down on my stomach. It hurt like hell. It hurt . . . it really, really hurt. I was gagged but I screamed, ''it hurts, it hurts''. And she said to me softly you know, ''It won't be long now, it won't hurt for long''. But it did. I was sore. For going to the toilet, I was sore, and I had marks, scratch marks on my legs and marks where I had things stuck into me.'
   'Things? What sort of things?'
   'They were sort of bullets, like a shot gun kind of bullet, with a brass thing, a suppository-type of thing, I used to have them twirled into me.'
   'Where into you?'
   'My bottom. Up on my legs.' She pulled up the skirt of her long dress she was wearing and showed me some curious round scars.
   'Did you ever wonder why they did that?'

Comment

Mary was abused in a very bizarre way which probably lay outside of the experience and knowledge base of those with responsibility for her care. If a child's hymen is still intact this does not mean that she has not suffered some form of sexual abuse. The acts of violence by adults towards children may be beyond belief but it is important to think the unthinkable and enter the child's world and to try to comprehend what they tell us.

Account continued

She shook her head. 'Perhaps to make me cry? But I didn't. I wouldn't cry . . .'
   'You are crying now; you are crying here.'
   'I wouldn't cry then', she repeated.

Comment

Children may be afraid to display emotions about the abuse. The abuse may have increased had she cried at the time. It is important to understand that children who have suffered repeated abuse may give an account in an unemotional or matter of fact way. This is one way of coping with the trauma.

Account continued

'Did your mother give you things afterwards?'

'Yes, sweeties and she was nice to me and she laughed. I can remember times when I had these games. I felt afterwards she loved me. I had a bag of chips and I wouldn't get hit. I remember her then as very pretty and she didn't call me names, and even taught me to knit. But then she ripped off all the stitches off and threw the stuff at me.'

Comment

Mary was loved and abused by the same mother. She didn't know or understand the difference between the two. She was emotionally abused as well as physically and sexually harmed.

Account continued

'How long did this horror go on?' I asked Mary,

'At Westmoreland Road', she said. 'And also in another room nearby, in Elswick Road, which I think belonged to her friend, Elsie. I think while I was small, you know, really small, four, five, six. After that she or Elsie would take me to rooms where old men lived and leave me.'

'And what would happen?'

She shrugged. 'Not that much. They'd touch me. They'd masturbate. I didn't care.'

Comment

Mary minimises the impact of the abuse. This is a common coping mechanism. For instance, children will say the abuser didn't mean it because they were drunk or stressed.

Account continued

She cared. And she demonstrated this in an extraordinary way when she was about seven going on eight she thinks. 'I told you about dad's friend Harry Bury, the rag-and-bone man who lived upstairs? He was brilliant. He called me his lucky mascot. And one day I went to his room and he'd probably had a drink and was lying on his back. And I went up and fiddled with his trousers . . . You know . . . I opened his buttons or zip or whatever and took it out.'

'You took his penis out? Why?'

'I wanted to see whether he'd be like all the others. And he shot up and he was absolutely disgusted and said, 'What the hell are you doing?' But then almost rightaway, he was like, 'its all right, it's all right. Let's go and have a cuppa tea and feed the cat.' And after that I was OK, you know. The next time it came up. I told my mother I wouldn't do it no more.'

Comment

Gitta Sereny located Harry Bury who confirmed this story. This inappropriate sexual behaviour might well be the first point of referral to children's services. Children who demonstrate sexually abusive behaviour may be repeating learnt patterns of abuse. Mary did not know she was doing anything wrong as she was acting out aspects of what she had experienced. This included her learnt pattern of behaviour of choking. She repeated this onto the children she murdered, without understanding that such choking could lead to a child's death, because she had survived such trauma.

Feedback: Group discussion.

Activity 16: Saturdays at Half Past Three: A Child Retracts

Aim: For participants to gain an understanding of the dynamics of disclosure and in particular the pressures that are on children to retract disclosures.

Delivery: Participants are given the roles as stated below and told to listen to the poem not as the professional but in their allocated role. They sit in a horseshoe around the trainer. Badges are provided stating the roles. The trainer reads the poem and plays the role of the child. The participants are given a few minutes to think about what has been said by the child (trainer). The trainer then points in turn to the participants starting with the 'mother' and works their way around the horseshoe taking each role in turn. The trainer asks them what they would like to say to her now that she has read the poem. They address her as the child author of the poem. The child (trainer) depending on responses received may well come back to particular participants to ask further questions and develop the exercise as an interaction between the participants and the trainer as the child. The trainer explains that this poem was written by a child and sent anonymously to a helpline. It was given to one of the authors for use in training.

Content

Roles

Those asterisked are essential roles because they are mentioned in the poem:
  Mother*
  Maternal grandmother*
  Maternal grandfather
  Paternal grandmother*
  Paternal grandfather
  Older sister
  Younger sister
  Uncle, father's brother
  Aunt, father's sister
  Teacher*
  Police officer*
  Social worker*
  Mother's best friend
  Neighbour
  Neighbour
Father* This role is played by the second trainer and is not identified until the end of the activity.
  Other roles may be added such as: father's friend, sports coach or church pastor.

Handout 14: Saturdays at Half Past Three

Once I had a lovely Daddy, smiled and took me on his knee.
Used to laugh with me and Mummy, Saturdays at half past three.
How I loved my lovely daddy, standing on a kitchen chair.
Watching from the window for him –'Put the kettle on, he's there.'

Then one day my lovely Daddy turned into a stranger man.
Just when Mummy'd gone out shopping, said he'd got a wizard plan.
Said we'd play, but I must promise not to tell my Mum or Gran.
What he did I'd try to tell you, but I just don't think I can.

Ever since he left me crying, now I never can be sure,
'Cos I've got a devil Daddy – Please don't do it any more.
Teacher asked at school on Monday what it was that made me cry.
Stranger men are sent to prison so I had to tell a lie.

If they take my devil Daddy, they take my lovely Daddy too.
Daddy, don't be angry now – I used to think so much of you.
Give me back my lovely Daddy, make it like it used to be,
When you laughed with me and Mummy, Saturdays at half past three.

Delivery and Feedback:

This exercise will vary each time – there will be a range of participant and trainer responses such as the following which are offered as examples;

Child	What are you feeling as the mother?
Mother	I'm very upset. I'm not sure what to think.
Child	Do you believe me?
Mother	Yes.
Child	So can you tell him to stop being a devil Daddy.
Mother	How can I do that?
Child	Just don't go shopping on Saturday at half past three any more.
Mother	OK, but I think I will need to tell the police about this.

Trainer moves on to next role . . .

Maternal grandmother	You can come and stay with me and granddad.
Child	Can Daddy come and visit me?
Maternal grandmother	Not at the moment
Child	Why not?
Maternal grandmother	I don't want him coming round until things are sorted out.
Child	Well you can speak to him and sort it out.

Trainer moves on to next role . . .

Paternal grandmother	My son would never harm any child of his. He was brought up properly.
Child	Do you think I'm telling lies?
Paternal grandfather	Well you do make up stories sometimes don't you?
Child	I'm not making this up. This is true.
Paternal grandfather	I don't believe you.

Trainer moves on to next role . . .

Older sister	He's done the same to me. I know what you are talking about.
Child	He said I was his special one. Why didn't you tell me?
Older sister	Because I thought I was special.
Child	Well you're not but I am.

Trainer moves on to next role . . .

Uncle: father's brother	You are a little liar. You are just making trouble for the family.
Child	Why don't you believe me? Do you do the same to your daughter?

Trainer moves on to next role . . .

Teacher	I believe you are being hurt. I'm going to report this to children's services
Child	I only want him to stop being a devil daddy on Saturdays.

Trainer moves on to next role . . .

Social worker	Tell me exactly what happened?
Child	I have told you. Didn't you listen?
Social worker	But I don't know what actually happened.
Child	I told you it's on Saturdays at half past three he is a devil daddy.
Social worker	What do you mean by devil daddy?
Child	He's not my normal nice daddy. Can you speak to him and tell him to stop being devil daddy?
Social worker	Not at the moment I'm going to have to tell the police and we can tell the police officer together. Is that alright?
Child	Why have you got to tell the police? They will lock him up.

Trainer moves on to next role . . .

Child	So are you going to lock him up then?
Police Officer	I'm going to go and speak with your Dad
Child	Will he go to prison? I don't want him to get hurt. I love my daddy. I just want him to stop.
Police officer	We need to speak to you to find out exactly what happened.
Child	I'm not going to tell you anything because I'll miss my nice Daddy if you put him in prison.

Trainer moves on to next role . . .

Neighbour	Your Dad is such a good Dad. But, if you want, you can always come and talk with me.
Child	Can your children still come and play at my house?
Neighbour	No. But you can come to our house anytime.

And so on . . .

The trainer/child continues and summarises the significance of the responses to the child. The trainer/child asks the second trainer, who is playing the father, what he is thinking now.

He says that he is a little worried but that there is nothing he cannot sort out. His response will vary depending on the contributions that have been made.

The trainer/child then decides to make life easier for everyone by retracting the statement. She says that she has lied and made it all up and that nothing ever happened at all. The trainer/child then goes around the group again asking what they are thinking in the light of the retraction and deals with the responses as before.

At the end the second trainer/father says that he is laughing because, whilst everyone is arguing, he can carry on abusing her as they are not there to protect her. His statement is made relevant to the contributions from the participants. He might say, for example, that the teacher is making it hard for him so he will have to think of ways to try and get in favour with the teacher.

The trainer points out that the child's retraction will remain on record and the next time the child tries to tell it will be even more difficult to be heard because professionals will think the child is 'crying wolf', inventing allegations and being a nuisance.

Presentation 11: The Child Abuse Accommodation Syndrome

The sexual abuse of children often follows a predictable pattern of stages.

Helplessness

Most offenders are trusted adults to the child and children will feel helpless within authoritarian adult/child relationships. This power dynamic makes disclosure very difficult.

Engagement or entrapment

The offender initiates the contact with the young person by offering bribes, rewards, special attention or affection. This is referred to as grooming the victim. Child sexual abuse is usually well planned by the offender who uses his/her close and trusted relationship to access the child. If left unprotected the child learns to survive as best s/he can. There appears no way out of the situation and the child learns to accommodate the reality of the continuing abuse. The child may convince themselves that they provoked the abuse and then lie to maintain the secret.

Sexual interaction stage

Once the child responds to the special attention, the adult begins some form of sexual activity. The interaction is usually progressive.

Secrecy stage

Sexual abuse usually happens when the child is alone with the offender. Secrecy is a source of fear and attempts to disclose are likely to be countered with an adult conspiracy of denial and disbelief. Many survivors never tell about having been sexually abused. Once the sexual activity has begun the adult imposes secrecy by threatening that:

- No one will believe them if they tell.
- The young person, family or pets will be hurt if they tell.
- Their family will be broken up.
- Something bad will happen to the offender.
- The young person will be removed from their family and blamed for the abuse.

Disclosure stage

Disclosure may take place:

- When a child is concerned for other children's safety.
- When they are in a situation of overwhelming family conflict.
- When a third party discovers the abuse.

© Liz Davies and Debbie Townsend. *Joint Investigation in Child Protection.* www.russellhouse.co.uk

- Following education by protective agencies raising their awareness of the nature of the abuse and means of reporting and gaining safety.

Following disclosure the child will be in crisis because of the anxiety caused by the telling of the secret, fear of the response of the authorities and impact on their lives.

Suppression stage

The child will carry the responsibility of destroying the family unit by telling which perpetuates the lie that nothing harmful has happened. Without adequate family or other support and fearing the threats of the offender the child may retract, withdraw or minimise the disclosure. It is very common for children to retract their disclosure after the initial telling. Children often face disbelief and denial from their family, friends and local community.

(Summit, 1983)

Presentation 12: Young People Who Sexually Abuse

A young person who sexually abuses other children must be considered as both an alleged perpetrator and a possible victim of child sexual abuse themselves. The protection needs of all the child victims of the alleged perpetrator must be assessed. *Working Together* provides the guidance. 'Evidence suggests that children who abuse others may have suffered considerable disruption in their lives, been exposed to violence within the family, may have witnessed or been subject to physical or sexual abuse, have problems in their educational development and may have committed other offences' (DfES, 2006: 11.32). They are essentially children in need and some will be children in need of protection. The criminal justice agencies must work closely with children's services in order to agree with the benefit of expert opinion, whether the behaviour is actually abusive or within the range of normal childhood activity. A therapeutic approach prepared in advance of a court hearing will often be acceptable to the court. Working together the agencies will need to decide:

- Any criminal proceedings
- Child protection procedures
- Child in need procedures

Masson and Erooga (1999) estimated between 25 per cent and 33 per cent of all alleged sexual abuse involves young mainly adolescent perpetrators.
  Factors associated with such behaviour are:

- Abnormal sexual environments: Families where sexual boundaries were too rigid or too relaxed.
- Sexualised models of compensation where sex is seen as a comfort in difficult times.
- A parental history of sexual or physical abuse.
- History of drug or alcohol use in the family.
- Parental loss.
- Social isolation, lack of confidence, lack of social skills and maladaptive coping skills.

(Calder et al., 1997: 51)

A link appears to exist between a history of sexual victimisation and subsequent sexual perpetration against other children. However, this is a not a straightforward 'victim to abuser' cause and effect. Studies also show that not all children who sexually abuse are victims and not all victims of sexual abuse go on to become abusers. Many adult sex offenders have not suffered sexual abuse as children. Factors which affect the development of abusive behaviour in abused children are; the age when abuse occurs, its duration, severity, the relationship between the victim and perpetrator and the use of physical force (Vizard, 2006: 4).

Professionals need to make judgments about the difference between sexual experimentation between children and sexual abuse of one child by another.

It is important, when working with young people who sexually abuse, to define the abuse as a pattern of behaviour which may be changed:

> *There is considerable confusion about what constitutes 'normal' sexual behaviour in children and adolescents, partly because of rapidly changing societal norms about children and sex and partly because of the ethical constraints in conducting research into childhood sexuality.*

> (Vizard, 2006: 2)

The child may suffer significant harm if the relationship is coercive or abusive. The harm may involve all forms of abuse. Any child under the age of 13 years cannot consent to sexual activity which would be an offence under the Sexual Offences Act 2003. Between the ages of 13 and 16 years, sexual activity with a child is also an offence. It is an offence for any adult who is in a position of trust or authority in relation to the child to have a sexual relationship with them if the child is under the age of 18 years. A strategy discussion will be needed in each case to debate what action is needed to safeguard the young people involved and in the majority of cases police will not pursue criminal action. The best interests of the child are paramount and children must be empowered to feel confident to access health and educational services.

In order to determine whether a relationship presents a risk of harm to a child the following needs to be considered:

- Whether the child is competent to understand and consent to the sexual activity (children under 13 are not legally capable of consenting to sexual activity).
- The child's living circumstances and school attendance.
- Whether there are age or power imbalances in the relationship. Power can result from differences in size, age, material wealth, physical, social, sexual development, ethnicity, sexuality and levels of sexual knowledge.
- Whether overt aggression, coercion or bribery was or is involved including misuse of alcohol or other substances as a disinhibitor.
- Whether the child's own behaviour places them in a position where they are unable to make an informed choice about the activity.
- Any attempts to secure secrecy by the sexual partner beyond what would be considered usual in a teenage relationship.
- Whether methods used to secure a child's compliance, trust and/or secrecy by the sexual partner are consistent with grooming for sexual exploitation. Grooming is likely to involve efforts by a sexual predator (usually older than the child) to befriend a child by indulging or coercing them with gifts or treats (i.e. money or drugs) developing a trusting relationship with the child's family, developing a relationship with the child, through the internet or other means, in order to abuse the child.

- Whether the sexual partner is known by one of the agencies as having or previously having had other concerning relationships with children (which presupposes that checks will be made with the police).
- Whether the child denies, minimises or accepts the concerns, and help by professionals.

(LSCB, 2007: 5.39.13)

Activity 17: Young People Who Sexually Abuse – Case Study

Aim: To provide an opportunity for participants to explore the complexities of child sexual abuse perpetrated by children.

Delivery: Participants volunteer to read out the scenario from a script and read the following roles:

Narrator
Designated teacher
Education social worker
Designated teacher
Local authority safeguarding manager
Police officer
Child psychiatrist
Children's services duty team manager

Handout 15: Young People Who Sexually Abuse

Scene 1: Secondary school discussion – pre-referral

Designated teacher
I must talk to you about Teresa Farrow. Do you remember her?

Education social worker
Didn't you speak to me about her six months ago because she was involved with a sixth form boy?

Designated teacher
Yes, looking back I think we should have tried to get her some help then.

Education social worker
She's in Year 8 and must be about 13 years old now. So what's it all about today?

Designated teacher
Nadia, Teresa's friend came to see me this morning. She is usually very loyal to Teresa but seemed to think this time things have gone too far. They were on the school bus going home from a trip to the museum yesterday. Teresa sat 'snogging' Jonathan on the back seat. Then Nadia saw Teresa put her hand into Jonathan's jeans and was, in her own words, 'wanking him off'. She said Jonathan was so embarrassed because the whole top of the bus got to hear about it and he has been having a terrible time. Teresa is boasting about it to her friends.

Education social worker
How old is Jonathan?

Designated teacher
He is 16. He studies very hard but has learning disability.

Narrator
Sixteen? At 16 surely the boy is entitled to some experimentation? I'm sure at 16 he knows his own mind.

Safeguarding manager
He may be nearly 16 but we protect children up to the age of 18 and his best interests are the prime consideration. These may differ from his wishes and feelings. Teresa is only 13 and her best interests also have to be paramount.

Education social worker
So what have you done since Nadia came to see you?

Designated teacher
I thought I'd better wait and talk it over with you.

Education social worker
I think we'd better call these young people into the office and put a stop to this nonsense. I want to see what they have to say for themselves.

Narrator

Hold it a minute, not so fast!

What are the dilemmas for the school at this stage? Should they move to school sanctions or is there sufficient for a child protection referral? I want to know more.

Is the school aware of previous concerns?

Has Teresa been sexually involved with any other boys and have they always been older than her?

Does she usually engage in sexual activity so publicly?

Is Nadia thought to be a reliable source of information?

What is the view of the teacher who was accompanying the young people on the bus?

Education social worker

I think I'm clearer now. The school can decide how to manage the situation within the school and also refer to children's services. Jonathan may well need some protection. The head teacher should speak to Teresa's parents and suggest she is kept out of school for a few days to take pressure off Jonathan.

Narrator

Wait a minute. If we speak to the parents so soon this could lead to pressure on Teresa and we don't know where she has learnt this behaviour from. Her parents may try to stop any investigation. Teresa's parents could also try to take their anger out on Jonathan and his parents.

Police officer (CID or CAIT)

This is not one of the most serious of cases. It isn't appropriate for police to get involved. A low key approach is more likely to keep these two young people safe from harm.

Education social worker

I want to stop the rumours going round the school and the name calling.

Yet if the police do want to be involved at a later stage my action in the school might contaminate important evidence. The police may wish to interview other children on the bus as witnesses.

Police officer (CID or CAIT)

No. I would not want to interview the other young people as the need to preserve evidence has gone because the young people have already talked to each other about the incident.

Education social worker

Well then how do we at the school protect Jonathan today? Teresa is at the school and there could be another incident. He is especially vulnerable.

Safeguarding manager

There needs to be a Section 47 strategy discussion and follow up strategy meeting. The school needs to consider how to monitor Teresa's behaviour meanwhile. Nadia witnessed the incident and Teresa has been bragging about it. The school staff should be informed so that the incident can be contained within the school.

Scene 2: Discussion – duty team manager and social worker

Duty team manager
The designated teacher made a referral this morning about a girl aged 13 and a boy aged 16 who has learning difficulties.

Social worker
Do you think that's abusive? He probably thinks he just got lucky. Are we going to investigate this? All young people experiment.

Duty team manager
It was a public display. If the girl is sexually active she will be vulnerable to being exploited herself. There is some background information. Teresa is cared for by her grandmother as her mother left home. She used to scratch herself and cut up her clothes. She wanted to live with her father and later moved in with him and his new partner. Can you make checks with the general practitioner? Jonathan is known to the Children's Disability Team can you also check with them?

We must try and get the general practitioner to attend the strategy meeting.

Scene 3: Duty team manager meets child psychiatrist

Duty team manager
Can I discuss Teresa Farrow with you?

Child psychiatrist
From what I know she is highly sexualised for her age and there have been other incidents at school. Some aspects are of concern. The incident was in public and so Teresa was wishing to draw attention to herself. She also has a history of self harm. You need to decide whether or not Jonathan has suffered sexual abuse as a result of this incident. Teresa may be younger than him but she has more power because of her level of sexual knowledge and also because of his learning disability. Both young people need help and support as well as sexual health advice.

Scene 4: Strategy discussion – duty social worker and police officer

Duty social work
I think we're going to have to speak with both young people's parents and the young people themselves.

Police officer (CID or CAIT)
Technically there is an incident of Section 10 of the Sexual Offences Act 2003 'causing or inciting a child to engage in sexual activity' by Teresa to Jonathan but I'm concerned as to whether or not she may be a victim herself.

Scene 5: Strategy meeting – duty social worker, team manager, police officer and designated teacher

Duty social worker

I visited Teresa's father and stepmother and they agreed for her to stay at home at the moment. Mr Farrow said Teresa is often out late. He has seen her out on a motor bike with a man aged 19. I also managed to speak to Jonathan's mother and informed her of this meeting.

Designated teacher

Jonathan went to his teacher and said he was dirty. He wanted to wash his hands all afternoon.

Duty social worker

The general practitioner said Teresa has been to see her to seek contraception and that Teresa is very well informed about sexual health.

Team manager

Jonathan has obsessional behaviour and the learning disability team have been trying to assist his family in managing this. He is sexually very naïve.

Police officer

It seems both young people are vulnerable. Although we technically don't need to gain parental consent I think we should get parental permission to interview both young people and then meet again.

There is now more information about Teresa. Concern has increased. We need to assess how protective her father and stepmother are able to be.

Strategy meeting decisions

Action	Timescale	Person responsible
Teresa to be kept out of school temporarily with parental agreement.	Immediately	Designated teacher
Visit Jonathan's parents	Within a week	Social worker
Achieving Best Evidence interview of Jonathan	Within a week	CAIT and social worker with advice from social worker from Children's Disability Team
Depending on outcome of interview with Jonathan, Teresa to be interviewed either under the Police and Criminal Evidence Act, 1984 as a suspect or as a possible victim of abuse (Achieving Best Evidence interview) or single agency interview.		
Child protection conference to be convened for Jonathan	Within 15 days	Social worker
Core assessment re Teresa to address: Self harm Level of sexual knowledge Risk to herself Risk to others Depending on outcome of investigation consider convening a child protection conference	To begin this week and conclude within 35 days	Social worker

Scene 6: Child protection conference re Jonathan

Social worker
Jonathan was distressed and embarrassed during the Achieving Best Evidence interview. It was thought that he had been confused by the incident but also excited by the attention. He said Teresa has said she would show him what to do. He also said other young people were teasing him. Jonathan clearly confirmed that the incident had taken place.

Police officer

Given the evidence provided by Jonathan, Teresa was interviewed under the Police and Criminal Evidence Act, 1984. She spoke little on interview and was obviously very embarrassed. Police discussed the case with the Crown Prosecution Service and a decision was made to refer the case to the Youth Offending Team to support her in keeping herself and others safe.

The conference members concluded that Teresa had been abusive towards Jonathan. It was thought that because of his vulnerability future incidents were likely. Jonathan was considered to be in need of a child protection plan which included a referral to Child and Adolescent Mental Health Service and to the health service for counselling.

Scene 7: Summary of action taken

Narrator

Three months later

Teresa has attended appointments at the Youth Offending Team. There have been no further incidents. The Farrows say she is coming in earlier. The general practitioner says that Teresa is still taking the contraceptive pill.

Six months later

Teresa was admitted to hospital after taking an overdose. She said she had a row with her boyfriend aged 20 years. He had beaten her up and she had got home at 2 a.m. Her father had thrown her out and she went to stay with Nadia's family. Nadia's mother found her the next morning having taken an overdose. A strategy meeting was held at the hospital. Teresa was placed with foster carers at her own request and with parental consent.

At the Looked After Review the foster carer reported Teresa's sexual behaviour towards her two sons. Her son Martin is aged 17 years and she found them kissing. Then her other son Jamie brought some friends over and she found them queuing for Teresa's attentions! She asked for a specialist residential establishment to be found or a foster placement where there were no other children.

In a new foster placement Teresa began to speak about being sexually abused by her father from the age of 8 years. This disclosure led to a Section 47 investigation and a child protection conference. Teresa then co-operated with the therapeutic programme at the Child and Adolescent Mental Health Service.

The focus of this case changed from Teresa as a young person with sexually abusive behaviour to older boys to her as a victim herself. The case presented dilemmas. It was difficult to deal with her abusive behaviour when the cause was unknown and there was initial ambivalence about whether the behaviour was defined as abusive or not. The criminal route was not pursued. The child protection procedures provided Jonathan with protection. Teresa herself did not gain protection until a later date.

© Liz Davies and Debbie Townsend. *Joint Investigation in Child Protection.* www.russellhouse.co.uk

Feedback

Trainers raise the following questions as a basis for discussion

- Did Teresa commit a criminal offence?
- Did this abusive behaviour gain the correct professional response?
- Would the outcome have been different if she had been a boy?
- Was there enough consideration of possible abuse of other young people?
- What action should have been taken about the older men involved in her life?

Presentation 13: Supporting the Non-abusive Carer

It is important to provide support for the non-abusive carer because:

- Survivors say that the support of a non-abusive carer is a very important factor for subsequent healing.
- The Crown Prosecution Service, in considering whether or not to proceed with a prosecution, will always wish to know where the child will gain the support they need to cope with the investigative processes and court hearing.
- Children who have support from a non-abusive carer will know that they have been believed and will make the best use of therapeutic processes.
- Disclosure is the beginning for a child and their family. The family will have to continue healing long after the professionals have gone and indeed for the rest of their lives.

Parent's emotional responses to the discovery of child abuse

Parents and carers will have three main questions when confronted with an allegation that their child has suffered abuse.

- Why didn't I know?
- Why didn't my child tell me?
- Why has it happened to my child?

One of the most commonly expressed feelings by carers is the sense of exposure. In this they obviously mirror the child's feelings but they also have their own dilemmas about who to tell. Professionals must be clear with the non-abusive carers about which professionals know about the abuse and the 'need to know' basis of respecting confidentiality.

Parents with children who have recently disclosed are under enormous pressure. They have to cope with their own grief, help their children to come to terms with what has happened and then feel the added burden of being judged and scrutinised. Some parents will have been abused themselves and their child's abuse will reopen their own wounds.

Parents whose children have suffered abuse are likely to go through emotional stages comparable to those commonly experienced during bereavement. Initially they may feel shock and disbelief, leading professionals to think that the parent is being uncooperative or unsupportive of their child. It is important to be patient and support the parent towards an acceptance of what has happened. Peake describes how just at the time, when the parent is stretched to their limits, they have to make every effort to prove to professionals that they are a model parent (Peake, 1997).

The following emotions are common: disbelief, shock, grief, shame, numbness, guilt, feeling isolated, anger (towards child for disclosing and towards abuser) depression, betrayal.

It is not uncommon for the disclosure of abuse by a child to have a ripple effect as others close to the child also disclose. Professionals often find themselves suddenly confronting a number of different abuse situations relating to the experiences of various family members.

Reasons why a parent or carer may not have known about the abuse their child was suffering

- The abuser is usually someone known to the parent and in a position of trust and responsibility. The parent would not suspect them of harming their child.
- The abuser often manipulates the parent/child relationship to undermine any closeness between them. The abuser may destroy the parent's sense of self esteem and confidence in parenting.
- The abuser will go to great lengths to demonstrate their concern for the child by buying gifts, taking them out and providing other favours which can deceive the vulnerable parent.
- Children find it extremely difficult to disclose the abuse to their parent because they may be threatened by the abuser or feel guilty and ashamed about the abuse. They may fear their parents' response or the break-up of their family.
- Even when a child shows signs of being abused, the abuser will give the parent many other plausible explanations for these signs, such as behavioural problems at school or illnesses. The parent may then lose trust in their own good judgement.
- The abuser may have targeted the child because of family instability which will make it more difficult for the child to gain parental protection.
- The abuser will be so cunning that child sexual abuse will be very difficult for a parent to detect.
- The parent may live with a violent partner and be afraid to acknowledge the abuse of their child. They may well be financially dependent on the alleged perpetrator and fear for their future.
- Parents want to believe that their children are safe and that they have brought them up in the right way so that abuse would and could not happen to them.

Assessment of the non-abusive parent or carer as an effective protector

Risk assessment of the non-abusive parent or carer will need to cover five key questions:

- Is the parent or carer also abusive?
- Is the parent or carer collusive with the abuser against the interests of the children?
- Can the parent or carer effectively protect and safeguard the children?
- Can they work with professionals to achieve positive change in order to protect the children?
- What is the child's view of the parent or carer's ability to protect?

Morrison (1998) outlines the seven steps of contemplation which is an excellent tool for assisting judgement about parental responses. He writes that, 'it is too easy to assume, either that clients must be motivated before they walk into the room if change is to happen or conversely to accept a vague promise that they will do whatever we ask as evidence of motivation. It is imperative to distinguish between ambivalence, compliance and change. Some children have suffered because professionals did not distinguish between compliance and change' (Morrison, in Adcock and White, 1998: 140–1).

Parents and carers cannot be forced into change. Rushing may increase their sense of failure and low self esteem and lead to defensiveness and non-compliance.

Family Group Conference (FGC)

The FGC is one way of involving the non abusive family and community network in protection planning. *Working Together* states that an FGC must not replace or remove the need for a child protection conference (DfES, 2006: 10.2). The FGC must always be held within child protection procedures if there is any risk of harm. An independent coordinator convenes the conference which may include family members, friends and people from the local community. The social worker presents concerns to the conference and the group then have private time to consider their responses to these concerns. Children may take part and have someone to support them. The group decision is then either approved or not approved by the social worker. The FGC may take place following Section 47 enquiries and protective action as a means of helping the protectors in the family respond to the child's need to be safe.

Activity 18: Practising Skills in Responding to Parents and Carers

Aim: For participants to have an opportunity to explore varying parent/carer responses to a child's disclosure and to evaluate their capacity to protect the child.

Delivery: Participants work in groups of four to play the following parts; parent, social worker, police officer, observer. Each group needs space to enact the role play ideally in separate small rooms.

A police officer and social worker are making a joint visit to inform the parents of Melanie, aged 9 years, that she has told her teacher that she has been sexually abused by her grandfather. Those playing the parents are only told how to respond and are not aware of the professional referral and task. The professionals are not party to the parental briefing.

Trainers should rotate the participants' roles to allow for practice. Therefore over the four role plays each participant plays every role once. Each role play lasts no longer than 10 minutes but, depending on content, it may be far less. The trainer is the time keeper and stops the role play. The observer then feeds back to the others in the group and makes note of significant observations.

Content: Participants are given the following information:

The girl told the teacher that her grandfather 'makes me touch his willy all white stuff comes out and goes over my hand. I don't like it.'

Role play 1: Angry

The parents are briefed that they must respond in an angry manner to whatever is said to them even to the point of not letting the professionals come past the doorstep. They might say:

'How dare you come here.'
'What do you want I'm right in the middle of something. It's not convenient.'
'Yes she's my daughter. What's happened?'
'I'm not letting you in until you tell me what's going on.'

The parents are told that if they feel comfortable with how they are being treated then they should let the professionals into the house. The responses might then be:

'Don't be stupid. She said what?'
'When, where?'
'She never told me.'
'She hasn't seen him for ages. He doesn't come round.'
'I'd know if something wasn't right.'

Role play 2: Me-Me-Me

The parents are briefed that the grandfather is the maternal grandfather and he lives with them in the house which he owns. They let the professionals in but do not listen to the concerns about the daughter as they are focused on their own needs about financial security and make comments such as:

'I don't own this house where will I go to live?'

'What will happen when the neighbours find out?'

'Is it going to get into the papers?'

'Oh no, what will happen now?'

'Who is going to help me with all this mess?'

Role play 3: Carpet

The parents are briefed to welcome the professionals into the house, to agree with everything the police officer and social worker suggest and ask them for advice as to what they should do next. They let the police officer and social worker walk all over them and make comments such as:

'Of course I'll help you all I can and she will too.'

'You know best. I'll do whatever you say.'

'If you say so.'

'OK, that's fine, no problem.'

'I'm sure this will be soon sorted.'

Role play 4: Mr or Mrs Professional

The parents are briefed that they are a high ranking professional such as a bank manager, barrister or magistrate. In this scenario Melanie attends a very exclusive private school. Comments made might be:

'I pay thousands of pounds for her education.'

'The head teacher should have called me.'

'I know the chief superintendent I don't need to speak to a constable.'

'My father was a renowned judge he would never do anything like this.'

'She is just attention seeking.'

'Who knows about this?'

Feedback: Each person in the observer role feeds back to the whole group to facilitate debate. Trainers draw out the emotional responses from the professional and parental roles and explore assumptions. They then explain that it is common for every role play to result in the child's interests being dismissed.

Focus on Perpetrators, Organised Abuse, Safe Practice and Whistleblowing

Presentation 14: Child Sex Abusers

The cycle of offending

A local probation officer should be invited to contribute to this presentation and activity which should cover learning about the cycle of offending behaviour.

Finkelhor (1986 adapted by Joe Sullivan, Principal Therapist, Lucy Faithfull Foundation) stated that there are four pre-conditions relating to child sexual abuse before abuse occurs:

- 'Wanting to'
  A potential offender needed to have some motivation to abuse a child sexually. Motivation might include arrested emotional development and inappropriate patterns of sexual arousal.
- 'Conscience'
  The potential offender had to overcome internal inhibitions against acting on that motivation. These might include alcohol use.
- 'Creating opportunity'
  The potential offender had to overcome external impediments to committing sexual abuse. This might include finding situations that may include social isolation, lack of supervision or opportunities to be alone with the child.
- 'Doing it and getting away with it'
  The potential offender had to overcome or undermine a child's possible resistance to sexual abuse through coercion, gaining the child's trust or bribing a child.

Activity 19: Child Sex Abusers – Distorted Thinking

Aim: For participants to be aware of the excuses and distortions of thinking used by child sex abusers for their abusive behaviour.

Delivery: Trainers ask the participants to call out any ideas they have about excuses child sex abusers may give for their abusive behaviour and write them on the board.

Content:
I only need to go so far and then I stop.
I only do it when I'm drunk.
I'll only do it one more time.
I need to reduce my tension.
She likes it and leads me on.
He won't remember when he is older.
She is too young to get pregnant.
She is better than having no one at all.
No-one will find out. He won't tell.
It's OK she is my daughter.
It's OK he isn't my son.
She likes me.
He wants my love, affection, attention.
I am lonely, I need love.
He likes being with me – we are close friends.
I am oversexed.
She didn't tell me to stop.
No one will see me.
I'm teaching her about sex.
It makes me feel better.
He wants me to do this.
I'm in love.
She puts her arms around me and sits on my lap.
I deserve to feel good.
She looks older than she is.
I can't stop myself.
He says 'No' but really means 'Yes'.
I'm not hurting her.
He is very mature for his age.
It happened to me at that age.
She does it for the money.
Some children like sex.

It's more exciting than sex with my partner.
It's OK she is asleep.
God told me to do it.
He does it with other boys.
In most ways I'm a good father/mother.
If she doesn't want me to I won't.
My sex life is no-one's business.

(Adapted from Willis, 1993: 50)

Feedback: Referring to the above list trainers add in any statements that have been omitted by participants and then discuss in the group how professionals might respond to these varying presentations.

Presentation 15: The Multi Agency Public Protection Arrangements (MAPPA)

Purpose of the MAPPA

- To consider the current circumstances of registered sex offenders and dangerous or potentially dangerous adults in the community.
- To develop a multi-agency risk management strategy to:
  - reduce the risk of further offending.
  - protect the public.

MAPPAs were established following the Sex Offenders Act 1997 (they do not apply to child sex offenders convicted prior to that date). The Act provided for:

- Sex offenders to register with the local police service.
- Sex offenders to register any change of address.
- Key responsibility on police to monitor compliance.

Subsequently a 'duty to cooperate' was included, which was to involve MAPPAs working with a wider range of agencies. The legislation involves cooperation between police, prison and probation services to:

- Establish arrangements for assessing and managing the risks posed by sexual and violent offenders.
- Review and monitor the arrangements.
- Publish an annual report on their operation.

There are three categories of offender:

1. Registered sex offenders (RSOs) that is those sexual offenders required to register under the terms of the Sex Offender Act (1997) and its amendments.
2. Violent offenders and those sexual offenders who are not required to register.
3. Any other offender who, because of the offences committed by them (wherever they have been committed) are considered to pose a risk of serious harm to the public.

(DfES, 2006: 12.15)

The length of time offenders remain within the MAPPA is determined by:

- The length of their sex offender registration requirement (a minimum of five years).
- The length of post release supervision licence.
- Their continuing to pose a risk of serious harm.

The MAPPA is responsible for:

- Cross-agency collation of information about adults in the community who are defined as a risk or potential risk to the public.
- Targeted monitoring and surveillance.
- Organisation of assessment and treatment.
- Investigation and planning to safeguard possible victims.
- Consideration and decision making about community notification.
- Records of meetings are only available to those attending and are not entered on client records. Referral to the MAPPA is through the appropriate agency representative.

Membership of the MAPPA

Chair: Detective Chief Inspector
Police Child Abuse Investigation Team/Public Protection Unit
Probation Service
Prison Service
Local Housing Authority
Local Education Authority
Youth Offending Team
Local Authority Children's Services
NHS Trusts, Primary Care Trusts and Strategic Health Authorities
Jobcentres Plus
Registered social landlords who accommodate MAPPA offenders
Electronic monitoring providers
Two lay advisors appointed by the Home Office

Activity 20: The Multi Agency Public Protection Arrangements – Role Play

Aim: To provide an opportunity for participants to consider their professional role in relation to the role and functions of the MAPPA.

Delivery: Participants role play a MAPPA meeting seated round a table. Trainers allocate roles give out labels and ask participants to quietly read their specific role. The participants must attempt to reach conclusions and recommendations in each case. The chairperson should ideally be someone from the local MAPPA who understands the process. The chairperson reads aloud the case history and also concludes each case with a set of decisions for comparison with those reached by the group and each case then concludes with a discussion and decision about the risk level posed – high, medium or low risk. If there are more participants than roles then some may perform the task of ' whisperers' and sit behind the role player to be available for consultation and advice.

Content:

Roles

Chairperson: Detective Chief Inspector
Police officer: Public Protection Unit (PPU)
Detective sergeant: Public Protection Unit (PPU)
Detective inspector: Child Abuse Investigation Team (CAIT)
Safeguarding manager: Local authority children's services
Team manager: Education social work
Manager: Local authority housing
Manager: Drug and Alcohol Counselling Service
Consultant psychiatrist: NHS trust
Manager: Youth Offending Team
Team manager: Mental health trust
Senior probation officer: Local Probation Board

Levels of risk to be considered in decision making

The panel concentrate their attention on those who pose the highest risk but assess risk as follows:

Low: no significant current indicators of concern.

Medium: identifiable indicators of risk of harm. The offender has the potential to cause harm, but is unlikely to do so unless there is a change in circumstances.

High: identifiable indicators of risk of serious harm. The potential event could happen at any time and the impact would be serious.

Very high: an imminent risk of serious harm. The potential event is likely to happen immediately and the impact is likely to be serious.

(DfES, 2006: 12.18)

Handout 16a: Case Study A

Category: Potentially Dangerous Offender

Name: Marsha Nash
Age: 50 years, White UK
Risk: High

Chairperson reads the case history

This person has been diagnosed as having a personality disorder. She says she wants to kill her father. She carries weapons and can be violent. Three months ago her father had a stroke, which it is thought, was a reaction to stress caused by her threats. Whilst he was in hospital she tried to smother him with a pillow. She was taken onto the psychiatric ward for the night and then discharged. Marsha has two sons. One son, Martin Nash, is married and when his wife Flora was about to have a baby. Marsha threatened to kill Flora to stop her having the baby. Two months ago she was arrested and charged in possession of knives on her way to see her father. She was sentenced to a one year community rehabilitation order with a condition of mental health treatment.

Mental health social work manager

You see Marsha at the weekly appointments but she still says her only wish is to kill her father because he sexually abused her as a child. The abuse she describes was repeated and violent. She won't speak about it in any depth and just repeats her wish to kill him. Last weekend she had to be admitted to the ward as she was in a very agitated state and was threatening to overdose unless she could go to kill him. You know she has been diagnosed as having a personality disorder but sometimes it seems as if she is hearing voices.

Drug and alcohol manager

Marsha comes to your groups but is drinking heavily and sometimes has to be excluded. The alcoholism will lower her ability to control her behaviour and increase the risk to her father. You consider that risk to be high. She rants and raves to other service users. One day she was having lunch and made stabbing movements with her fork saying 'they won't stop me'.

Police officer, PPU

You interviewed Marsha recently on a home visit. She lives in a block of flats. Her flat was quite clean but there was no food in the cupboards. She was well dressed. She told you that her grandchild, Max, is born now and this has increased her sense of anger to her father. You went to visit Martin and Flora. You are convinced that Max is well protected by them. You think the risk to the baby is very low.

The risk to her father though remains very high indeed in your view. You have visited and provided all the necessary home security for him but he can't live like a prisoner. There are his human rights to consider.

You interviewed the father about her allegations, he said nothing happened and that she says things because she is drunk. He said she used to come home drunk as a young teenager and 'touch him up'. He told me that, when she was aged 6 years, a childminder interfered with her and maybe this is what she is on about. You wonder if Marsha has made it all up to gain attention.

Safeguarding manager

You believe that Marsha was sexually abused by her father Mr Phillip Nash. You had a call from the disability team who said that the grandmother had spoken to the home carer about her husband's sister also having made allegations of him sexually harassing her when young. She had told the home carer in confidence and doesn't know that this was referred.

You have also checked Marsha's file and there is reference to a teacher being concerned that Marsha wasn't eating and was cutting her arms. She was referred to the Child and Adolescent Mental Health Service and saw a child psychiatrist who thought she might have been sexually abused, but nothing could be proved. She also did some sexualised drawing at school and had outbursts of aggression to her teachers, sometimes resulting in her being excluded.

You recently convened a strategy meeting (Section 47) to discuss the safety of Max. The reports about the baby are all good but you did hear that Marsha tried to take the baby out in the pram the other day and didn't take kindly to being prevented by her son. After the meeting you told Marsha that she can't be on her own with the baby at all and you put this in writing. You are quite sure she won't comply with the decision of the meeting and you will have to evaluate Martin and Flora's ability to protect Max. You are convening a child protection conference next week and intend to make a plan to include no contact for the baby with the grandfather or mother and to recommend that Martin and Flora leave the area. If they don't comply you will consider commencing care proceedings.

The social worker tells you that Martin and Flora are very reasonable and quite frightened of Marsha but they don't believe her story about the abuse. They really like the grandfather.

Education social work team manager

You have checked your files and discovered that Flora's older sister was abused as a child. Your authority dealt with the allegations of child sexual abuse by a teacher. He was taken to court but not convicted. Flora didn't believe her sister was telling the truth as she got on well with the teacher who took her out at weekends.

Detective sergeant, PPU

You are worried that the parents still take the baby to see the grandfather. You are not happy about this at all. You think the baby is in danger.

Consultant psychiatrist

You see Marsha when she attends your appointments. You have also read the history from the social work and child psychiatric files. You tell the meeting not to underestimate the risk to the baby. Marsha may not state her intentions and is very unpredictable. She is very determined. There must be a child protection conference immediately. She is not mentally ill but has a personality disorder which is untreatable. She is not on any medication.

You really don't think the social worker's warning to Marsha is good enough. You think she shouldn't have access to Max at all. It is far too dangerous. She still abuses alcohol. You think the plan should be to offer to re-house this family away from the area for safety. When she was on the ward last weekend Marsha spoke incessantly about wanting to murder her father, described how she would do it in detail and how she wanted to see him suffer first.

Housing manager

You can offer them something but think that they will probably refuse. You ask why Martin and Flora can't be prevented from visiting the father given the sexual abuse allegations by Marsha? You think that the baby is at risk of being abused and that children's services should get a Prohibited Steps Order (CA 1989.S8) to stop the visits.

Detective inspector, CAIT

You are sympathetic to Marsha. You think that Marsha's anger can be resolved if she makes a statement to your team about the abuse. You offer to see Marsha to ask if she will make a statement about the grandfather. You think she deserves some justice which might help her to stop taking the law into her own hands. You have dealt with many similar cases like this before and once the person feels that they have been heard and have a chance to gain justice their behaviour changes dramatically. Currently you have 25 cases of historic abuse being investigated. The Crown Prosecution Service would definitely run with this one given all that history on record to corroborate her story and the sister could be interviewed too.

Senior probation officer

As part of the conditions of the community rehabilitation order you see Marsha regularly. She does keep her meetings with you but you can't get through to her at all. She is keeping to her mental health and alcohol counselling appointments but sometimes smells strongly of alcohol when she comes to see you. She told you the baby would have to die to stop it being abused. You may have to place her in breach of the order if she continues to misuse alcohol.

Group discussion

Planning to assess risk to:

- baby
- parents
- grandfather
- Marsha
- Anyone else?

Chairperson makes recommendations

- The plan is to review in one month and to review the outcome of the child protection conference.
- The baby must be safeguarded immediately by insisting the parents do not allow access to either the grandfather or Marsha.
- Marsha has to be told by police that she cannot visit the grandchild unless supervised. A police officer will be provided to assist children's services in supervising contact arrangements. This might give an opportunity to test the relationship and Marsha's progress.
- Marsha to be told by police that she cannot go anywhere near her father.
- Martin and Flora Nash to be offered re-housing outside the area. The Sex Offender Unit to assess whether the parents are proactive protectors of Max. The child protection conference should seek their agreement to this.
- Police officer, CAIT to offer to take statement from Marsha about the abuse. This might help her resolve the issue and lead her to begin treatment and healing.

Participants in the role play then make a decision about the level of risk.

Handout 16b: Case Study B

Category: Sex Offender

Name: Mr. Henry Heinrich
Age: 45 years, White European
Risk: High

Chairperson reads the case history

Mr Heinrich has been providing accommodation to children leaving care in this authority and also to young asylum seekers. Two boys have made an allegation that he came into their rooms unannounced and indecently assaulted them at night. He also, they say, smokes cannabis. He has been arrested for indecent assault but not yet charged. The investigation is ongoing.

Detective sergeant, PPU

You think this is a real mess. You have discovered that this man was running his own Housing Association and he has previous convictions for sexual offences (gross indecency 10 years ago) against boys aged 16 years. You cannot believe children's services were placing their most vulnerable children in his care. If this gets out to the media there will be a fine show down! It seems as a landlord he is not subject to regulations, other than the usual health and safety. What a loophole!

Police officer, PPU

You did some intelligence checks and you have located the record of a Henry Heinrick with the same date of birth, who was investigated for allegedly touching a boy in a playground five years ago. The boy was learning disabled and couldn't communicate very well verbally. The case never went to court. You think this is the same person despite the difference in spelling of his name.

Housing manager

You are very concerned as you know that other vulnerable people were also housed through this association, Caring Housing Ltd. They are not on your list of recommended associations to use, but word went round and when the agencies were really stuck you passed the information on to them. You knew other Boroughs were using it and trusted that they had made the relevant checks. You have told all your staff not to recommend it any more. Vulnerable people have been placed there from a wide area and they included the mentally ill, learning disabled, young offenders, asylum seekers and young people leaving care. You have to admit some of the young asylum seekers were only aged 15 years which is against the protocols.

You tell the meeting that Mr Heinrich has properties over a wide area. They are mainly bedsits and often in groups. This has caused problems sometimes such as when a person with mental health problems was placed next door to a young vulnerable care leaver. Mr

Heinrich moves residents around all the time from flat to flat saying they have caused a disturbance. This has been of concern to your department and social workers have complained about this approach seeming unreasonable. This authority currently has 25 people placed through this association.

Safeguarding manager

There was a strategy meeting last week, following the allegations, and later the two boys were interviewed on video and gave good evidence. It seems Mr Heinrich had a copy of all the keys and there was also a rule that tenants should not lock their doors, supposedly in case of fire. The boys also spoke of being harassed in the accommodation by other residents. One man with learning difficulties, who was very lonely, came in their rooms to get company but he was incontinent. One night a woman, in the room next door, was taken to hospital urgently as she had slashed her wrists. These young people have been exposed to many traumas in these flats. Both boys have now been re-housed.

You have discussed this case with the Director of Children's Services who has notified councillors as this may well become a media issue and heads might have to roll!

You want to offer the two boys therapy but will seek police advice about this.

Detective inspector, CAIT

You are horrified that a man like this is running all these flats and making a fortune without having been police checked. He has previous convictions for gross indecency against boys aged 16 years. This was in the context of a residential establishment he worked in. He was placed on probation for a year. He smoked cannabis with these current youngsters and said he'd report them to the police if they told about the abuse. He also said he would move them on to another flat in a worse area. Fortunately they had a good relationship with their leaving care social worker and told her what was happening. The two boys interviewed well and were very brave. They did not require medical examinations. The social worker feels devastated for having placed them in these flats. She had just assumed they were checked out. Now she has gone off sick.

Probation manager

You have spoken to the Probation officer who dealt with Henry Heinrich before and she told you that he was a very astute person. He bribed the young people with privileges so that they wouldn't tell. He allowed them to go out late at night or have alcohol on the unit. She told you that he was married at one time and had four children but they were all removed from his care. The mother left him. The files are with another authority, but it seems there were concerns about him abusing the children.

Consultant psychiatrist

You are concerned for the safety of Henry Heinrich post his arrest. There is a high risk, in your opinion, of vigilante action if this information gets out to the local communities. This matter involves a number of authorities. You ask the police what action they are taking to safeguard him meanwhile. Also, once confronted he is likely to be a suicide risk. You ask if anyone has thought to refer him to a psychiatrist for assessment as he also has rights.

Education social work team manager

You say that you will circulate all head teachers and college heads to inquire whether they are aware of any young people living in this accommodation as they may have been referred through other routes.

Group discussion

Planning to assess risk to:

- Henry Heinrich
- tenants
- the two young boys who made the referral
- the professionals with responsibility in the case.

Chairperson makes recommendations

- Review in one month.
- There must be a strategy meeting under organised abuse procedures (DfES, 2006: 6.7) with safeguarding managers, housing managers and police from all the authorities who have people placed with Caring Housing Ltd. You are quite sure they will all want their lawyers and press officers present!
- Each authority must be notified immediately to re-house their tenants and after the meeting plans must be made to interview all of them. You suggest that CAIT and children's services take the lead to ensure consistency of questioning.
- The MAPPA will write to all the Directors of Children's Services and the chairs of the local MAPPAs to emphasise the seriousness of this matter and the urgency of response required.
- Mr Heinrich to be offered an appointment with the forensic psychiatrist for a risk assessment to himself and others.
- The two boys to be offered therapeutic support within the Achieving Best Evidence Guidance (CJS, 2007)

Participants in the role play then make a decision about the level of risk.

Handout 16c: Case Study C

Category: Sex Offender

Name: Tomasz Zabrinski
Age: 33 years, White European
Risk: Medium

Chairperson reads the case history

Mr Zabrinski was arrested and cautioned a year ago for taking indecent photographs of children and attempting to take indecent photographs of children as well as being a public nuisance. His name is on the Sex Offenders Register.

Police officer, PPU

Mr Zabrinski was arrested at the local swimming pool when girls reported seeing a video camera pointing under the changing room door. He was actually caught in possession of the camera and the film confirmed the girl's story that pictures of girls had been taken. He admitted the offence and was therefore cautioned. It was a first offence.

Mental health social work manager

You question the wisdom of the caution as now Mr Zabrinski has not had to participate in any therapy programmes and is on the loose to repeat the offence.

Detective inspector, PPU

You support the police decision to caution this man and as he is still reviewed under the MAPPA he can receive unannounced visits from the police and be monitored. You also have good relationships with the local chemists, who have been alerted to inform you, should he bring a film in for developing. There is also a CCTV camera on the shop fronts below Mr Zabrinski's flat. This will be reviewed from time to time to check that no young people are going in and out of the flat.

Safeguarding manager

You report that you have met with the leisure department managers and have been informed that there are now CCTV cameras installed in the corridor approaching the changing rooms to ensure the safety of the young people. This was one of a number of similar incidents at the pool and security has been tightened as a result. The staff have also had child protection training. The girls were offered therapeutic support but declined.

Housing manager

You inform the meeting that Mr Zabrinski has recently requested a housing transfer outside of the authority. You need to know if this is advisable or not, though he does have rights to do so. During the interview with the housing officer, Mr Zabrinski said he now has a new job working at a computer company. This worries you.

Detective inspector, CAIT

You have heard from a local neighbourhood watch member that Mr Zabrinski was seen loitering in the park near the children's playground.

Education social work team manager

You have had a report from a head teacher that some parents were given cards at the school gates advertising a local photographer who specialises in photographs of young children. She passed the card to you and you inform the meeting that it is the same address as Mr Zabrinski but the name on the card states, 'Pretty Pictures Ltd.' It says the pictures can be taken in the child's home in their own comfortable surroundings. The head teacher is well informed on child safety issues and has sent a letter to all parents warning them against using photographers who were not recommended by the school. So far, the parents have not made the link with Mr Zabrinski himself, but word travels fast on that estate. He may become subject to vigilante action now that the head teacher has gone ahead with this letter before seeking advice.

Consultant psychiatrist

Only when you hear the report from housing about Mr Zabrinski getting a job in computers, and other reports about Mr Zabrinski's recent behaviour, do you advise the meeting that this is extremely worrying. You see a pattern of escalation in his offending behaviour. Mr Zabrinski is constructing opportunities for himself to extend his sexually abusive behaviour. How will he be stopped before another allegation comes to light? You suggest we speak with his general practitioner to see if he will be persuaded to go into therapy voluntarily.

Group discussion

Planning to assess risk to:

- Mr Zabrinski from any punitive action by his employer or the local community
- Local children
- Victims of his possible computer offences at his work

Chairperson makes recommendations

- There is evidence of escalation in behaviour and Mr Zabrinski is taking surprising risks, given his previous arrest and a police warning of unannounced visits.
- The head teacher's action was well meaning but should have been agreed through the MAPPA as it might escalate his behaviour further.

- There is a need for caution here as Mr Zabrinski has not offended again, as far as is known, and he does have human rights. The meeting needs to discuss whether or not we as a panel inform his new employer and run the risk that he will be sacked. He may well then become more difficult to track and monitor, especially as he may move home as well. He may go underground and this will be more dangerous for children. It is important for him not to disappear from view.
- The employer may help with monitoring.
- A few things need to be considered such as if and how the employer is informed, what advice is given to housing and whether the doctor is spoken to about the need for therapy.

Participants in the role play then make a decision about the level of risk.

Handout 16d: Case Study D

Category: Violent Offender

Name: Mr. Kalra
Age: 38 years, Asian
Risk: High

Chairperson reads the case history

There has been a history of domestic violence in the family for five years. His wife Kirti and two daughters, aged 10 and 8 years, have suffered repeated trauma. Mr Kalra was recently arrested for breach of the peace, common assault on his wife, harassment and breach of an injunction. Most recently, he was sentenced to a two year Community Rehabilitation order and a two year Restraining Order.

Detective Sergeant, PPU

You have had to deal with some of the incidents. They are quite bizarre. Mr Kalra does not sleep at night and sets fire to bits of paper in the house. One time he disconnected the hose to the oven and the family had to leave the home until it was fixed, he had been drinking heavily at the time. He also made a lot of noise all night long keeping the family awake by singing very loudly and put the TV on at high volume.

At the time of the assault he had threatened to set fire to the house. You do not know how the family have put up with it for so long without reporting it. The wife was not badly injured but had bruising on her arm and was very shocked.

Probation officer

You are supervising this man and describe him as a difficult character. He will not comply with any of the conditions of the order. He is residing at a local bed and breakfast hotel and must not have contact with his ex-wife, children, extended family, friends of the family, children's friends, school or his ex-wife's workplace. He must not go within half a mile of the victim's address. He must co-operate with the psychiatric assessment. So far, after one month, you can report that he is staying with his parents but has been seen loitering around the school fence. He has been in the supermarket which is outside the half mile limit but where they do their weekly shopping. So far they have not seen him. He also frequents the local cinema and leisure centre where he thinks they may go. The result is that this family are housebound for fear of meeting him. So far you have not got proof enough to breach him but you will at the first opportunity. To be frank, you really can't work with this person at all, he is rude to you and confrontational all the time.

Safeguarding manager

You convened the child protection conference after reports from the school that the children were saying unusual things about their father's behaviour. On investigation the mother would say little at first as she remained loyal to her husband. This inquiry took a long time. Slowly, details emerged that he would go out at night and buy food to eat because he would never eat anything she had cooked. The family would be kept awake with the sounds from the kitchen.

Later he was sending the family obscene letters and making obscene phone calls.

Housing manager

You have offered to re-house Mr Kalra from the area but he will not agree to this. He is determined to stay in the area and continue his activities. The tenancy for the family home is now in Kirti's name. You have also offered her a new home outside the area but she does not want to disrupt the children's schooling. The youngest daughter is under hospital treatment for her asthma and Kirti does not want to change doctors. The doctor has been very supportive to her and has referred her to a specialist asian women's counselling service which has been very helpful.

Police officer, PPU

You dealt with the harassment calls. Mr Kalra constantly dialled 999 and the family endured endless visits from police, fire and ambulance crews. He is currently awaiting trial for this as evidence of the calls was found on his mobile phone.

Detective inspector, CAIT

This is a clear case of non-compliance. You offer to allocate an officer to watch him for a week to see where he is going and what he is doing. This might give probation the evidence they need to take him back to court for breach of the order.

Consultant psychiatrist

You think the police/probation view is limited to containment of the behaviour and suggest that the problem will continue to reoccur until he has treatment. You agree to interview him again. You have only seen him once and he did not co-operate. You ask the mental health social worker to visit and bring him to your hospital to see you or even arrange a home visit. You know that research indicates that when one sibling commits suicide there is a high risk of another doing the same. Mr Kalra's brother committed suicide.

Education social work team manager

You receive many calls from the head teachers of both the children's schools. They are very anxious indeed. They find Mr Kalra to be intimidating and are afraid of him coming into the school. In the past he has been quite drunk and upset parents and children by throwing things about in the cloakroom. They have been informed that he must not go near the schools and know to inform police if this happens. They report both girls as withdrawn. They have both been seeing the school nurse in her drop-in time for counselling. They are still very afraid of their father and this is affecting their schooling. The mother is doing her best but seems quite depressed lately. She feels very guilty for reporting him to the children's services and police. She feels very sorry for him, as before the sudden death of his brother, he was a good husband to her. His brother killed himself by jumping under a train. This was a terrible shock to the family. These girls have had a lot to deal with.

Mental health social worker

You respond to the psychiatrist's suggestion that you visit Mr Kalra and organise a psychiatric assessment. You think this is a waste of time unless it is a condition of a court order.

Group discussion

Planning to assess risk to:

- The children
- The mother
- Mr Kalra – assessing the risk to himself and others

Chairperson makes recommendations

- Case to be reviewed in one month.
- Children must have child protection plans. It is important to hear the children's views via the school nurse if they are having any contact with their father.
- One week of police surveillance of Mr Kalra.
- Housing to make enquiries about the bed and breakfast accommodation and any reports about his behaviour there, so that the safety of the other residents can be considered.
- Mental health social worker to arrange mental health assessment as soon as possible. Even if this fails, it will strengthen reports for a court instruction for psychiatric assessment, should he be breached.

Participants in the role play then make a decision about the level of risk.

Handout 16e: Case Study E

Category: Sex Offender

Mr Neville Tracey
Age: 29 years, African Caribbean
Risk: Medium

Chairperson reads the case history

Mr Tracey was convicted of indecent assault eight years ago, on a girl aged 11 years. He took her to his home address and indecently assaulted her on a number of occasions. He was sentenced to three years imprisonment and placed on the Sex Offenders Register.

He also has a conviction for sexual intercourse with a girl under the age of 15 years, for which he had received a suspended sentence. He had worked at the local tennis club and had befriended her.

Police officer, PPU

This case has come to attention following a report from Mrs James. She and her husband had gone out for the evening dancing and hired a babysitter called Francine. During the evening there had been a burglary and a lot of possessions had been taken. The babysitter was hired through, 'Nicest Nannies', a local agency. Police realised Francine's partner was Neville Tracey. The James family knew him as he had offered to walk their dog a number of times and sometimes collected their daughter Emma, age 11 years, from school. The James family had become quite good friends with Francine and Neville. They also have a young son called Harry aged seven. Police found no stolen goods at the home of Francine and Neville. You visited the home address of Neville and Francine yesterday and he was clear that he had changed his ways. He had told Francine that he had been in prison but she seemed to think it was for burglaries. She had no idea what it was really for and was very shocked when you told her. They have a baby, a little boy of three months old and he looked fine. Neville works part time for a voluntary organisation as a sports coach for disabled adults.

Detective sergeant, PPU

You contacted the nanny agency. They think very highly of Francine, who is reliable and well thought of. They did not know her partner was helping families as well and they had no idea of his convictions. They have suspended Francine while the investigations are in progress.

Detective inspector, CAIT

Your team intend to interview Emma and Harry. At the moment the parents are not giving their consent. This might take time or children's services may need to obtain an

Emergency Protection Order, (CA 1989 Section 44) with a condition of interview attached. It is not unusual for parents to need time to agree to such interviews.

Safeguarding manager

A strategy meeting has been held on the James children but not a conference because they have been protected by their parents, from any future contact with Neville, future harm is not likely. Reports about the children were positive and there are no signs that they have suffered abuse. You await the outcome of the interviews. You did not know, until today, that there was a baby in the sex offender's household; now there has to be a conference on this baby. Probably, it will be decided that the mother has to demonstrate how she can protect the baby from him.

Consultant psychiatrist

You have not had any contact with this case but you advise that Neville will always present a risk to children. Just because in the past he has abused older girls, does not mean he will not also abuse a baby boy. He needs a full risk assessment. He did not have any therapy and no-one knows what risk he poses to this baby. It seems he is still targeting families in order to gain an opportunity to abuse. He might take a year or so to gain the trust of the family before the abuse begins. It is probable, this time, that Emma has not yet been abused. The baby should not be living with him at all unless a risk assessment verifies that he has changed his ways. Francine will have to choose between him and the baby. He could have supervised contact. This will probably have to go to court.

Education social work team manager

You have checked the records for both Emma and Harry. There are no difficulties at school and their development is fine. Harry had told his teacher about Neville taking him for walks with the dog. You found records on Francine which showed that she was abused in foster care.

Probation officer

You have heard from another sex offender, who is friendly with Neville, that he attends a local church. He seems quite involved and is studying to be a lay preacher. You ask the meeting to consider what might be done to alert the minister to this.

Group discussion

Planning to assess risk to:

- The baby
- Harry and Emma
- Church congregation and sports club members

- Neville and Francine
- Children at the school where Mr Tracey collected Emma.

Chairperson makes recommendations

- Case to be reviewed in one month.
- Child protection conference to be convened with regard to the baby.
- Sex offender risk assessment on Neville as requirement of the child protection conference. Non-compliance to lead to court proceedings.
- Francine to be taken through evidence from his previous convictions to inform her of the risk. This will be a task for the PPU officer.
- Harry and Emma to be interviewed and offered therapeutic support if necessary. There must be no future contact with Neville. Social worker may need to consult with the child psychiatrist about appropriate means of informing the children of the risk.
- Police and social worker to visit church minister and sports club to implement protective strategy.
- Consider discretionary disclosure issues in notifying the church and sports club.

Participants in the role play then make a decision about the level of risk.

Handout 16f: Case Study F

Category: Sex Offender

Name: Jonathan Matthews
Age: 15 years, White UK
Risk: High

Chairperson reads the case history

Jonathan Matthews is currently at a young offender institution. He will be released on licence to the Youth Offending Team. He was convicted for indecently assaulting a woman in the High Street by touching her breasts and he received eight months imprisonment. His name is on the Sex Offenders Register.

Youth offending team manager

Jonathan lives with his grandmother and baby sister. His mother deserted him some years ago and he has unresolved anger about this. He was emotionally abused. You want a full psychological assessment on release. You will also organise Connexions to offer him training opportunities. You know he is interested in working in a record shop but there will be problems about his contact with women. He will need to join a therapeutic group before any career option can be agreed.

Housing manager

On release you will place him in a hostel for men, it is not ideal but he has not been in care so does not get an allocation under leaving care provision. You cannot put him in a group home for young people as it may place young women at risk.

Police officer, PPU

Jonathan has constantly been in trouble in the young offender's institution. There have been a number of fights and he has been placed on high security.

Safeguarding manager

You know that Jonathan was the subject of a child protection plan because of emotional abuse and his grandmother tried hard to care for him. He was close to her and his little sister. You do not see him as presenting a risk to the immediate family and the grandmother wants him home again. However, measures must be in place to safeguard him from his mother who still occasionally calls round and causes trouble. Jonathan reminded her of his father who was violent to her. You think it is outrageous that he is now labelled a sex offender. You are minded to reconvene the child protection conference to consider his needs as a victim of abuse.

Education social work team manager

It is your view that there is no way Jonathan can return to school. It came to your attention that a welfare assistant reported that Jonathan had touched her breasts but she did not want to make a fuss. She thought he was a nice boy who just missed his mum.

Group discussion

Planning to assess risk to:

- The sister
- Grandmother
- Mother
- Women generally
- Jonathan

Chairperson makes recommendations

- Case to be reviewed in one month.
- On release Jonathan should be placed on the young sex offender's programme at the Youth Offending Team.
- A decision needs to be made about his housing and an evaluation about whether he is safe enough to return to his grandmother's home.
- There needs to be clarity about what has to happen in order to remove his name from the Sex Offenders Register.

Participants in the role play then make a decision about the level of risk.

Handout 16g: Case Study G

Category: Potentially Dangerous Adult

Name: Matthew Perkins
Age: 55 years, White UK
Risk: Undecided

Chairperson reads the case history

Matthew Perkins was named by the US Federal Bureau of Investigation as having downloaded abusive images of children from the internet. He used his credit card on pay for view sites. His computer was seized and is being examined. He works in a local bank. He is married to an occupational therapist. Their son and two grandchildren visit frequently. Matthew and his wife run a local scout troop and have done so for years. His wife is also a part time magistrate in a neighbouring area.

On interview he denied that he had done this deliberately, he said that his credit card number had been misused and that police would find nothing on his computer hard drive to incriminate him. Police did, however, on a search of his house, find in his address book, the number of a well known local child sex offender who had previously worked in the scouts.

Group to discuss

Whether or not Matthew's actions, as yet unproven in court, should impact on his and his wife's career, activities and his grandchildren's visits.

Planning to assess risk to:

- Matthew
- Matthew's wife
- Matthew's grandchildren
- Children in scout group

Participants in the role play then make a decision about the level of risk.

Handout 16h: Case Study H

Category: Alleged Sex Offender

Name: Carolyn Martin
Age: 44 years, White UK
Risk: Undecided

Chairperson reads the case history

Ms Martin was arrested for indecency with children over the period of three months. The victim was a boy aged 14 years. A young girl had been interviewed about unlawful sexual intercourse by a man living with Carolyn. During her interview she stated that whilst in the house, she had seen Carolyn having sex with the boy.

Detective inspector, CAIT

The boy, on interview, denied the offence so the case could not proceed. He said the girl had lied and that she always boasted about her sexual encounters with men, which he said were rubbish.

Police officer, PPU

On interview, Carolyn said that she had never had sexual intercourse with the alleged victim but did admit that her flatmate had been in bed with the girl with the agreement of her parents. She said she had not known the girl was only aged 12 years. She thought she was aged 16 years.

Safeguarding manager

This case will go nowhere criminally but Carolyn has a severely disabled daughter aged 11 years who lives at the address. A conference will be held to evaluate the risk to the daughter. She has a social worker in adult services who says she communicates using Makaton communication system.

Housing manager

You have had reports from neighbours complaining about noise at night and people coming and going to and from the property. There has been some talk about drugs, and a lot of young people visit the address.

Education social work manager

The local head teacher has noticed some of the school children visiting this address. Some parents have said there are drugs being passed around. Carolyn sometimes teaches reading at the school. She gets on well with the staff and the children have got to know her.

Group discussion

Planning to assess risk to:

- The alleged victim
- Carolyn's daughter
- Young people visiting the household
- Children at the school

Participants in the role play then make a decision about the level of risk.

Presentation 16: Organised Abuse

Definition of organised abuse

Abuse involving one or more abuser and a number of children. The abusers concerned may be acting in concert to abuse children, sometimes acting in isolation, or may be using an institutional framework or position of authority to recruit children for abuse.

(DfES, 2006: 6.7)

When any agency reports a situation of organised abuse, named officers from the police and children's services will be appointed to co-ordinate the case. A special strategy meeting will be urgently convened involving senior managers. Organised abuse may involve numbers of child victims and numbers of perpetrators. These investigations are complex and often cross local authority boundaries. Sometimes abuse networks extend outside the country.

Indicators of organised abuse

Early indicators may include the following:

- Child gives clues, verbal or non-verbal, about sexual activities.
- Inexplicable breakdown of the child's world e.g. suspension from school following emotional or aggressive outbursts, atypical parental 'over-reactive' behaviour, or child withdraws from peer group.
- Child exposed to inappropriate sexual material.
- Child introduced to adult activities such as alcohol, drugs, crime, abusive images of children or adults.
- Child goes missing or runs away and there is little understanding of the whereabouts.
- Child shows unpredictable and inexplicable fears.
- Involvement of known 'risk to children' individuals in the child's life.
- Child has access to 'rewards' such as money or clothes.
- Child seeks out abusive images.
- Child has intimate knowledge of adults' lives which extends beyond the expected boundaries of the relationship.

Medical presentations of organised abuse may include the following:

- Evidence of forced injection or ingestion or other application of drugs, especially muscle relaxants, hallucinogens or anaesthetics.
- Evidence of the forced ingestion or external application of non-food substances such as human or animal faeces or urine.
- Evidence of the use of implements in the abuse.
- Indication of violence such as strap marks to wrists, ankles or marks around the throat.

- Forensic or medical evidence of more than one perpetrator having been involved in the abuse.
- Child extremely afraid of the medical examination or forensic photographer.
- Evidence of sexual activities with animals e.g. animal's hair, blood, semen.

Other indicators of organised abuse may include the following:

- Disclosures from the child.
- Allegations received from the family, community, professionals.
- Police intelligence about abusive images of children or known 'risk to children' individuals.
- Evidence obtained through police surveillance or searches such as photographs or videos.
- Child sexually abused in group context: young people abusing other young people in a group or in the presence of adults or young person.
- A young person encouraging other young people to become involved.
- Use of photography, video or online abusive images in the abuse.
- Abuse takes place in a number of different locations.
- Adults attempt to change child's name or obtain possession of the child's passport.
- Child has heightened level of fear and/or other indicators of sexual abuse such as attempted suicide, self harm, dissociation, eating disorders, danger seeking behaviour, substance abuse, involvement in criminal activities or arson.
- Known connections between child sex abusers and family members.
- The child, family or professionals are victims of threats.
- Suspected adult breaks normal rules and boundaries of relationship in order to access the young person.
- Adult takes child to isolated places such as caravans or boats.
- Child repeats adult terminology and statements indicative of adult power over child.
- Child has confused sexual identity, e.g. may say they are not gay and yet be involved in homosexual relationships.
- Sexual activities involving animals.
- Sexual activities involving the use of rituals, costumes or chanting.
- Evidence of cult involvement.

Presentation 17: Child Sexual Exploitation

Working Together to Safeguard Children Involved in Prostitution (DoH, 2000) is national guidance on this aspect of child abuse. The identification of a child involved in prostitution should trigger local procedures to ensure the child's safety and enable the police to gather evidence about abusers and coercers. There are strong links between sexual exploitation of children, running away from home, substance misuse and human trafficking. Interventions require 'a careful, caring and concerted inter-agency approach that may have to be sustained for a long period of time' (DoH, 2000: 2.4).

The emphasis must be to prevent the entry of children into prostitution and, where they are already involved, to protect them from further abuse. Targeting abusers may involve prosecution for a range of offences. The police must be robust in seeking evidence to support charges such as grievous bodily harm, unlawful wounding, actual bodily harm, kidnapping, abduction, sexual crimes, false imprisonment as well as drugs offences and benefit or tax fraud, (DoH, 2000: 3.4).

The United Nations Convention on the Rights of the Child states that children should be protected from sexual exploitation and abuse including prostitution and involvement in pornography.

Article 34 states that all appropriate measures will be taken to prevent:

- The inducement or coercion of a child to engage in any unlawful sexual activity.
- The exploitative use of children in prostitution or other unlawful sexual practices.
- The exploitative use of children in pornographic performances and materials.

Article 35 states that children have a right to protection from being abducted or sold.

(United Nations, 1989)

Sexual Offences Act 2003 (enforced from 1st May 2004)

The law has been tightened to protect young people from broader methods of sexual exploitation and more severe penalties have been introduced.

The following are now an offence:

- Grooming.
- Trafficking and moving children in, out of and within the UK for sexual purposes.
- Whatever is an offence offline is also an offence online.

The Act includes consensual and non-consensual offences against children and vulnerable adults. There is no defence of a belief that the young person was over the age of 18 years though such a belief may influence sentencing as a mitigating factor.

A child under the age of 13 years does not under any circumstances have the legal capacity to consent to any form of sexual activity. All penetrative sex (including penetration of the mouth) of a child under the age of 13 years will be automatically classified as rape with a maximum penalty of life in prison.

It is an offence:

- To buy the sexual services of a child, e.g. Payment by cash, goods or services, drugs or waiving of debts.
- To recruit, induce or compel a child into commercial sexual exploitation.
- To participate in, facilitate or allow the commercial sexual exploitation of a child.
- To receive money or other reward, favour or compensation for the commercial sexual exploitation of a child.

The Protection of Children Act (1999) states it is an offence to take, make, permit to take, distribute, show, possess with intent to distribute or to advertise, indecent photographs of under 16s. This offence now applies to images of 16 and 17-year-olds.

Presentation 18: Cheryl – Case Study

This case study is based upon a true case. Many details were in the public arena at the time but the name has been changed. Cheryl died as a result of a methadone overdose. She was found dead by her apparent boyfriend. She had been sexually exploited. It is important to replace terms like punter, pimp and prostitute with abusing adult, child sex abuser and child victim. When Cheryl died there were two contrasting attitudes in the public arena.

1. ChildLine

Can we correct one thing while we're talking about it? This child wasn't a prostitute. She was an under-aged young person who was being sexually abused by adults who paid to do that, not a prostitute. It's very important that we get that right and that we target the adults who are after under-age young people rather than calling young people prostitutes.

2. Press headlines

Drug death of girl 13	*Death of vice girl 13*
Prostitute dies of overdose at 13	*13 year old child prostitute*
Just a child	*Tragic child prostitute*
Inquiry into a girl's death	*Grim death of Cheryl age 13*
Prostitute dies at 13	*Tragic girl*
Sad Cheryl	*Death of prostitute age 13*
Prostitute age 13	*Drug girl*
Tragic vice girl junkie and prostitute age 13	*Child hooker*
Tragic Cheryl	*Girl addict*

- Cheryl was known to 240 professionals during her 13 years of life.
- She was missing 61 times in the last year of her life.
- She experienced 68 changes of carer and had 17 different foster carers. In the last year of her life she was placed with 3 foster carers and in 3 residential placements.
- In the last year of her life she had 7 sexually transmitted infections.
- She was known to 13 general practitioners.
- She attended 8 schools.
- She had two cultures/religions – Muslim and Christian.

Known to children's services since birth, the first years of her life were characterised by neglect and exposure to an unstable, sometimes violent, home environment. Her mother was very caring but unable, through mental ill health, to look after Cheryl properly. When Cheryl was aged 9 years she was placed in the care of her birth father. At this time her life changed from that of a Christian to a Muslim, including a change of name and school.

Her father took her abroad for long periods of time which disrupted her education. She made many allegations of physical abuse, sexual abuse and neglect by different perpetrators over several years. She disclosed the abuse to teachers, police, social workers, counsellors, medical staff at the Genital Urinary Medicine clinic, general practitioner, residential care staff, foster carers, hospital staff, family and friends. In the last year of Cheryl's life she had an allocated social worker who worked extremely hard and was the recipient of many of the messages from the child via other professionals. The social worker informed her managers of her concerns. Managers finally sought secure accommodation but Cheryl died before the placement was arranged.

Some issues of professional dangerousness may be applied to this case (see page 127).

The child's statements did not elicit a protective response, as Cheryl was described by professionals as bubbly and sparking. She was defined as able to care for herself, even though she was so young, because she appeared capable. She spoke about the abuse in a matter of fact way minimising the impact. Professionals meeting her had the **rule of optimism** and they allowed themselves to believe her façade of being in control of the situation. In reality she was entrapped by a number of child sex abusers. Her messages to professionals were also through her behaviour – she was running away, self harming and taking drugs. These behavioural messages were interpreted as behaviour which required management rather than leading to action to target the perpetrators of the crimes. She frequently made allegations and then swiftly retracted them. The professionals did not understand the dynamics of child abuse to recognise that retractions add to statement validity and often indicate a child who is fearful of the consequences of disclosure. Her continual retractions became interpreted as another issue requiring behaviour management. The **professional accommodation syndrome** mirrored the **child abuse accommodation syndrome** in this case as professionals held to strategies of intervention that did not provide a protective response to the abuse. As a result of her response, Cheryl was pathologised by professionals and gained the labels of manipulative, rude, disruptive and prostitute.

Because the mother was caring, the **rule of optimism** also led to a belief that she could care for Cheryl in between placements or when permission was provided for overnight stays at home. This led to a gap in the protective system. **The false compliance** of the carer, allowed the network of abusers to take control. The mother was a non-abusive carer but she was not a proactive protector. The father was defined as an appropriate carer but could be quite intimidating to professionals. **Stockholm syndrome** applied as professionals tended to identify with him as a good carer and applied **cultural assumptions** that his disciplinarian approach to her was justified in cultural terms.

It was also assumed that, when at the age of 11, she spoke of her boyfriend aged 15 years that he was a true boyfriend. Professional's **rule of optimism** again interfered with proper analysis and checks being made with the relevant authority.

There was **non-compliance with statutory procedures.** Cheryl was defined as a child needing a care placement and not a child victim of sexual exploitation. She was moved from placement to placement in an attempt to provide her with stability but there was no attention to removing the child abusers from her life. There was a lack of formal child protection procedures. There were no strategy meetings and there was no child protection conference. The residential and foster placements broke down because no service could compete with the influence of the abusers on Cheryl's life. As each placement ended there was no formal multi-agency review of the reasons for the breakdown and information gathered by each placement did not inform the next. The perception of the case as a child in need of care, rather than protection, persisted, leading to **assessment paralysis.** There was no managerial review of the lack of protective interventions and as Cheryl's behaviour continued the professionals maintained their fixed view of the situation. Strategies were not subjected to re-evaluation over time. **Rigid belief systems** prevailed, beliefs that Cheryl made up abuse allegations, that her parents could protect her and that the care system could provide her with safety from the abuse network.

Some **protectors and carers went unheard** because of their low status – **the exaggeration of hierarchy.** Her family expressed concern and her friends held the most information about her activities. Some of them were also being abused. Professionals did not appreciate the friends as a crucial source of information about the abuse networks.

Her chaotic lifestyle which was responsive to the abusers demands made conventional services such as the Child and Adolescent Mental Health Service (CAMHS) inaccessible to her. Yet some professional decisions included **concrete solutions** such as 'appointment with CAMHS' or 'counselling' which were not helpful in the context of Cheryl's lifestyle controlled by the abusers. She herself was defined as capable of providing the solution to her situation by compliance with professional decisions, but the abuse network remained unseen.

Given the lack of statutory procedures and formal child protection processes there was no chronology completed which would have highlighted patterns. Key information was only collated after her death. **Priority was given to recent, emotional and vivid information** and highly relevant old information on the files was not available to the professional network. Professionals did not share information through formal procedures leading to **role confusion.** There was lack of clarity about each professional role in the protection process. For instance the school sent Cheryl home for not wearing uniform at a time when the police and social workers were looking for her when she had gone missing. The social worker was preoccupied with trying to find the missing child and to identify appropriate placements. Because of the lack of formal protocols the social worker was acting largely alone without the support of a multi-agency team of professionals. Under the weight of numerous reports of child abuse in this case, she rushed to and fro trying to do her best. She mirrored the child's **flight behaviour.** With good supervision she might have been able to reflect on her own responses to the case and realised that she had become **enmeshed** with the child's emotional responses to the abuse.

Although Cheryl spoke of abuse within her family she did not disclose the abusers outside the family network. It still remains unclear who was exploiting her. After her death only one perpetrator was convicted when some abusive images of her were found. She was clipping, which involved offering men sexual activity in return for money and then running away. This provided her with quick money for purchasing drugs. She was also found by police all over the country and it is not known how she got to these places or what she was doing there. After her death it became clear that there was much more information available about her activities, that if collated, may have protected her and targeted the perpetrators.

Activity 21: Protecting a Sexually Exploited Child

Aim: For participants to consider what might have helped to protect Cheryl.

Delivery: Participants work in mixed groups to consider protective strategies and to list these under the headings provided in the guidance.

Content:

- Recognise the problem.
- Treat the child primarily as a victim of abuse.
- Prevent further abuse.
- Provide child with exit strategies.
- Investigate and prosecute those who coerce, exploit and abuse children.

(DfES, 2006: 6.2)

Feedback: Group discussion based around what professional intervention should have been implemented in this case.

- **Recognise the problem:** Cheryl should not have been pathologised as a child but professional attention should have focused on the perpetrators. Cheryl should have had the benefit of child protection procedures with a detailed protection plan involving education, health, children's services and police.
- **Safeguard the child and promote their welfare:** A formal assessment of her parent's capacity to protect would have allowed fewer gaps in the protective systems for abusers to exploit.
- **Prevent further abuse:** Section 47 investigation through organised abuse procedures would have identified police officers responsible for collating intelligence about the perpetrators and evaluating the information provided by the numerous Police 78 forms (when a child comes to the attention of the police). Proactive strategies to investigate what was happening to Cheryl would have been in place. Foster carers and residential workers had daily logs including names, places, car and phone numbers of alleged perpetrators. An organised abuse strategy would have put in place a system for ongoing evaluation of this evidence.
- **Provide child with exit strategies:** Cheryl could have been offered a safe house but there is only one such resource in the UK for children. This was the key resource identified by her friends as necessary for their protection from harm. Another resource they would have used would have been a local helpline.
- **Investigate and prosecute those who coerce, exploit and abuse children:** Organised abuse procedures should have been implemented as there was more than one alleged or known perpetrator. Police and social workers working together through organised abuse procedures would have been likely to identify those sexually exploiting Cheryl and the drug dealers and remove them from the life of the child.

The Multi-Agency Public Protection Arrangements should have had a role in monitoring the activities of known offenders in her life. This would also have provided protection for other child victims of the abuse network.

Activity 22: Responding to the Protection Needs of Sexually Exploited Children

Aim: For participants to learn about the dynamics of sexual exploitation of children and to practice responses to a young person entrapped within an organised-abuse network.

Delivery: Two videos are shown.
Barnardo's (1998) *Whose Daughter Next?* Essex: Barnardo's.

Barnardo's (2001) *No son of mine.* Essex: Barnardo's.

Both videos address the sexual exploitation of young people. After the videos there is discussion followed by a carousel.

The participants form two circles. The outside circle faces inwards and the inside circle faces outwards to form a carousel. The participants on the outside play the part of sexually exploited children and are given cards each with one question on it. They ask the question of the person opposite them in the inner circle who plays the part of an adult to provide a clear, sensible and age appropriate response to the question. After a short while, the trainer tells the participants to move round and the outside circle move once to the left to ask the same question of the next adult. The people in the inner circle remain stationary throughout. The trainer should allow about one minute for each question. It is useful to have a bell or whistle to signify the need to move round. Once the participants have completed a whole rotation they reverse places in the carousel. Those that played children become the adults and those that played adults become the children.

Feedback: Discussion of the issues raised by the activity.

Handout 17: Practising Responses to Sexually Exploited Young People

- How do you know you have been raped?
- What's AIDS?
- I want to have a kid.
- You know nothing about my life.
- I just want someone to love me.
- I hate myself.
- Clipping's better than selling.
- Bet you don't know what buggered means?
- How do you know if you are gay?
- Do I walk like I'm gay?
- The condom burst, it doesn't matter just once does it?
- Can I tell you a secret?
- I'm really frightened.
- Do you think meeting someone from the internet is okay?
- My friend says that you don't get pregnant if you do it standing up.
- What's a pimp?
- What's a punter?
- Do you think I look sexy?
- My boyfriend gave me this ring, do you like it?
- My friend's boyfriend makes her do stuff with other men.
- What's cottaging?
- Is oral sex dangerous?
- Sleeping with someone for a place to stay isn't prostitution, is it?
- I'm disgusting and dirty.
- He was really kind to me and I liked the sex.
- He was my knight in shining armour. He's got a car instead of a horse.
- Older men make much better lovers, what's that to you?
- They're going to get my family if I stop going round there.
- Everyone I know takes crack.
- (Silence)
- I've got awful stomach pains.
- When I see the blood run I feel calmer.
- Why should I tell you? I've told hundreds of times already.
- I can't stand this place, my worker's a nonce.
- Being on the streets is better than at home.
- I don't need any help, I can look after myself.
- I've done it loads of times but they just got too heavy.
- Kiss my arse.
- What else is there to do, being stuck in this shithole?

- He gets me to wear my trousers back to front.
- He calls us his bum boys
- I'm ugly, I can't look in the mirror.
- I get dolled up by his girlfriend.
- Can women be pimps?
- He filmed us in our school uniform.

Presentation 19: Investigation of Organised Abuse

Reference is made to the organised abuse procedures in *Working Together* (DfES, 2006: 6.7) and the Home Office Guidance (2002) in context of Activity 20 which concerns allegations of abuse by a teacher.

Particular considerations to highlight:

> Those managing the investigation need to be aware that there may be attempts to sabotage the investigation, destroy materials or to interfere with or intimidate staff. Appropriate steps must be taken to minimise these risks.

(Home Office, 2002: 14)

An organised abuse investigation must include setting up:

1. A Strategic Management Group
2. An Investigation Management Group
3. An Operational team
4. A senior level strategy group

Set up a Strategic Management Group to:

- Establish the terms of reference and take leadership of the investigation, considering cross boundary issues if the young people or alleged perpetrators are from outside the authority.
- Agree staffing of the investigation and membership of the investigation management group for the conduct of the investigation and separate Section 47 enquiries.
- Agree protocols for managing the investigation, identifying and supporting victims and witnesses, sharing information and staff safety.
- Ensure current risks to children are acted on immediately with regular review.
- Collation of known information about the alleged perpetrators.
- Collation of information about any previous allegations or suspicions, inspection reports, employment record.
- Mapping the methods of abuse including venues, patterns of grooming, bribes, favours and threats as well as identifying and profiling other possible perpetrators.
- Overview processes for gathering corroborative and additional evidence.
- Ensure effective working together.
- Ensure allocation of resources and administrative support and office space.
- Arrange access to legal advice.
- Establish a policy for questions of financial compensation to victims.
- Monitor and review collation of evidence to safeguard against allegations of prompting witnesses.
- Ensure appropriate recording processes including the security of the investigation, such as numbered documents.
- Manage media contact and appoint spokesperson to consider health and social care needs of victims and adult survivors, particularly if acting as witnesses including accommodation needs.

- Ensure interviews are conducted according to Achieving Best Evidence guidance (CJS, 2007).
- For children's services to provide accommodation for young people if required, as well as medical, physical and emotional support. Consideration of health needs of victims such as screening for sexually transmitted infections and HIV.
- Agree communication with, and support of, carers of the young people involved.
- Liaise with the Crown Prosecution Service in respect of prosecutions.
- Set up operational teams to conduct the individual Section 47 investigations with clear review processes.
- Identify policy and training implications.

An **Investigation Management Group** should be set up under the Strategic Management Group to:

- Provide a forum where professionals can meet, exchange information and implement strategy on a daily basis.
- Co-ordinate the inter-agency approach and investigation.
- To include representatives from the local authority children's services, police, health, education and probation.
- Provide a safe reporting channel for whistleblowers.

Operational team to:

- Make decisions about immediate safety of the young people.
- Conduct video recorded interviews which may need to be simultaneous to prevent contamination of evidence.
- Arrange medical consultations.
- Organise forensic retrieval.
- Organise any search of premises and computers.
- Interview any corroborative witnesses.
- Assess photographic and visual evidence.

The **senior level strategy group** to review outcome of the operational teams and consider in sequence:

- Enquiries and assessment by children's services about whether a child is in need of protection or in need of services.
- A police investigation of a possible criminal offence.
- Consideration by an employer of disciplinary action in respect of the individual.

The employers responsible for disciplinary action should await the outcome of the child protection investigation and any police action before progressing to formal disciplinary proceedings. This does not prevent the employee being suspended pending the outcome of the investigations (DfES, 2006: Appendix. 5.2).

Activity 23: Investigating Organised Abuse – Case Study

Aim: Participants to explore the dilemmas and complexities of investigating a case of organised abuse.

Delivery: Participants divide into two mixed professional groups. Trainers give both groups the scenario and each group has a distinct task.

Group A

To plan a joint investigation strategy and draw a flow chart to illustrate this strategy.

Group B

To discuss the above case and prepare a list of key issues for consideration in planning a joint investigation.

Handout 18: Investigating Organised Abuse – Scenario

Mrs Paterson, mother of Carl, aged 13 overheard him speaking with a school friend called Martin from the local independent boarding school which both boys attend. It was the start of the summer holidays. She heard Martin say to Carl that he should not tell about the photos and she later challenged Carl about it. Carl explained that he is especially fond of one teacher, Mr Green. He and about ten other boys go to his flat after school. They have a great time. They play music, dance and Mr Green provides the vodka. Sometimes they stay all night. Carl said that Mr Green took him to another man's house a few miles away. The friend, whom he calls John, showed Carl a photo of Mr Green and Martin cuddling naked on Mr Green's bed. John asked Carl if he would like to earn some money like the rest of Mr Green's special boys. Mrs Paterson knows that Mr Green is the Chair of a local charity and as a local councillor sits on the Adoption Panel. She also knows that his wife teaches part-time at the school. The nine other boys seemed to come from outside the area. Mrs Paterson found some muscle relaxant pills in her son's pocket and she went to the local police station where the officer on duty contacted the CID. A decision is made by senior level police and children's services managers that there will be a joint police/children's services investigation.

Feedback: Trainers in discussion with the group draw comparisons between the outcome of each group's work.

Trainers may recommend the following for further information about organised abuse:
Wolmar, (2000) *Forgotten Children*. An analysis of institutional abuse in children's homes.
Gallagher, (1998) *Grappling with Smoke*. Research concerning organised abuse.
Gosling and D'Arcy, (1998) *Abuse of Trust*. An analysis of the Leicestershire children's
    home scandal.
Oliver and Ramsey, (1993) *Lambs to the Slaughter*. An account of Operation Orchid, the
    investigation of the murders of boys in South-east England.

Presentation 20: Ritual Abuse

In 1994, the Ritual Abuse Investigation Team at Scotland Yard completed a research project into 40 cases of ritual child sexual abuse. Michael Hames, former Superintendent and head of the team, stated that 'it would be wrong to dismiss all allegations of ritual abuse as fantasy'. He suggests that in such cases professionals listen, retain objectivity and examine each piece of evidence patiently, working towards a conclusion. 'An investigator has to remember that at the heart of an allegation there may be acts that did take place but they may be rendered distorted or unbelievable by misinformation' (Hames, 2000: 184). Unfortunately, this important police research was not made public.

Following the death of Victoria Climbié, Eleanor Stobart investigated cases of child abuse linked to accusations of possession and witchcraft (Stobart, 2000). She found that a belief in possession is widespread and not confined to particular cultures, countries, religions or to recent migrants. The abuse of children mainly occurred when the child was exorcised and abuse included, beating, burning, semi-strangulation, cutting, being tied up and starvation. In the context of certain African religions, Angus Stickler, a BBC journalist, investigated such abuse of children and one of his videos can be accessed online at; www.news.bbc.co.uk/2/hi/africa/4677969.stm.

Jean La Fontaine, an anthropologist, wrote a report for the Department of Health in 1994 in which she claimed that there was evidence of some child sex abusers using the paraphernalia of witchcraft to frighten children. There is no doubt that child sex abusers harm children in a range of ritualised contexts. What is needed is an objective study by specialist police and social work investigators to examine evidence from historic and current cases.

Presentation 21: Whistleblowing: Professionals Protecting Children

Working Together guidance states:

> *Clear procedures and support systems should be in place for dealing with expressions of concern by staff and carers about other staff or carers. There should be a guarantee that procedures can be invoked in ways which do not prejudice the whistleblower's own position and prospects.*

> (DfES, 2006: 11.6)

An organisation that supports whistleblowers and provides advice, is Public Concern at Work (www.pcaw.co.uk).

If children's voices are to be heard then professional voices must be heard when they are carrying the message for the child. Child abuse is essentially the abuse of power. Powerful adults abuse children and networks of perpetrators extend to the highest levels of society. It can be difficult and even frightening to carry the message forward to ensure that children gain protection. It may require individuals, organisations or processes to be challenged. Child abuse is perpetuated by secrecy and silence, that silence must be broken but it may be very difficult to do so.

> *Child advocacy involves a willingness to engage in creative conflict with adult interests because the rights of the child are unequally represented in our society.*

> (Richardson, 1991: 19)

The Waterhouse Inquiry into abuse in children's homes in Wales stated that child abuse would have been prevented if workers had voiced concerns but that staff who did voice concerns were disbelieved and vilified for speaking out.

> *There were no procedures in any of the establishments to enable members of staff to voice matters of concern and in many of them complaints by staff were strongly discouraged.*

> (Waterhouse, 2000: 201)

Both children and professionals are commonly met with denial when they do disclose. The child abuse accommodation syndrome becomes the professional accommodation syndrome with dynamics that mirror those of the child. Professionals may experience threats and pressure to be silent. There have been many social workers, police officers, doctors and other professionals who have suffered public vilification for speaking out about child abuse. Alison Taylor was a residential social worker in Wales. She spent 15 years disclosing the abuse of children in children's homes and was dismissed from her job. She has spoken of being repeatedly accused of manipulating children, exaggerating the abuse and even organising a nationwide conspiracy of false allegations for personal gain (Taylor in Hunt, 1998: 41–64). The Waterhouse Inquiry report made the following recommendation:

> *Every local authority should establish and implement conscientiously clear whistleblowing procedures enabling members of staff to make complaints and raise matters of concern affecting the treatment or welfare of looked after children without threats or fear of reprisals in any form.*

(Waterhouse, 2000: 216)

The following overview by Freedom to Care (www.freedomtocare.org) of common organisational responses to professionals exposing poor practice is helpful and would be amusing if they were not so tragic for the victims.

Hot air

The authorities will appear at first to share one's concern. Many words will be generated, insubstantial memoranda may fly about, a meeting may be convened, and promises will be made. No action will be taken, except perhaps the most trivial. At a later date any conversation not recorded on paper may be strenuously denied.

Sent to Coventry

A change of mood comes over certain managers and colleagues. Initially this is quite subtle. Greetings, smiles and friendly banter are less frequent. At first you brush it off then it becomes more pronounced. Eyebrows are raised mysteriously, you are avoided and left out of events and decisions and sarcastic comments are made. If you mention it you may find that your mental health is questioned.

Close ranks

It is clear that what you said to one colleague or manager has been passed on, and possibly distorted, to his or her peers. When you approach a manager further up the line, it is clear that they have been forewarned. Your concern has somehow created an anti-you group. You are identified as a 'trouble-maker' by most people with any authority, and any attempt to raise your concern is now pre-empted and prejudged. Some of your colleagues feel that your complaint demeans them by implication.

Stonewall

When you raise your concerns formally you find that your letters are unanswered and the manager is never available. Promises to 'get back to you' are broken, you are passed on to someone who eventually sends you a letter saying something like 'your concern has been investigated, nothing is amiss, and the matter is now closed'. You may be told directly not to send any more memos or letters.

Biomedical diagnosis

It is suggested that you have been under a 'lot of stress lately' and that you ought to visit the occupational health department, a counsellor or your general practitioner. You are asked if you are 'coping'. It emerges, unknown to you, that you have been informally diagnosed as anxious, depressed, paranoid, having a personality disorder, or as being 'neurotic', too old or too fat.

Spying

A colleague is passing on information about you and has, perhaps, been asked to do so. You are the object of close observation, fault-finding, and perhaps your mail is being opened and your telephone bugged. Some of your work goes wrong or astray and you wonder about sabotage. If you mention this, it is taken as further evidence that you are unable to cope or 'paranoid'.

Grind down

Work becomes more difficult. Your workload increases, you get the tough end of the rota, you are transferred to the most difficult work area. You may find that demotion looks more probable than promotion, you do not get your holidays when you want, you are asked to share an office or move out of the one you have and your phone line is put on 'internal calls only' or taken away.

Sticks and carrots

An intermediary, usually a union official, will call you aside for 'a chat' in which offers are made to you concerning promotion, a generous severance package or some other benefit. These will be linked in coded terminology with your concern – the suggestion being that you drop it in return for the benefit. Alternatively, or if you refuse to accept the carrot, veiled threats will be made such as, 'Are you sure you wouldn't be happier working elsewhere?' These become overt threats such as 'You are jeopardising your future' and 'You won't be working here much longer'. If you raised concerns about colleagues, such as their abuse of patients, you may find that you receive hate mail and threats of violence.

Character assassination

Aspersions will be cast on your character, your personal conduct, your personal past, your political views, your class, ethnic origin, or your sexual orientation. These may progress to accusations of abuse of clients, theft of documents, lying, disloyalty, breach of confidentiality, and the like.

First strike

Official counter-complaints may be formulated against you in a disciplinary hearing before your own concerns are addressed or instead of addressing them. You may be made a scapegoat. Disciplinary or grievance procedures may be used as a pre-emptive or retaliatory measure. The authorities will attempt to get their revenge in first.

Make redundant

Your presence is no longer tolerable. You may be suspended and then dismissed or there may be a reorganisation in which your post is made redundant. You will proceed to an industrial tribunal. If you win you are paid a fixed sum – which the authorities consider cheap at the price.

Cosmetic reshuffle

If your concerns were of a serious nature, especially if an inquiry took place, then there will be some changes at your workplace of a cosmetic nature. Some posts may be reshuffled, but it is unlikely that policies will be revised or that managerial heads will roll. Certainly no acknowledgement will be made that there is any connection between your raising a concern and the changes which followed.

   (Hunt, 2007) available online http://www.freedomtocare.org/ page64.htm#shooting%20the%20messenger

The Public Interest Disclosure Act, 1998 provides statutory protection from victimisation and dismissal to workers who speak out against corruption and malpractice at work. It refers to any disclosure of information which in the reasonable belief of the worker making the disclosure tends to show one or more of the following:

- A criminal offence has been committed or is likely to be committed.
- A person has failed, is failing or is likely to fail to comply with any legal obligation to which they are subject.
- That a miscarriage of justice has occurred, is occurring or is likely to occur.
- That the health or safety of any individual has been, is being or is likely to be endangered.
- That the environment has been is being or is likely to be damaged.
- That information tending to show any matter falling within any one of the preceding paragraphs has been, is being or is likely to be deliberately concealed.
- It does not apply if the person making the disclosure commits an offence by making it.

The person must:

- Make the disclosure in good faith.
- Reasonably believe the information to be substantially true.
- Not make the disclosure for personal gain.
- Believe at time of disclosure that he will be subject to detriment by his employer.
- Believe evidence relating to the relevant failure will be concealed or destroyed if he makes a disclosure.

Also:

- A worker has the right not to be subjected to any detriment by any act, or any deliberate failure to act by his employer done on the ground that the worker has made a protected disclosure.
- A worker will be regarded as unfairly dismissed if the reason for the dismissal is that the employee made a protected disclosure.

Activity 24: Who to Tell?

Aim: To provide participants with an opportunity to consider who they might tell and to experience what emotions and considerations are aroused by the possibility or act of telling about a serious matter relating to child protection.

Delivery: The carousel format is used. On the inside circle participants hold cards stating a range of people they might tell.

The outer circle use the relevant scenario to their profession and move around the inner circle deciding at each point what to say, if anything.

Content

Outer circle

Social workers

You heard a social work colleague in a bar boasting about how she likes sex with teenage boys. You subsequently learn that she owns a boating club for teenagers. You know that your manager and the Local Safeguarding Children Board manager volunteer in the same club.

Police officers

You arrested a man for the rape of two young girls. When you searched his property you found that his computer and all the evidence had gone. Someone had tipped him off but this could only have been your colleague.

Inner circle

Church leader, Local councillor, MP, *Daily Mail* journalist, Director of Children's Services, Police Commander, Trade Union official, BASW/Police Federation representative, Trusted colleague, Close friend, Family, Agency representative on Local Safeguarding Children Board, general practitioner.

Feedback:

The trainers facilitate a discussion on the pros and cons of telling, to whom and in what circumstances and how this was experienced. The key message is to inform participants to seek advice from the organisation, Public Concern at Work or a professional body. This exercise commonly leads to participants telling of their personal experiences of child protection issues being dismissed by organisations.

It is important to revisit the ground rules of the need to anonymise cases but also to state that issues of concern may be taken forward from the training with participants agreement and full involvement.

The Public Interest Disclosure Act, 1998 states that a disclosure must be reasonable. This is open to interpretation. It is expected that a professional will go through the usual channels provided by management.

Although prior to the legislation, in the Islington Child Abuse Scandal in the 1990s the whistleblower wrote 15 reports for the children's services managers. She then reported, with her colleagues from all the agencies, to the Area Child Protection Committee. This committee decided there was no evidence. The local councillor, MP's and trade unions were contacted to no effect. Finally the social workers reported probable crimes to the police. The police investigated and also used the media to expose the abuses. It was only as each aspect was exposed in over 100 media articles, as well as radio and TV coverage, that there was public pressure to bring about the 13 inquiries which followed. The social worker was vindicated by her professional body because, before the matter was in the public arena, she had first pursued all available channels to expose the abuse. Whistleblowing is not without risk; some of the whistleblowers in this case received very serious threats and were dismissed from their posts. The key residential social work whistleblower had his name placed on the Protection of Children Act List as an abuser although there had never been any investigation into the allegations. It took 10 years for his name to be finally removed and for him to be able to resume work with children. In contrast 32 professionals who were identified by the inquiry as unsuitable to work with children did not have their names placed on the Protection of Children Act List. (Fairweather, 1998 in Hunt, 1998 and White and Hart, 1995).

Presentation 22: Arena of Safety

Ray Wyre used the concept of the arena of safety to describe:

> *A safety zone of relationship, integrity and respect for others and yourself. A position where morale and confidence is enhanced and where both adults and children can feel safe. It is a place of appropriate attitude, behaviour, lifestyle, regime and cultural practices. Whatever we do we must remember that there will always be those who are motivated to abuse and will do so whatever systems are in place, whatever level of staff selection, registration, supervision, treatment and monitoring, supportive institutions and appropriate protocols we have. However, there is a duty to do whatever we can to reduce the risk and manage the risk.*

Wyre emphasised that the vast majority of people who work with children will not abuse them but that organisations need to have an aware culture and provide clear messages about the unacceptability of child abuse and the expectations of safe practice by staff. Protocols in themselves do not protect, the staff must put the protocols into operation and to do this effectively they need training, supervision, good management and safe working conditions. Low level breaches of the codes of practice must be confronted and debated within a staff group and management must take action against abusive behaviour.

> *The aware culture and the arena of safety is as much to do with helping staff feel safe from the possibility of false allegation as it has to do with making children and vulnerable adults feel safe.*

(www.raywyre.uk.com)

251

Activity 25: Sounding the Alarm

Aim: For participants to learn from an example of whistleblowing.

Delivery: A video is shown which describes a case of whistleblowing and the dilemmas involved.

Content: Video – Barnardo's (1998) *Sounding the Alarm*. Essex: Barnardo's.

Feedback: Discussion. Trainers can draw attention to the judgment of the Care Standards Tribunal concerning Lisa Arthurworrey, social worker for Victoria Climbié.

The judge upheld that child protection work is a complex and specialist task and that Ms Arthurworrey was inexperienced, untrained in child protection, had a high workload, poor supervision and worked to flawed policies. (Care Standards Tribunal, 2005). Also Munro (2005) provides a very useful systems based analysis of professional responsibilities in protecting children. Jones (2001) writes about the pressures on social workers in an increasingly managerialist culture. For two recent cases of whistleblowing see Waugh (2007) where six social workers in Wakefield who were sacked for raising issues concerning child sexual abuse gained a settlement from the council and Ahmed (2007) concerning Simon Bellwood, a social worker in Jersey, who raised issues concerning children aged as young as 11 years being kept in solitary confinement for extensive periods of time.

Presentation 23: Therapeutic Healing Stories

Nancy Davis has written a large number of stories for a wide range of situations that children may experience. The stories work through metaphor teaching new attitudes and belief systems. They are non-threatening and engage both the conscious and the unconscious, encourage independence and bypass resistance to change, thus mobilising problem solving and healing. The stories are not interpreted but simply read. The stories may be adapted to be more particularly relevant to a child's circumstances such as by including the name of a child's toy or pet.

The stories are to:

- Empower and treat the symptoms of child abuse and other traumatic experiences.
- Develop healthy emotional reactions, thinking, perceptions, beliefs, self-image and social skills.
- Help reduce fear and support disclosure.
- Help with problems related to parents, siblings, adoption, foster care and divorce.
- Help with death, loss or illness.
- Aid sleep.

(Davis, 1999)

More information is available on Nancy Davis's website. (www.therapeutic-stories.com).

Activity 26: Practising Storytelling

Aim: Participants to experience listening to a story being read to them and to reflect on the impact.

Delivery: Participants work in groups of three taking turns to read a story to the others. The listener must not interrupt at all. Each group will need sufficient space to allow for concentration on the subject and not to be distracted by the others.

Content: Three stories

Feedback: There is no discussion after reading the stories but it is recommended to have a short break afterwards as for some participants the stories will have had a strong emotional impact. If they have felt abused by the course content or if they have suffered child abuse themselves the stories will have a healing effect.

Handout 19a: The Burned Tree

Once upon a time there was a tree in the forest that didn't look green and alive like other trees. It looked as if it had been struck by lightening and had stopped growing – like someone had come and cut its branches back to stubs. Most of the trees in that part of the forest thought it was dead, because some trees are able to stand long after the life has gone out of them. But they were wrong, because deep down inside, this tree was alive. It just didn't know how to grow and develop into a beautiful tree with leaves as the other trees had done because it had been hit by lightening and badly burned. Sometimes after being burned a tree goes into shock and gives up the will to grow and to live and to be like other trees. And sometimes the shock of the lightening and the storms makes a tree believe that it can't grow and that it has to stay the same, looking burned and ugly and dead.

One day a beaver came along and, thinking that this tree was dead, began to chew on it.

'Hey! Ow!' yelled the tree.

Startled, the beaver looked around and exclaimed, 'Who's there? Who's talking to me?'

'It's **me**,' said the tree. 'You're hurting me! Quit biting me!'

'I can't believe it!' said the beaver. 'You didn't look alive. You looked deader than a doornail. You looked burned and pitiful. Why, your branches are broken and you don't even have any leaves. Now, I'm a pretty responsible beaver and I don't cut down live trees, because I'd feel bad about that. I just figured you were dead.'

'I'm not dead,' said the tree. 'I'm not even sick'.

The beaver gave her a puzzled look. 'Well, if you're not dead and you're not sick, why do you look so awful?'

Sadly the little tree replied, 'I don't know how to grow. I don't know how to get leaves. I don't know how to look alive again, because the lightening hit me so many times and there have been so many storms in my life that I lost the knowledge about how to grow.'

The beaver, which had much experience with trees decided to help, and explained that she must first remove the burned ends of the limbs. Climbing in and out of the branches, she chewed away at the burned ends until all the dead parts were gone and new life could start growing. The tree was surprised that it hardly hurt at all. Next the beaver found some special fertiliser for trees and put it all around the trunk. She made sure that the tree got all the sunshine and water it needed. In a very short time the little tree discovered that it **did** know how to grow and it **did** know how to develop, and it **did** know how to look beautiful and full of green leaves just like the other trees. It began to sprout new leaves and to grow and develop, and before long there was no sign that it had ever been hit by lightening or burned. The tree and the beaver became very close friends after that.

Because the beaver had helped the tree grow to be so beautiful and healthy, the tree decided to do something special for the beaver. She asked the beaver to carve a sign about their friendship. It was placed in front of the tree so that everyone who passed would realise just how much difference a trusted friend can make in the way your life goes.

Handout 19b: The Butterfly and the Spider

Once upon a time there was a spider. As spiders do, this spider built a very big web. The spider was determined to catch any unsuspecting flying thing – insects or butterflies – unlucky enough to come within reach. Now the spider knew that insects were attracted to flowers, so it spun the web between the two flower bushes. It then settled back to wait for something appealing to come by looking for the sweet juicy nectar in the flower. It knew that it had created a good trap.

The web was invisible to the eyes of most insects unless it was covered with raindrops or morning dew, then it sparkled like jewels in the light. This made the web even more dangerous because unsuspecting insects would not see the trap and the destruction it represented until it was too late. Sometimes insects would see the spider but, not understanding how spiders live their lives, would fly directly into the trap of the web. Now spiders wrap up their victims and keep them alive until they are ready to use them, and this spider was no different. It was proud of its web and felt no guilt at all about the way it lived its life.

One day a blue butterfly happened by, flying from one colourful flower bush to another. The unsuspecting butterfly was attracted by the glistening web that sparkled in the sunlight, and suddenly was caught fast in the spider's trap. Terrified, the butterfly tried to free itself, pulling and twisting and fighting, but the more he moved the tighter he was caught. The spider counted on the terror of those it caught to make the prison of the web even tighter.

Now a wise little ladybug who had learned about spiders from experience saw the trapped butterfly and made a decision to help him escape. The spider, busily spinning on the other end of the web, was so sure that the butterfly was helplessly trapped that it did not even hurry to make sure that it could not get away. Carefully the ladybug flew near the butterfly and whispered, 'Stop fighting the web. That will only make it a tighter prison than ever.'

'But I am so scared!' cried the butterfly

'Then use your fear to give you power,' the ladybug went on. 'Understand how the web has trapped you, and use your mouth to free yourself. **You have the power to be free.**'

So the butterfly calmed himself down and stopped struggling against the web. Concentrating on what the ladybug had said, he thought about the best way to escape from the spider's trap. He used all that he had learned to figure out a way to free himself. Once he was free, he noticed that his wings were torn from being trapped in the web. As time went on, however, the butterfly was able to find a way to heal the hurt that he had experienced because of the spider. Soon he was once again a whole, blue butterfly who loved to fly from flower to flower. But as he flew, he was aware of spiders and their webs and their traps. He made sure that he was always smarter than spiders, and in this way he continued to be free.

Handout 19c: The Bear and the Thorn

Once upon a time in a forest not far away there lived a very fuzzy bear. Now bears usually go lumbering through the forest on all four legs, but this bear always seemed to be limping, as if something was wrong with his right front paw. Other animals would question why he walked with a limp and the bear would reply, 'I don't limp!' or, depending on how he felt at the moment, 'I don't know why I limp.' Sometimes the bear could sense pain deep down inside his paw and he would hold it up and look at it, but he saw nothing unusual. It looked just like his other paws, with scarcely any signs of scars or cuts or problems that would cause him to limp.

Now this bear also had problems getting along with the other bears in the forest. He didn't want to tumble and play with the others, and didn't understand why any bear would want to tumble with another bear. He didn't even enjoy getting honey out of trees. Often the bear felt a deep sadness within him, but he wasn't quite sure why. He seemed unable to feel the feelings that other bears told him they had or to enjoy life as other bears seemed to.

One day as he was walking down a path, with nowhere in particular to go, the bear came upon a little cub who had fallen into a clump of prickly bushes and now had a huge and sharp thorn lodged in his paw. The little cub was whimpering and crying because it was very afraid and did not seem to know what to do to get rid of its pain. Gently the bear held the little cub and pulled the thorn out of the paw. The cub whimpered and cried for some time after the thorn was removed, and the bear watched and comforted the cub as the bleeding stopped and the wound began to heal.

All at once as the bear looked down at the young cub, from deep within him in the hidden corners of his memory, a picture from the past began to appear – a picture from a time when he too had fallen into a prickly bush and lodged a huge thorn deep within the pad of his right front paw. The memory became clearer as he realised that when he was younger he didn't know how to get anyone to help him. So, gradually the skin on his paw grew around the thorn, covering up the thorn and also covering up the knowledge that it was even there. But the sharp object, lay deep within his paw, surrounded by infection that spread throughout his whole body, leaving only numbness instead of feelings of being a bear.

As he found his memory, the bear understood what he had to do. He soon helped the little cub find its mother and then set off to find other bears in the forest and ask for their help in removing the thorn. Before long, he managed to find a bear who had much experience in thorn removal. 'This is going to hurt some' said the wise bear. 'Its been buried so long that as we bring it up you may wonder if you shouldn't leave it in place so you won't have sharp pain now.' 'But,' she went on, 'this thorn has hurt you far more than you now understand. It must come out so that the infection that it caused in your body can be healed.' Then, using pressure and persuasion, the wise bear eased the sharp thorn nearer and nearer to the surface of the lonely bear's paw until at last it was visible and could be removed. The other bears helped too and before long every bit of thorn was out.

Getting all of the pieces of the thorn out after such a long time was painful, but the bear understood that in order for his pain to be completely gone every bit of the long embedded thorn had to be released from his paw. As he began to heal his paw sometimes hurt, but he noticed that each day he felt better and better. It was amazing – he was experiencing feelings in a new way and seeing the world through the eyes of a bear who was healthy and who, at last, loved being a bear. And to make sure he learned from his experience he told other bears how powerful a mind can be to hide the pain of a thorn buried deep in a paw. For he understood the lesson of the thorn that pain not remembered can be the most destructive pain of all.

Activity 27: Stop, Start and Continue

Aim: To draw together key learning points from the week.

Delivery: Participants sit quietly to reflect on learning from the course.

Content: Participants to answer each of the following in open forum to the whole group:

- Something they will now stop doing.
- Something they will start to do.
- Something they will continue to do.

Feedback: Trainer can write up the responses onto a flip chart commenting on similarities and differences.

Activity 28: The Umbrella

Aim: For participants to identify strategies to support themselves in safe practice.

Delivery: Each participant writes in the umbrella what they need to be in place to ensure their safe practice.

Content: Umbrella drawing.

Feedback: Participants share their drawings with the group.

Handout 20a: The Umbrella

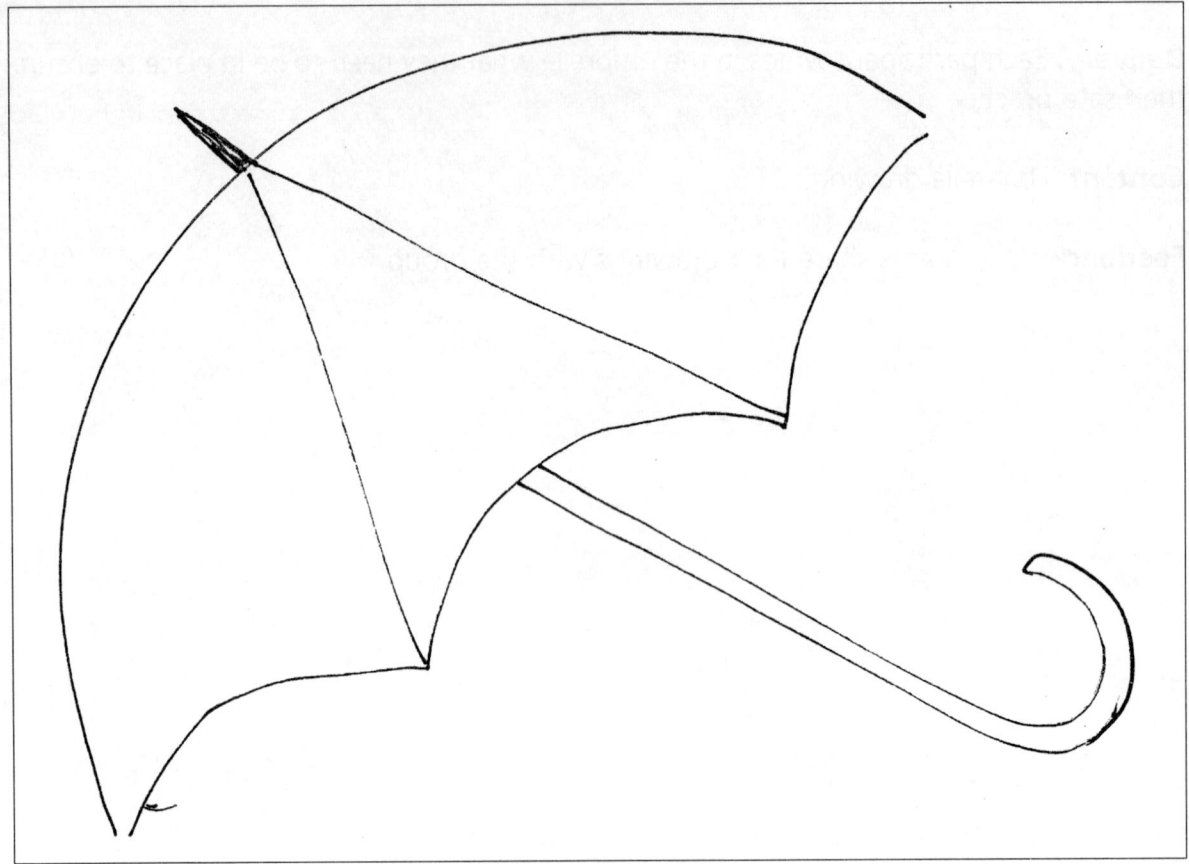

Handout 20b: The Umbrella

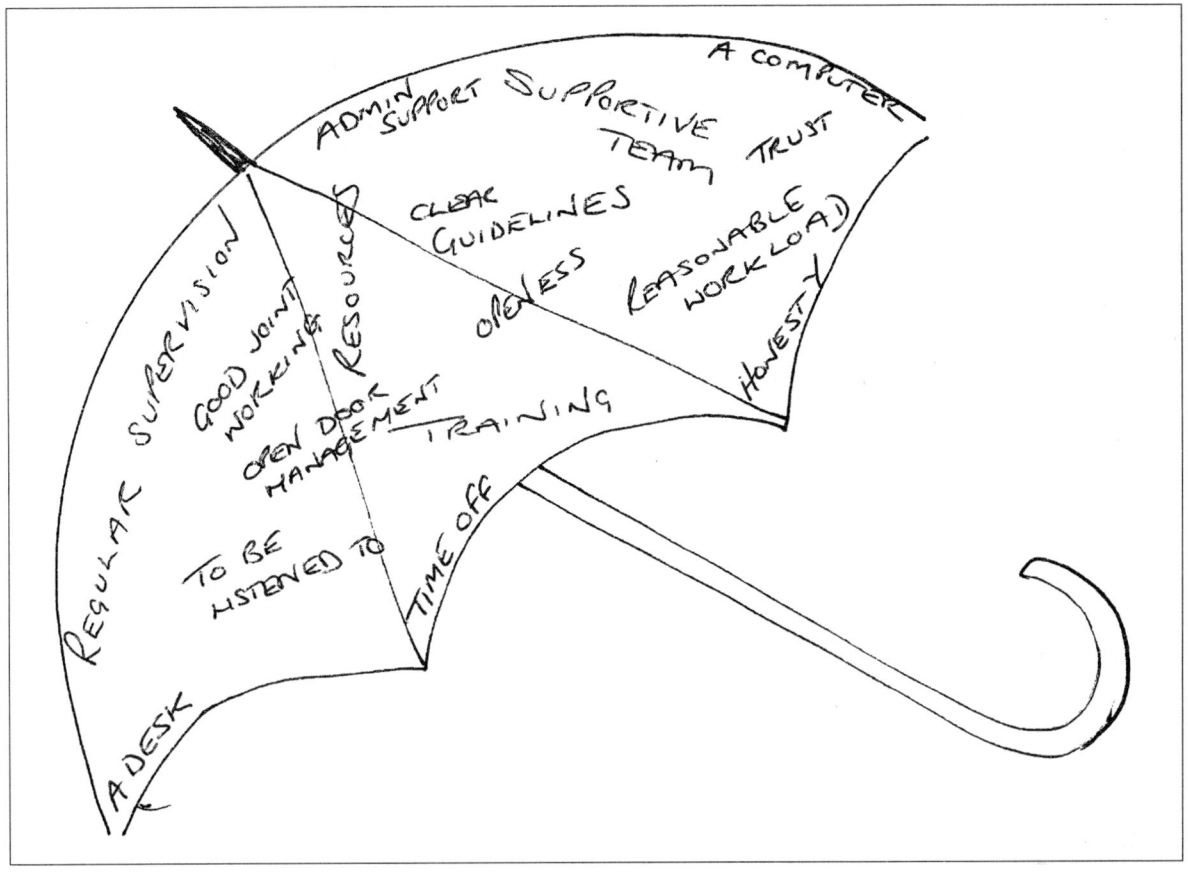

Activity 29: The Toolkit

Aim: For participants to identify ways of looking after themselves.

Delivery: Each participant writes statements in the outlines of the tools describing their own ways of looking after themselves.

Content: Drawing of toolkit

Feedback: Participants share their statements with the group.

Handout 21a: The Toolkit

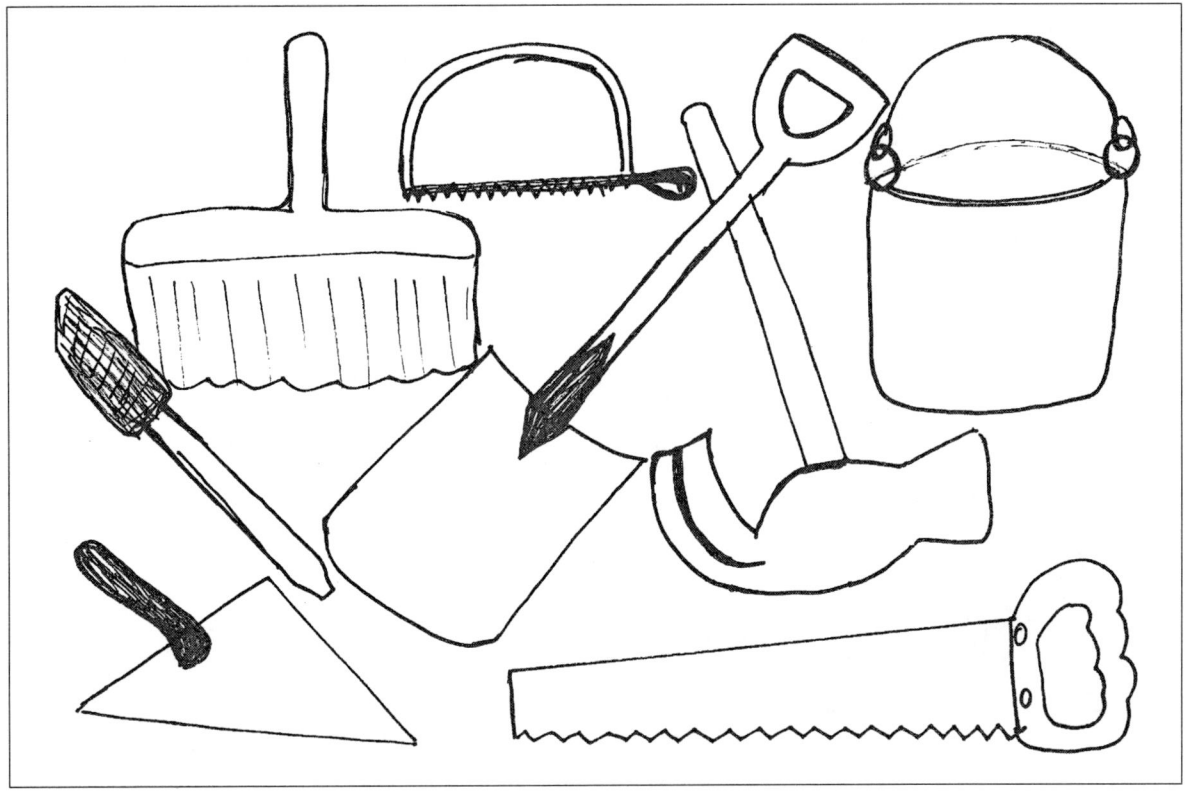

Handout 21b: The Toolkit

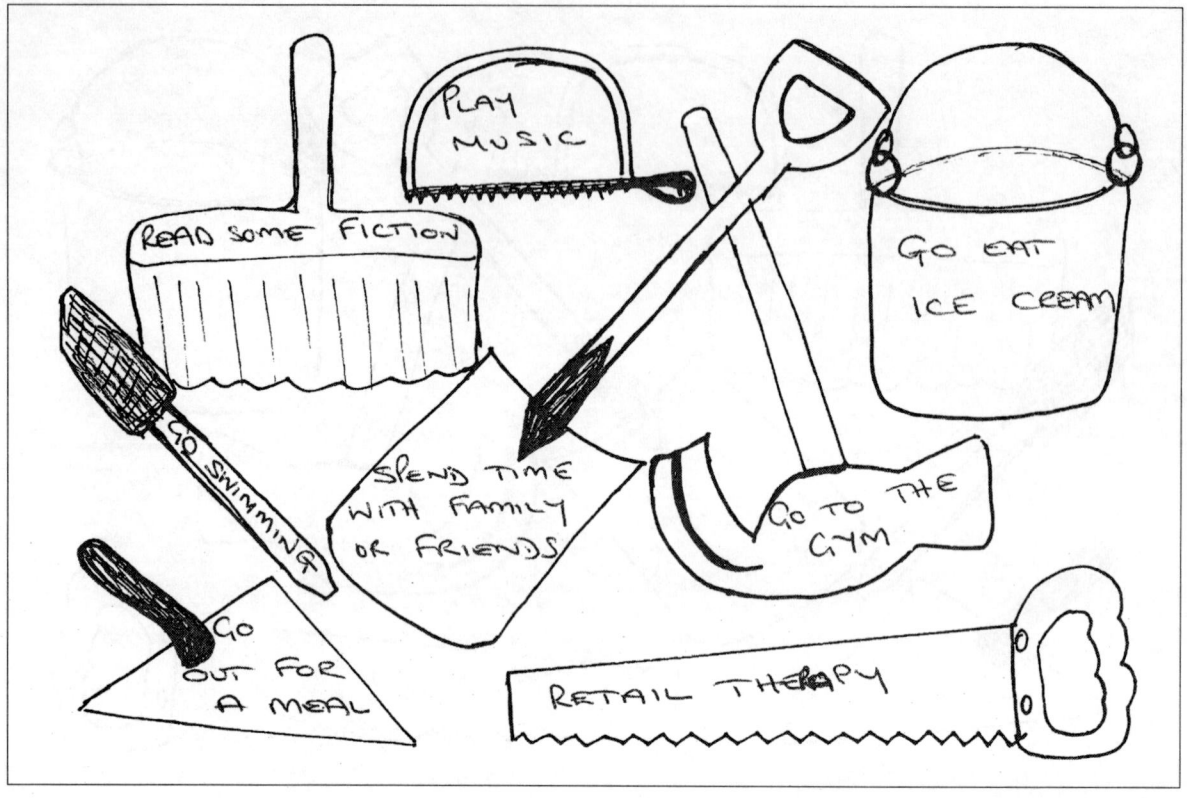

Activity 30: Evaluation

Students are given evaluation forms to complete to enable quality assurance and certificates of attendance to be provided.

Brickwall evaluation

This style of evaluation enables the participant to assess their learning around the key themes in the course. It may be given to them at the beginning and the comparison may be made with the scores at the end. Child protection training often raises more questions than answers and a reduction in score after the week of training may be a positive sign that the participant is recognising their need to learn further and has a more realistic view of their level of knowledge.

1 = LOW 5 = HIGH

listening to the child 1.2.3.4.5		making judgements to keep children safe 1.2.3.4.5	
inter-agency working 1.2.3.4.5		child abuse categories 1.2.3.4.5	
joint S 47 investigation 1.2.3.4.5	the MAPPA 1.2.3.4.5		child protection planning 1.2.3.4.5
survival skills 1.2.3.4.5		working with the non abusive carer 1.2.3.4.5	
whistleblowing 1.2.3.4.5	organised abuse 1.2.3.4.5		sexual exploitation of children 1.2.3.4.5

References

Abel, G. et al. (1985) Sexual Offenders: Results of Assessment and Recommendations for Treatment. In Ben-Aron, H. (1985) *Clinical Criminology.* Toronto: M M Graphics.

Adcock, M. and White, R. (1998) *Significant Harm. Its Management and Outcome.* London: Significant Publications.

Adoption and Children Act 2002. London: HMSO.

Ahmed, M. (2007) Social Worker Blows the Whistle on Jersey. *Community Care,* 7th September 2007. www.communitycare.co.uk/.../2007/09/07/105628/exclusive-uk-social-worker-blows-the-whistle-on-jersey.htm

Armstrong, H. and Hollows, A. (1989) *A Positive Model: Standards for the Development and Evaluation of Materials For Training in Child Sexual Abuse.* London: National Children's Bureau.

Association of Chief Police Officers (2005) *Guidance on Investigating Child Abuse and Safeguarding Children.* Hampshire: National Centre for Policing Excellence.

Baker, A. and Duncan, S. (1985) Child Sexual Abuse: A Study of Prevalence In Great Britain. *Child Abuse and Neglect,* 9.

Barnardo's (1998) *Sounding the Alarm.* Essex: Barnardo's. Video

Barnardo's (1998) *Whose Daughter Next? Children Abused Through Prostitution.* Essex: Barnardo's. Video and Book

Barnardo's (2001) *No Son of Mine.* Essex: Barnardo's. Video and Book

Barter, C. (1998) *Investigating Institutional Abuse of Children.* London: NSPCC.

Barter, C. (1999) *Protecting Children From Racism and Racial Abuse: A Research Review.* London: NSPCC.

Batty, D. (2003) Catalogue of Cruelty. *The Guardian* 27.01.2003 http://society.guardian.co.uk/print/0,3858,4271108-108861,00.Html

Batty, D. (2006) Q & A The Sex Offenders Register. *The Guardian* 18.01.2006 http://education.guardian.co.uk/schools/story/0,,1689261,00.Html

Beddoe, C. (2007) *Missing Out. A Study of Children Trafficked in the North West, North East and West Midlands.* London: ECPAT.

Ben-Aron, H. et al. (Eds.) (1985) *Clinical Criminology.* Totonto: MM Graphics.

Bentovim, A. and Williams, B. (1998) Children and Adolescents: Victims who Become Perpetrators. *Advances in Psychiatric Treatment,* 4:101–7.

Bichard, M. (2004) *The Bichard Inquiry Report.* HC653. London: TSO. http://www.homeoffice.gov.uk/Pdf/Bichard_Report.Pdf

Bichard, M. Lord (2004) *The Bichard Inquiry Report.* HMSO Norwich www.thebichardinquiry.org

Biehal, N. and Wade, J. (2000) Going Missing from Residential and Foster Care. *British Journal of Social Work,* 30: 2, 211–25.

Biehal, N. et al. (2002) *Lost From View. Missing Persons within the UK*. Bristol: Policy Press.

Birchall, E. and Hallett, C. (1995) *Working Together in Child Protection*. London: HMSO.

Bird, B. (2002) To Safeguard Children We Need Joint Police-Social Work Teams. *Society Guardian*. 20th November http://society.guardian.co.uk/print/0,,4550147-111194,00.html

Blake, N. (2006) *The Deepcut Review. A Review of the Circumstances Surrounding the Deaths of Four Soldiers at Princess Royal Barracks, Deepcut, Between 1995 and 2002*. London: TSO.

Bonomi, B. (2006) *Report on Yarl's Wood Calls for Complete Overhaul of Child Detention*. London: Institute of Race Relations. 10th August. www.irr.org.uk/2006/August/Ak000006.Html.

Bostock, L. et al. (2005) *Managing Risk and Minimizing Mistakes in Services to Children and Families*. London: SCIE.

Bowker, L. (1988) On The Relationship Between Wife Beating and Child Abuse. In Yllo, K. and Bograd, M. (Eds.) *Feminist Perspectives on Wife Abuse*. California: Sage.

Brandon, M., Belderson, P., Warren, C., Howe, D., Gardner, R., Dodsworth, J. and Black, Jane (2008) *Analysing child deaths and serious injury through abuse and neglect: what can we learn? A biennial analysis of serious case reviews 2003–2005*. London: DCSF.

Bray, M. (1997) *Poppies on the Rubbish Heap: Sexual Abuse, The Child's Voice*. London: Jessica Kingsley.

Breslin, R. and Evans, H. (2004) *Key Child Protection Statistics. Sex Offenders and Sex Offences against Children*. www.nspcc.org.uk/inform/statistics/keycpstats/12.Asp

Bridge Child Care Consultancy (1996) *Heather and Charmaine West, Serious (Part 8) Case Review*. Gloucestershire: ACPC.

Bruzzone, C. (1996) *All About Me*. Surrey: Small Publishing.

Burchall, K. (2007) *Kimberley Baker: It Could Happen Again*. http://www.thisiswiltshire.co.uk/display.var.1387449.0.kimberley_baker_it_could_happen_again.php.

Butler-Sloss, Lord Justice E. (1988) *Report of the Inquiry into Child Abuse in Cleveland 1987, CMND.412*. London: HMSO.

Cairns, K. (2006) *Surviving Paedophilia – Traumatic Stress after Organised and Network Child Sexual Abuse*. Gloucester: Akamas.

Calder, M. et al. (1997) *Juveniles and Children who Sexually Abuse: A Guide to Risk Assessment*. Lyme Regis: Russell House Publishing.

Care Standards Tribunal (2005) *Lisa Arthurworrey v The Secretary of State for Education and Skills (2004) 355.PC*. available from www.carestandardstribunal.gov.uk/documents/digest6.doc

Carr, J. (2005) No Funds to Tackle Child Porn. *The Guardian*, 01.11.2005

Cawson, P. et al. (2000) *Child Maltreatment in The United Kingdom: A Study of the Prevalence of Child Abuse and Neglect*. London: NSPCC.

Charles, M. and Hendry, E. (Eds.) (2000) *Training Together to Safeguard Children: Guidance on Inter-agency Training*. London: NSPCC.

Child Exploitation and Online Protection: CEOP (2007) *A Scoping Project on Child Trafficking in The UK*. London: Home Office.

Childline (2007) *Calls to Childline about Sexual Abuse*. London: Childline. www.Childline.org.uk/Casenotes.Asp

Children Act 1989. London: HMSO.

Children Act 2004. London: HMSO.

Children and Young Persons Act 1933. London: HMSO.

Children's Rights Alliance for England (2006) *The State of Children's Rights in England*. London: CRAE.

Children's Rights Alliance for England (2007) *The State of Children's Rights in England*. London: CRAE.

Clyde, Lord (1992) *Report of the Inquiry into the Removal of Children from Orkney in February 1991,H0C195*. London: HMSO.

Commission for Social Care Inspection (2005) *Safeguarding Children: The Second Joint Chief Inspector's Report*. Newcastle: CSCI.

Cooper, T. (2008) *Trust No One. One Girls Harrowing and Disturbing Tale of Institutional Abuse*. London: Orion.

Corby, B. (2006) *Child Abuse. Towards a Knowledge Base*. Berkshire: OUP.

CPS and DoH With Home Office (2001) *Provision of Therapy for Child Witnesses Prior to a Criminal Trial. Practical Guidance*. London: Crown Prosecution Service.

Criminal Justice System (2007) *Achieving Best Evidence in Criminal Proceedings: Guidance on Interviewing Victims and Witnesses and Using Special Measures*. London: TSO.

Crittenden, P.M. (1999) Child Neglect: Causes and Contributors. In Dubowitz, H. (Ed.) *Neglected Children: Research, Practice and Policy*. CA: Sage.

Davidson, J. et al. (2006) Child Victims of Sexual Abuse. Children's Experience of the Investigative Process in the Criminal Justice System. *Practice*. 18: 4, 247–62.

Davies et al. (1995) *Videotaping of Children's Evidence. An Evaluation*. London: Home Office.

Davies, G., Marshall, E. and Robertson, N. (1998) *Child abuse. Training Investigating Officers*. Police research series paper 94. London: Home Office.

Davies, L. (2007) Is Protection Working? *Community Care* 15 November 2007: 6.

Davis, N. (1999) *Once Upon A Time: Therapeutic Stories to Heal Abused Children*. USA. Psychological Associates.

Department for Children, Schools and Families (2007) *National Statistics, Referrals, Assessments and Child Protection and Young People Who are the Subject of a Child Protection Plan or are on Child Protection Registers, England Ending 31st March, 2007*. London: DCSF. http://dcsf.gov.uk/rsgateway/DB/SFR/S000742/Index.Shtml

Department for Children, Schools and Families (2007) *Local Safeguarding Children Boards. A Review of Progress*. Nottingham. DCSF.

DfES (2003) *Keeping Children Safe*. London: TSO.

DfES (2005) *Common Core of Skills and Knowledge for the Children's Workforce*. London: HMSO.

DfES (2006) *Working Together to Safeguard Children. A Guide to Inter-Agency Working to Safeguard and Promote the Welfare of Children*. London: TSO.

Dhanda, P. (2007) written parliamentary question no.117707. 05.02

DHSS (1982) *Child Abuse. A Study of Inquiry Reports 1973–1981*. London: HMSO.

DHSS and the Welsh Office (1988) *Working Together. A Guide to Arrangements For Inter-Agency Co-Operation For The Protection of Children From Abuse*. London: HMSO.

Dirie, W. (2005) *Desert Flower. The Extraordinary Journey of a Desert Nomad*. London: Virago.

DoH (1991) *Child Abuse. A Study of Inquiry Reports 1980–89*. London: HMSO.

DoH (1991) *Working with Child Sexual Abuse. Guidelines for Trainers and Managers in Social Services Departments*. Lancashire: Health Publications Unit.

DoH (1995) *Messages From Research*. London: HMSO.

DoH (2000) *The Framework for the Assessment for Children in Need and Their Families*. London: HMSO.

DoH (2000) *Towards Safer Care. Training Pack*. London: HMSO.

DoH (2000) *Working Together to Safeguard Children Involved in Sexual Exploitation*. London: TSO.

DoH, Home Office, DES, Welsh Office (1991) *Working Together. A Guide to Arrangements For Inter-Agency Co-Operation For The Protection of Children From Abuse*. London: HMSO.

DoH, Home Office, DfEE (1999) *Working Together to Safeguard Children. A Guide to Inter-Agency Working to Safeguard and Promote The Welfare of Children*. London: TSO.

Downey, R. (2002) Victims of Wonderland. *Community Care*, 7–13th March.

Doyle, P. (2002) *The God Squad*. London: Corgi.

Dustin, D. and Davies, L. (2007) Female Genital Cutting and Children's Rights. Implications for Social Work Practice. *Child Care in Practice*, 13: 1.

Elliot, M. et al (1995) Child Sexual Abuse Prevention: What Offenders Tell Us. *International Journal of Child Abuse and Neglect*, 19: 579–94.

Fairweather, E. (1998) The Islington Child Abuse Scandal. In Hunt, G. *Whistleblowing in the Social Services*. London: Hodder Arnold.

Falkov, A. (2006) *Study of Working Together 'Part 8 Reports'*. London: DoH.

Female Genital Mutilation Act 2003. London: HMSO.

Fever, F. (1994) *Who Cares? Memories of a Childhood in Barnardo's*. London: Times Warner.

Finkelhor, D. (1986) *A Sourcebook on Child Sexual Abuse*. London: Sage.

Fitch, K. (2007) *Sex Offender Management*. London: NSPCC. http://www.nspcc.org.uk/inform/policyandpublicaffairs/sexoffendermanagement_Wdf50066. Pdf

Fitzgerald, J. (1999) *Child Protection and the Computer Age: Sharing Information between Agencies by Computer*. London: Bridge Publishing House.

Ford, H. (2006) *Women who Sexually Abuse*. London: Wiley.

Frampton, P. (2003) *Golly in the Cupboard*. Manchester: Tamic.

Gallagher, B. (1998) *Grappling with Smoke. Investigating and Managing Organised Child Sexual Abuse. A Good Practice Guide*. London: NSPCC.

Garnham, N. (2003) Opening Statement to The Victoria Climbié Inquiry http://www.victoria-climbie-inquiry.org.uk/evidence/archive/sept01/260901latestp4.Htm/

Ghate, D. and Daniels, A. (1997) *Talking About My Generation: A Survey of 8–15 year olds Growing Up in the 1990s.* London: NSPCC.

Gibbons, J. et al. (1995) *Operating the Child Protection System.* London: HMSO.

Glennie, S. and Horwath, J. (2000) Inter-agency Training: Broadening The Focus. *Child Abuse Review*, 9: 148–56.

Goddard, C. and Mudaly, N. (2003) *The Truth is Longer than a Lie.* London: JKP.

Goldson, B. and Coles, D. (2005) *In the Care of the State? Child Deaths in Penal Custody in England and Wales.* London: Inquest.

Gorin, S. (2004) *Understanding What Children Say about Living with Domestic Violence, Parental Substance Misuse or Parental Mental Health Problems.* York: Joseph Rowntree Foundation. http://www.jrf.org.uk/knowledge/findings/socialpolicy/514.Asp

Gosling, P. and D'Arcy, M. (1998) *Abuse of Trust. Frank Beck and The Leicestershire Children's Home Scandal.* London: Bowerdean.

Greater London Authority (2003) *Young People, Big Issues.* London: GLA.

Grubin, D. (1998) *Sex Offending against Children: Understanding the Risk.* Police Research Series Paper 99. London: Home Office.

Hames, M. (2000) *The Dirty Squad. The Inside Story of the Obscene Publications Branch.* London: Little Brown.

Harris, J. and Grace, S. (1999) *A Question of Evidence? Investigating and Prosecuting Rape in the 1990s.* London: Home Office.

Hendry, E. (1995)The Inter-Agency Child Protection Trainer: A Developing Role. *Child Abuse Review*, 4: 227–9.

HM Chief Inspector of Prisons for England and Wales (2006) *Annual Report.* London: TSO.

Holton, J. and Bonnerjea, L. (1994) *The Child the Court and the Video: A Study of The Implementation of The Memorandum of Good Practice on Video Interviewing of Child Witnesses.* London: HMSO.

Home Office (2002) *Achieving Best Evidence in Criminal Proceedings for Vulnerable and/or Intimidated Witnesses including Children.* London: Home Office Publications.

Home Office (2007) *Keeping Children Safe from Sex Offenders. How Sex Offenders are Managed.* London: Home Office. http://www.homeoffice.gov.uk/documents/child-safe/

Home Office and DoH (1992) *Memorandum of Good Practice on Video-recorded Interviews with Child Witnesses for Criminal Proceedings.* London: HMSO.

Home Office and DoH (2002) *Complex Child Abuse Investigation – Inter Agency Issues.* London: Home Office. www.dh.gov.uk/publicationsandstatistics/publications/publicationspolicyandguidance/Fs/En

Hood, R. et al. (2002) *Reconviction Rates of Serious Sex Offenders and Assessments of Their Risk. Findings 164.* London: Home Office.

Horwath, J. (2007) Working Effectively in a Multi Agency Context. In NSPCC (2007) *Safeguarding Children a Shared Responsibility.* London: NSPCC.

House of Lords – Gillick V West Norfolk and Wisbech Area Health Authority (1985) 3 All ER 402/Gillick V West Norfolk and Wisbech Area Health Authority (1986) AC 112.

Howard League for Penal Reform (2007) *Press Release. UK Government Flouting United Nations Convention on The Rights of The Child* 21st June 2007.

Howard League (2008) Growing Up, Shut Up. www.howardleague.org/fileadmin/ howard_league/user/pdf/Press_2008/Growing_Up_Shut_Up_2_July_2008.pdf

Hughes, B., Parker, H. and Gallagher, B. (1996) *Policing and Child Sexual Abuse. The View From Police Practitioners*. London: Home Office.

Humphreys, M. (1996) *Empty Cradles*. London: Corgi.

Humphreys, C. and Mullender, A. (1999) *Children and Domestic Violence: A Research Overview of the Impact on Children*. Dartington: Research in Practice Available from www.rip.org.uk

Hunt, G. (1998) *Whistleblowing in the Social Services*. London: Hodder Arnold.

Jacob, M. and Hobbin, H. (2006) *Competence Matters. A London Multi Agency Safeguarding Children Programme*. Formerly available on London Safeguarding Children Board website.

Jones, C. (2001) Voices from the Front Line: State Social Workers and New Labour. *British Journal of Social Work*, 1: 31, 547–62.

Kaufman, J. and Zigler, E. (1993) The Intergenerational Transmission of Abuse is Overstated. In Gelles, R.J. and Loseke, D.R. (Eds.) *Current Controversies on Family Violence*. London: Sage.

Kelly, L., Regan, L. and Burton, S. (1991) *An Exploratory Study of the Prevalence of Sexual Abuse in a Sample of 16–21 Year Olds*. London: University of North London.

Kelly, Sir C. (2004) *Serious Case Review 'Ian Huntley' for North Lincolnshire Area Child Protection Committee*. 21.07.04.

King, M. (2002) Sexual Molestation of Males: Associations with Psychological Disturbance. *British Journal of Psychiatry*, 181: 153–7.

La Fontaine, J. (1994) *The Extent and Nature of Organised and Ritual Abuse*. London: DoH.

Laming, Lord (2003) *The Victoria Climbié Inquiry. Report of an Inquiry by Lord Laming*. London: HMSO.

Laville, S. (2007) Met Chief: Put Gang Siblings on Protection Register. *The Guardian* 03.05.2007, P4

Lawson, E. (1989) *Liam Johnson Review*. London: London Borough of Islington.

Leadbetter, M. (2002) *Submission of the Association of Directors of Social Services (ADSS) to Phase Two of The Victoria Climbié Inquiry*. www.adss.org.uk/pres/2002/ Climbie4.Shtml

London Safeguarding Children Board (2007) *London Child Protection Procedures*. London: LSCB.

Lovell, C. (2007) Restraint methods used on children in custody. http:// www.communitycare.co.uk/Articles/2007/12/19/106848/restraint_methods_used_on_ children_in_custody_suspended.html

Masson, H. and Erooga, M. (1999) Children and Young People who Sexually Abuse Others: Incidence, Characteristics, Causation. In Erooga, M. and Masson, H. (Eds.) *Children and Young People who Sexually Abuse Others. Challenges and Responses*. London: Routledge.

Masson, H. and Erooga, M. (1999) *Children and Young People who Sexually Abuse Others. Challenges and Responses.* London: Routledge.

McNulty, T. (2007) Written answer to parliamentary question by Annette Brooke M.P. Hansard 5th February 2007.

McVeigh, K. (2007) Youth Shot for Living in The Wrong Place. *Guardian* 17th November. www.guardian.co.uk/gun/story/0,,2212636,00.Html

Metropolitan Police and London Borough of Bexley (1987) *Child Sexual Abuse, Joint Investigative Programme. Bexley Experiment.* London: HMSO.

Metropolitan Police, UK Immigration Service, ADSS, NSPCC and London Borough of Hillingdon (2004) *Operation Paladin Child. A Partnership Study of Child Migration to the UK via London Heathrow.* London: Reflex.

Milner, P. and Carolin, B. (Eds.) (1999) *Time to Listen to Children.* London: Routledge.

Morgan, R. (2004) *Safe From Harm. Children's Views Report.* Newcastle. CSCI. Available on www.Right4me.Org

Morrison, B. (1998) *As If.* London: Granta Books.

Morrison, T. (1997) Training and Change in Child Protection Work: Towards Reflective Organisations. *Social Work Education*, 16: 2, 20–43.

Morrison, T. (1998) Partnership, Collaboration and Change under the Children Act. In Adcock, M. and White, R. (1998) *Significant Harm: Its Management and Outcome.* Surrey: Significant Publications.

Mudaly, N. and Goddard, C. (2006) *The Truth is Longer than a Lie. Children's Experiences of Abuse and Professional Interventions.* London: Jessica Kingsley.

Mullender, A. and Katz, A. (Ed.) (2003) *Stop Hitting Mum: Children Talk about Domestic Violence.* Surrey: Young Voice.

Munro, E. (1995) Common Errors of Reasoning in Child Protection Work. *Child Abuse and Neglect*, 23: 8.

Munro, E. (1996) Avoidable and Unavoidable Mistakes in Child Protection Work. *British Journal of Social Work*, XXVI: 795–810.

Munro, E. (2002) *Effective Child Protection.* London: Sage.

Munro, E. (2005) A Systems Approach to Investigating Child Abuse Deaths. *British Journal of Social Work*, 35: 4, 531–46.

Munro, E. and Calder, M. (2005) Where has Child Protection Gone? *The Political Quarterly*, 76: 3, 439–45.

National Criminal Intelligence Service (2003) *UK Threat Assessment of Serious and Organised Crime. Sex Offences Against Children Including Online Abuse.* www.ncis.co.uk

Nazer, M. and Lewis, D. (2004) *Slave: The True Story of a Girl's Lost Childhood and her Fight for Survival.* London: Virago.

Nelson, S. (2002) Physical Symptoms in Sexually Abused Women: Somatisation or Undetected Injury? *Child Abuse Review.* 11: 1, 51–64.

Nelson, S. (2004) *Neighbourhood Mapping for Children's Safety.* Edinburgh: Womanzone.

Nelson, S. (2008) *Hear Us, See Us. Schools Working with Sexually Abused Children.* Dundee: Violence in Preventable.

Nobes, G. and Smith, M. (1997) Physical Punishment of Children in Two Parent Families. *Clinical Child Psychology and Psychiatry*, 2: 271–81.

NSPCC (1997) *Childhood Matters. National Commission of Inquiry into the Prevention of Child Abuse*. London: NSPCC.

NSPCC (1997) *Turning Points. A Resource Pack for Communicating with Children*. London: NSPCC.

NSPCC (2007) *Safeguarding Children a Shared Responsibility*. London: NSPCC.

Ofsted (2007) *Narrowing The Gap: The Inspection of Children's Services*. London: DfES.

Oliver,T. and Ramsey, S. (1993) *Lambs to The Slaughter*. London: Times Warner.

Parton, N. (2005) *Safeguarding Childhood*. Hampshire: Palgrave Macmillan.

Peake, A. and Fletcher, M. (1997) *Strong Mothers*. Lyme Regis: Russell House Publishing.

Peake, A. and Rouf, K. (1998) *My Body, My Book*. London: The Children's Society.

Plotnikoff, J. and Woolfson, R. (2004) *In Their Own Words.The Experiences of 50 Young Witnesses in Criminal Proceedings*. London: NSPCC and Victim Support.

Press Association (2007) Teenager Killed in Street Shooting. *The Guardian*. 04.08.07
http://www.guardian.co.uk/uklatest/story/0,,-6826875,00.Html

Protection of Children Act 1999. London: HMSO.

Public Interest Disclosure Act 1998. London: HMSO.

R (The Howard League for Penal Reform) versus The Secretary of State for The Home Department (2002)

Reder, P. and Duncan, S. (1999) *Lost Innocents. A Follow-up Study of Fatal Child Abuse*. London: Routledge.

Reder, P. and Duncan, S. (2004) Making the Most of the Victoria Inquiry Report. *Child Abuse Review* 13: 95–114.

Reder, P., Duncan, S. and Gray, M. (1993) *Beyond Blame. Child Abuse Tragedies Revisited. A Summary of 35 Inquiries Since 1973*. London: Routledge.

Rees, G. and Lee, J. (2005*) Still Running II: Findings from the Second National Survey of Young Runaways*. London: The Children's Society.

Renold, E., Creighton, S.J. with Atkinson, C. and Carr, J. (2003*) Images of Abuse: A Review of the Evidence on Child Pornography*. London: NSPCC.

Richardson, S. (1991) *Child Sexual Abuse: Whose Problem? Reflections from Cleveland*. Birmingham: Venture.

Robertson, M. (1996) Open About Mistakes. *Community Care*. Letters. 21.01.1996.

Salter, D. et al. (2003) Development of Sexually Abusive Behaviour in Sexually Victimised Males: A Longitudinal Study. *The Lancet*, 361: 471–6.

Saunders, H. (2004) *29 Child Homicides*. London: Women's Aid.

Sereny, G. (1999) *Cries Unheard. The Story of Mary Bell*. London: Macmillan.

Sex Offenders Act 1997. London: HMSO.

Sexual Offences Act 2003. London: HMSO.

Shardlow, S. et al. (2004) *Education and Training For Inter-Agency Working: New standards*. Manchester: Salford Centre for Social Work Research.

Shepherd, J. and Sampson, A. (2000) Don't Shake the Baby: Towards a Preventive Strategy. *British Journal of Social Work*. 30: 721–35.

Sillen, J. and Beddoe, C. (2007) *Rights Here, Right Now. Recommendations for Protecting Trafficked Children*. London: UNICEF and Ecpat UK.

Smith, P. and Clarke, C. (1994) *Child Protection Training Needs Across Agencies. A Sample Survey of London Social Services Staff Views and Comparison With a Metropolitan Police Survey*. London: Training for Care and the Professionals Development Foundation.

Social Exclusion Unit (2002) *Report: Young Runaways*. London: ODPM.

Social Work Inspection Agency (2005) *An Inspection into the Care and Protection of Children in Eilean Siar*. Edinburgh: Scottish Executive.

Spence, P. and Wilson, C. (1994) *Team Investigation of Child Sexual Abuse*. London: Sage.

Stainton Rogers, W. and Worrel, M. (1993) *Investigative Interviewing with Children*. Milton Keynes: Open University.

Stephenson, O. (1998) *Neglected Children: Issues and Dilemmas*. Oxford: Blackwell Science.

Stevenson, O. (2000) The Mandate For Inter-Agency and Inter-Professional Work and Training: Legal, Practical, Professional and Social Factors. in Charles and Hendry (2000) *Training Together to Safeguard Children*. London: NSPCC.

Stobart, E. (2006) *Child Abuse Linked to Accusations of 'Possession and Witchcraft' Research Report 750*. London: DfES.

Striker, S. and Kimmel, E. (2004) *The Anti-Colouring Book*. New York: Scholastic.

Stuart, M. and Baines, C. (2004) *Safeguards for Vulnerable Children: Three Studies on Abusers, Disabled Children and Children in Prison. Progress on Safeguards for Children Living Away From Home. A Review of Actions Since The People Like Us Review*. York: Joseph Rowntree Foundation.

Sullivan, P.M. and Knutson, J.F. (2000) Maltreatment and Disabilities: A Population Based Epidemiological Study. *Child Abuse and Neglect*, 24: 10, 1257–73.

Summit, R. (1983) The Child Sexual Abuse Accommodation. Syndrome. *Child Abuse and Neglect*, 7, 177–93.

Sunday Herald (2003) *Slipping Through the Net*. 19.01.2003 http://xuk.biz/UKLR/ Landslide/Library/44/Sunday per cent20Herald.Htm

Svedin, C. and Bach, K. (1996) *Children who don't Speak Out about being Children Being Used in Child Pornography*. Sweden: Radda Barnen.

Swansea LSCB (2006) *Executive Summary Aaron Gilbert*. Swansea: Swansea LSCB.

Taylor, A. (1998) Hostages to Fortune; The Abuse of Children in Care. In Hunt, G. (1998) *Whistleblowing in the Social Services*. London: Hodder Arnold.

Thoburn, J. et al. (2000) *Family Support in Cases of Emotional Maltreatment and Neglect*. London: TSO.

Tomison, A.M. (1995) Spotlight on Child Neglect. *Issues in Child Abuse Prevention*, 4 (Winter).

Treasury, The (2003) *Every Child Matters*. London: TSO.

Triangle (2001) *Two Way Street. Communication with Disabled Children*. Sussex: Triangle Publications.

Turning Point (2006) *Bottling It Up. The Effects of Alcohol Misuse on Children, Parents and Families.* London: Turning Point.

UNICEF (2003) *More precious than gold.* Video available on line. www.endchildexploitation.org.uk

United Nations (1989) *United Nations Convention of The Rights of The Child.* Geneva: United Nations.

United Nations (2003) *Optional Protocol to the Convention on The Rights of the Child to the Involvement of Children in Armed Conflict.* New York: United Nations.

Utting, W. (1997) *People Like Us. The Report of the Review of the Safeguards for Children Living Away from Home.* London: DoH.

Utting, W. (2005) *Progress on Safeguards for Children Living Away from Home.* York: Joseph Rowntree Trust.

Vizard, E. (2006) Sexually Abusive Behaviour by Children and Adolescents. *Child and Adolescent Mental Health.* 11: 1, 2–8.

Walker, A. (1993) *Possessing the Secret of Joy.* New York: Vintage.

Walker, A. and Parmar, P. (1996) *Warrior Marks: Female Genital Mutilation and Sexual Blinding of Women.* Harvester: San Diego.

Walmsley, J. Baroness (2007) *Child Protection Debate in The House of Lords.* 24th October 2007 www.publications.parliament.uk/pa/Ld200607/Ldhansrd/Text/71024-0007.htm

Waterhouse, Sir R. (2000) *Lost in Care.* London: TSO.

Wattam, C. (1990) Working Together. *Social Work Today.* 13th September.

Waugh, R. (2007) Sacked Whistleblowers Win £1 Million Payout From Council. *Yorkshire Post* 14th August 2007. www.yorkshirepost.co.uk/news?articleid=3107592

Weightman, C. (2006) *Serious Case Review Executive Summary, Alexander Gallon.* Newcastle: Newcastle LSCB.

Weightman, C. (2006) *Serious Case Review Executive Summary, Baby O.* Newcastle: Newcastle LSCB.

West, A.M. (1995*) Out of the Shadows.* London: Simon and Schuster.

White, I. and Hart, K. (1995) *Inquiry into the Management of Child Care in Islington.* London: Borough of Islington.

Williams, D. (1991) Beat Abuse. *Social Work Today*, 24th October.

Willis, G. (1993) *Unspeakable Crimes.* London: The Children's Society.

Willow, C. and Hyder, T. (2004) *It Hurts you Inside. Young Children Talk about Smacking.* London: CRAE and Save The Children.

Wolmar, C. (2000) *Forgotten Children: The Secret Abuse Scandal in Children's Homes.* London: Vision.

Websites

www.anationalvoice.org. A national organisation run by and for children who are in or leaving care

www.bichard.gov.uk The Bichard Inquiry website

www.careleavers.com The Care Leavers Association

www.carestandardstribunal.gov.uk Care Standards Tribunal

www.ceop.gov.uk Child Exploitation and Online Abuse – investigates online abuse and provides a service for reporting

www.childline.org.uk ChildLine. Free and confidential helpline for young people

www.childrenareunbeatable.org.uk Children are unbeatable alliance. Campaign against the physical punishment of children

www.cica.gov.uk Criminal Injuries Compensation Authority

www.cps.gov.uk Crown Prosecution Service

www.crae.org.uk Children's Rights Alliance for England is a coalition of organisations committed to the full implementation of the United Nations Convention on the Rights of the Child.

www.dcsf.gov.uk The Department for Children, Schools and Families

www.ecpat.org.uk Campaign to End Child Prostitution, Child Pornography and the Trafficking of Children for Sexual Purposes

www.everychildmatters.gov.uk The *Every Child Matters* website

www.edcm.org.uk *Every Disabled Child Matters* is a campaign group to ensure inclusion of disabled children within the *Every Child Matters* agenda

www.frg.org.uk The Family Rights Group campaign

www.forwarduk.org.uk FORWARD. Campaign against female genital mutilation

www.freedomtocare.org Whistleblowers website

www.homeoffice.qov.uk The Home Office website

www.howardleague.org Howard League for Penal Reform

www.iwf.org.uk Internet Watch Foundation. Includes a hotline for reporting child abuse on the internet

www.lscb.gov.uk The London Safeguarding Children Board

www.missingpeople.org.uk Missing People is a charity working with young people who go missing

www.napac.org.uk National Association of People Abused in Childhood

www.norm-uk.org National Organisation of Restoring Men. Campaign against male genital cutting

www.no2abuse.com No to Abuse. Survivors website

www.nspcc.org.uk/Inform The NSPCC Inform website is a free child protection resource providing research, statistics, news and information.

www.pcaw.org Public Concern at Work. Advice and support for whistleblowers www.rights4me.org Office of the Children's Rights Director for England

www.southallblacksisters.org.uk Campaign against the policy of no access to public funds for asylum seekers

www.stand4children.org Campaign against the deportation of children

www.stopitnow.org.uk Stop it Now. Information and awareness campaign regarding the subject of child sexual abuse

www.survivorsswindon.com Survivors group in Swindon

www.swia.org.uk Social work inspection agency – Scotland

www.therapeutic-stories.com Nancy Davis website for survivors of all ages who have experienced trauma

www.thesurvivorstrust.org Organisation for over 120 voluntary sector agencies

www.victoria-climbie-inquiry.org.uk Victoria Climbie Inquiry website

National Occupational Standards (NOS) for Police Work

(www.skillsforjustice.com)

These are the NOS relevant to this area of police work.

Common NOS across the Justice sector

Diversity units
AA1 Promote equality and value diversity
AA2 Develop a culture and systems that promote equality and value diversity

Communication units
AB1 Communicate effectively with people
AB2 Support individuals to communicate using interpreting and translation services

Inter-agency and team working
AC1 Contribute to the quality of team working
AD1 Develop and sustain effective working with staff from other agencies
AD2 Develop, sustain and evaluate joint work between agencies

Personal development
E1 Maintain and develop your own knowledge, skills and competence

NOS for Witness Care

DE6 Establish details and contact regarding new or repeat victims and witnesses
DE7 Undertake needs assessments of victims and witnesses
DE8 Establish requirements for special measures at court
   DE8.1 Determine circumstances requiring the arrangements of special measures
   DE8.2 Present a case for special measures to be provided
DE9 Monitor and arrange support for victims and witnesses towards ensuring attendance at court
DE10 Notify victims and witnesses of the outcomes of cases and address their reactions

NOS for Policing and Law Enforcement (2003)

2H1 Interview victims and witnesses
   2H1.1 Plan and prepare interviews with victims and witnesses
   2H1.2 Conduct interviews with victims and witnesses
   2H1.3 Evaluate interviews with victims and witnesses

NOS for Policing and Law Enforcement (2008)

GC11.1 Respond to allegations or suspicions of child abuse
(http://www.skillsforjustice.com/websitefiles/O27NGC11.pdf)

GC11.1 Respond to allegations or suspicions of child abuse

Summary

This unit is concerned with responding to allegations or suspicions of the abuse of children and young people.

The unit covers all types of abuse – physical abuse, neglect, emotional abuse and sexual abuse. You are expected to evaluate the signs and symptoms of possible abuse, make judgments about the sufficiency of evidence and determine the actions required to safeguard and promote the welfare of children and young people. You must know how and to whom allegations or suspicions of abuse must be reported, liaise effectively with staff in other agencies and access appropriate personal support. This unit is appropriate for personnel involved with the investigation of abuse of children and young people. The competences described in this unit should be considered in conjunction with other units covering, for example, investigation and interviewing.

There is one element: GC11.1: Respond to allegations or suspicions of abuse.

Performance criteria

To meet the standard, you:

1. Respond calmly and without delay or prejudice to allegations or suspicions of **abuse**.
2. Evaluate signs and symptoms of abuse using all available **information** to identify their significance.
3. Communicate with the child where appropriate, at a pace, manner and level that is suitable to the **circumstances**.
4. Ask only sufficient questions to assess the welfare of the child and the necessity for formal interview ensuring that a full record is made.
5. Offer timely, appropriate and accurate information to the individual(s) responsible for the child whilst taking account of **relevant factors**.
6. Assess all available evidence relating to the allegation or suspicion of **abuse** and determine whether there is sufficient evidence to initiate a full investigation.
7. Make considered judgements about the actions required to safeguard and promote a child's welfare and, take steps to ascertain the child's wishes and feelings.
8. Take actions which are appropriate to the significance of the signs and symptoms of **abuse** and child safeguarding procedures.
9. Make accurate, legible and complete records about the possible **abuse** of children.
10. Make appropriate referrals immediately following any concerns of possible **abuse** and confirm in writing the information provided.
11. Provide prompt, accurate, complete and signed **reports** about the possible **abuse** of children to the **relevant people** in accordance with current policy and legislation.
12. Discuss cases as soon as possible with the **relevant people** in a manner which enables them to form a picture of the case and the issues inherent within it.

13. Access and use common information and data sharing systems where they exist.
14. Manage your own feelings generated by the case in a way which supports the right to such feelings, minimises any undue affects on the child, and does not impact on the investigation.
15. Deal with individuals in an ethical manner, recognising their needs with respect to race, diversity and human rights.
16. Fully document all decisions, actions, options and rationale in accordance with current policy and legislation.

Range

1. Abuse

    a. neglect
    b. physical
    c. emotional
    d. sexual

2. Information

    a. from internal sources
    b. from external sources

3. Circumstances

    a. the level of understanding of the child
    b. the stage of development of the child
    c. the nature of the allegations or suspicions
    d. the culture and background of the child

4. Relevant factors

    a. the risk to the child
    b. the nature of the allegations or suspicions
    c. compromise to evidence
    d. the requirements of safeguarding procedures

5. Reports

    a. for use for intelligence purposes
    b. for use in safeguarding processes

6. Relevant people

    a. internal to your organisation
    b. in external organisations or agencies
    c. the lead professional

Knowledge and understanding

To meet the standard, you need to know and understand:

Legal and organisational requirements

1. Current, relevant legislation, policies, procedures, codes of practice and guidelines for safeguarding children.
2. Current, relevant legislation, policies, procedures, codes of practice and guidelines for responding to allegations and suspicions of abuse of children.
3. Current, relevant legislation, codes of practice and organisational requirements in relation to sharing information regarding the possible abuse of children with other individuals and agencies.
4. The restrictions that apply to the disclosure of confidential and sensitive information.
5. Current, relevant legislation and organisational requirements in relation to race, diversity and human rights.
6. Current, relevant legislation and organisational requirements in relation to health and safety.

Safeguarding children

7. The principles of development and attachment in children.
8. The factors that can contribute to vulnerability of children and young people to abuse.
9. The factors that can contribute to the development of resilience.
10. The concept of children's rights and the importance of empowering children to exercise those rights; the external factors and constraints that make it difficult for children's rights to be promoted.
11. The forms which abusive behaviour make take.
12. The short-term and long-term impact of different forms of abuse on physical, emotional and behavioural development.
13. The signs and symptoms of possible abuse.
14. Methods of preventing the occurrence or re-occurrence of abuse.
15. The importance of active listening, and ways of communicating effectively with children and young people including indicators of readiness to communicate and how to interpret non-verbal communication.
16. The range of actions that can be taken to safeguard children and the reasoning processes involved in determining the most appropriate options for the individual(s) concerned.
17. Safeguarding procedures relating to the monitoring and reporting of possible abuse of children and how to ensure that the correct procedures are adhered to.
18. The potential impact of allegations or suspicions of abuse on family members and/or those responsible for the child, including the effect on their rights and responsibilities as set out in safeguarding procedures.
19. How to record, evaluate and present different types of information from various sources; the importance of distinguishing between directly observed evidence,

evidence from reliable sources, opinion and hearsay; safeguarding procedures relating to recording, evaluating and presenting of information.

20. How situations with a potential conflict of interest can be identified and resolved.
21. The importance of giving the child the opportunity to participate in decisions affecting them in accordance with the circumstances of the case.
22. The purpose of the Common Assessment Framework for Children and Young People (CAF) and its role in aiding communication between practitioners.

Working with others

23. The role of your organisation and its services regarding safeguarding children and how they relate to other agencies and services in the justice sector.
24. How to report and refer cases of possible abuse to others internal and external to your organisation.
25. How to liaise with staff in other agencies, and how to challenge their understanding and assumptions where necessary.

Individual practice and development

26. Your own role and responsibilities and from whom assistance and advice should be sought if you are unsure.
27. Your responsibility for safeguarding children, the information you are required to provide to others and the reasons for providing this information (including its use in case conferences and court proceedings).
28. How you apply the principles of equality, diversity and anti-discriminatory practice to your work.
29. How to identify and access support to manage your own feelings in order to ensure the welfare of all involved in the case.
30. When and how to relinquish control of a case to others whilst ensuring continuity of the case and integrity of evidence.
31. How to identify and meet your training needs in relation to safeguarding children and ensure that you always work within the scope of your competence.

The National Occupational Standards for Social Work

These standards provide a benchmark of best practice in social work competence across the UK and form the basis for the social work degree. (www.skillsforcare.org.uk)

Key Role 1: Prepare for, and work with individuals, families, carers, groups and communities to assess their needs and circumstances

Unit 1: Prepare for social work contact and involvement

1.1 Review case notes and other relevant material

1.2 Liaise with others to access additional information that can inform initial contact and involvement

1.3 Evaluate all information to identify the best form of initial involvement

Unit 2: Work with individuals, families, carers, groups and communities to help them make informed decisions

2.1 Inform individuals, families, carers, groups and communities about your own, and the organisation's duties and responsibilities

2.2 Work with individuals, families, carers, groups and communities to identify, gather, analyse and understand information

2.3 Work with individuals, families, carers, groups and communities to enable them to analyse, identify, clarify and express their strengths, expectations and limitations

2.4 Work with individuals, families, carers, groups and communities to enable them to assess and make informed decisions about their needs, circumstances, risks, preferred options and resources

Unit 3: Assess needs and options to recommend a course of action

3.1 Assess and review the preferred options of individuals, families, carers, groups and communities

3.2 Assess needs, risks and options taking into account legal and other requirements

3.3 Assess and recommend an appropriate course of action for individuals, families, carers, groups and communities

Key Role 2: Plan, carry out, review and evaluate social work practice, with individuals, families, carers, groups, communities and other professionals

Unit 4: Respond to crisis situations

4.1 Assess the urgency of requests for action

4.2 Identify the need for legal and procedural intervention

4.3 Plan and implement action to meet the immediate needs and circumstances

4.4 Review the outcomes with individuals, families, carers, groups, communities, organisations, professionals and others

Unit 5: Interact with individuals, families, carers, groups and communities to achieve change and development and to improve life opportunities

5.1 Develop and maintain relationships with individuals, families, carers, groups, communities and others

5.2 Work with individuals, families, carers, groups, communities and others to avoid crisis situations and address problems and conflict

5.3 Apply and justify social work methods and models used to achieve change and development, and improve life opportunities

5.4 Regularly monitor, review and evaluate changes in needs and circumstances

5.5 Reduce contact and withdraw from relationships appropriately

Unit 6: Prepare, produce, implement and evaluate plans with individuals, families, carers, groups, communities and professional colleagues

6.1 Negotiate the provision to be included in the plans

6.2 Identify content and actions and draft plans

6.3 Carry out your own responsibilities and monitor, co-ordinate and support the actions of others involved in implementing the plans

6.4 Review the effectiveness of the plans with the people involved

6.5 Renegotiate and revise plans to meet changing needs and circumstances

Unit 9: Address behaviour which presents a risk to individuals, families, carers, groups and communities

9.1 Take immediate action to deal with the behaviour that presents a risk

9.2 Work with individuals, families, carers, groups, communities and others to identify and evaluate situations and circumstances that may trigger the behaviour

9.3 Work with individuals, families, carers, groups and communities on strategies and support that could positively change the behaviour

Key Role 3: Support individuals to represent their needs, views and circumstances

Unit 11: Prepare for, and participate in decision making forums

11.1 Prepare reports and documents for decision making forums

11.2 Work with individuals, families, carers, groups and communities to select the best form of representation for decision making forums

11.3 Present evidence to, and help individuals, families, carers, groups and communities to understand the procedures of and the outcomes from, decision making forums

11.4 Enable individuals, families, carers, groups and communities to be involved in decision making forums

Key Role 4: Manage risk to individuals, families, carers, groups, communities, self and colleagues

Unit 12: Assess and manage risks to individuals, families, carers, groups and communities

12.1 Identify and assess the nature of the risk

12.2 Balance the rights and responsibilities of individuals, families, carers, groups and communities with associated risk

12.3 Regularly monitor, re-assess, and manage risk to individuals, families, carers, groups and communities

Key Role 5: Manage and be accountable, with supervision and support, for your own social work practice within your organisation

Unit 14: Manage and be accountable for your own work

14.1 Manage and prioritise your workload within organisational policies and priorities

14.2 Carry out duties using accountable professional judgment and knowledge based social work practice

14.3 Monitor and evaluate the effectiveness of your programme of work in meeting the organisational requirements and the needs of individuals, families, carers, groups and communities

14.4 Use professional and managerial supervision and support to improve your practice

Unit 17: Work within multi-disciplinary and multi-organisational teams, networks and systems

17.1 Develop and maintain effective working relationships

17.2 Contribute to the identifying and agreeing the goals, objectives and lifespan of the team, network or system

17.3 Contribute to evaluating the effectiveness of the team, network or system

17.4 Deal constructively with disagreements and conflict within relationships

Key Role 6: Demonstrate professional competence in social work practice

Unit 18: Research, analyse, evaluate, and use current knowledge of best social work practice

18.1 Review and update your own knowledge of legal, policy and procedural frameworks

18.2 Use professional and organisational supervision and support to research, critically analyse, and review knowledge based practice

18.3 Implement knowledge based social work models and methods to develop and improve your own practice

Unit 19: Work within agreed standards of social work practice and ensure own professional development

19.1 Exercise and justify professional judgements

19.2 Use professional assertiveness to justify decisions and uphold professional social work practice, values and ethics

19.3 Work within the principles and values underpinning social work practice

19.4 Critically reflect upon your own practice and performance using supervision and support systems

19.5 Use supervision and support to take action to meet continuing professional development needs

Unit 20: Manage complex ethical issues, dilemmas and conflicts

20.1 Identify and assess issues, dilemmas and conflicts that might affect your practice

20.2 Devise strategies to deal with ethical issues, dilemmas and conflicts

20.3 Reflect on outcomes

Unit 21: Contribute to the promotion of best social work practice

21.1 Contribute to policy review and development

21.2 Use supervision and organisational and professional systems to inform a course of action where practice falls below required standards

21.3 Work with colleagues to contribute to team development

Relevant Academic Standards

(www.qaa.ac.uk/academicinfrastructure/benchmark/honours/socialpolicy.asp#1)

These are extracted from *Academic Standards – Social Work* in the *Subject benchmark statements* for *Social Policy and Administration* in the *Quality Assurance Agency* (QAA) *Academic Infrastructure*.

3.1.1. Social work services and service users

- Explanations of the links between definitional processes contributing to social differences to the problems of inequality and differential need faced by service users
- The nature of social work services in a diverse society
- The relationship between agency policies, legal requirements and professional boundaries in shaping the nature of services provided in inter-disciplinary contexts and the issues associated with working across professional boundaries and within different disciplinary groups

3.1.2. The service delivery context

- The issues and trends in modern public and social policy and their relationship to contemporary practice and service delivery in social work
- The significance of legislative and legal frameworks and service delivery standards
- The implications of modern communication and information technology for service delivery

3.1.3. Values and ethics

- The moral concepts of rights, responsibility, freedom authority and power inherent in the practice of social workers as moral and statutory agents

3.1.5. The nature of social work practice

- The nature and characteristics of skills associated with effective practice, both direct and indirect, with a range of service users and in a variety of settings including group-care
- The factors and processes that facilitate effective inter-disciplinary, inter-professional and inter-agency collaboration and partnership
- The processes of reflection and evaluation, including familiarity with the range of approaches for evaluating welfare outcomes, and their significance for the development of practice and the practitioner

The subject skills highlighted to demonstrate this knowledge in practice include:

3.2.2. Managing problem solving activities
3.2.2.1 Managing problem solving activities
3.2.2.2 Gathering information
3.2.2.3 Analysis and synthesis
3.2.2.4 Intervention and evaluation

3.2.3. Communication skills

- Listen actively to others, engage appropriately with the life experiences of service users, understand accurately their viewpoint and overcome personal prejudices to respond appropriately to a range of complex personal and inter-personal situations
- Follow and develop an argument and evaluate the viewpoints of, and evidence presented by, others;
- Make effective preparation for, and lead meetings in a productive way; and
- Communicate effectively across potential barriers resulting from differences (for example, in culture, language and age).

3.2.4. Skills in working with others

- Involve users of social work services in ways that increase their resources, capacity and power to influence factors affecting their lives;
- Consult actively with others, including service users, who hold relevant information or expertise;
- Act co-operatively with others, liaising and negotiating across differences such as organisational and professional boundaries and differences of identity or language;
- Act with others to increase social justice by identifying and responding to prejudice, institutional discrimination and structural inequality;
- Act within a framework of multiple accountability (for example, to agencies, the public, service users and others); and
- Challenge others when necessary, in ways that are most likely to produce positive outcomes.

5.1.1. Knowledge and understanding

- Ability to use this knowledge and understanding in an integrated way in specific practice contexts;
- Ability to use research and enquiry techniques to collect, analyse and interpret relevant information;
- Capacity for critical evaluation of knowledge and evidence from a range of sources.

BSc Module Handbook

LONDON
metropolitan
university

LONDON NORTH CAMPUS

Department of Applied Social Sciences

Graduate Diploma/BSc (Honours) Specialist Social Work (working with children)

The joint investigation of child abuse and investigative interviewing of children

Module Code: SW3017N

Module Handbook 2007–2008

Undergraduate Centre location for course:

Ground Floor, room G20
Ladbroke House,
62–66 Highbury Grove,
London, N52AD.

Introduction to the Module

This Module, the joint investigation of child abuse and investigative interviewing of children, is within the Graduate Diploma/BSc (Honours) Specialist Social Work (working with children). This handbook will provide you with information specifically regarding this Module, and needs to be read in conjunction with the course handbook. The main source of information for this module is available on Weblearn. We hope you will enjoy studying with us.

The module will teach the skills required for the investigation of child abuse according to the statutory guidance *Working Together to Safeguard Children* (DfES, 2006) and the investigate interviewing of children according to the statutory guidance *Achieving Best Evidence in Criminal Proceedings: Guidance for Vulnerable or Intimidated Witnesses, including Children* (CJS, Office 2007). It will require the demonstration of competence in both these areas of advanced level child protection work.

Prerequisite: Agencies will be responsible for the initial selection of candidates. Candidates must be social work qualified and currently registered with the GSCC. Completion of the Protecting Children course or equivalent.

Location and staff contact

The course is located in North Campus, London Metropolitan University, 62–66 Highbury Grove, Ladbroke House, London N5 2AD. Telephone: 020 7423 0000. Fax: 020 7753 5763.

The module is led by the Module Convenor, Liz Davies, who is responsible for the day-to-day organisation of the course. The Academic Director has overall responsibility for the programme, and teaching staff and tutors are responsible for providing the workshops, tutoring of candidates, and liaison with the Module Convenor and Academic Director to ensure course quality.

Academic Leader	Stephen Fox
Module Convenor	Liz Davies
Teaching Staff	Debbie Townsend

Module Convenor:
Liz Davies: Room 240 Ladbroke House
e.davies@londonmet.ac.uk
020 7133 5110

Aims and learning outcomes of the module

This module aims to provide students with the knowledge and skills required to promote competence in the multi-agency investigation of child abuse and the investigative interviewing of children. The course will present current legislation, policy and practice guidance in a context of the paramountcy of the child's welfare and partnership working with families and carers. A child rights approach will be central to course content. There will also be emphasis on the professional as a specialist practitioner and the involvement of service users in the delivery.

By the end of this module students should be able to:

- Have knowledge of how to investigate child abuse under Section 47 CA 1989 and seek justice for children within a context of current legislation, policy and practice guidance.
- Work together within a multi-agency context to effectively protect children from actual or likely significant harm and in the preparation, planning and conduct of a child interview.
- Analyse and evaluate child protection investigations and interventions.
- Plan and set objectives for a child interview, to communicate effectively with children of different ages and backgrounds and have the technical capability to ensure accurate and effective recording of a child interview.
- Work within the key principles of the child's best interests being paramount, partnership with families and carers and anti-oppressive practice.
- Recognise the emotional impact of the work and the importance of safe working environments.

Syllabus

The syllabus includes:

- A child's right to seek justice – the child's perspective and childism
- Knowledge and skill in investigation of child abuse including complex forms of abuse
- Child protection legislation and policy – analysis of current trends
- Effective intervention through inter-agency 'working together' to protect children
- Communication with vulnerable children and partnership working with families
- The professional response – safe practice issues

Credits and learning time

Module level: H
The module attracts 15 CATS points at level 3.
The module consists of 10 days of University based learning
London Metropolitan University recommends that employers provide a minimum of 3 days study leave to complete the module.

Module structure

The course will delivered by a two week course. The first week will focus on the joint investigation of child abuse and the second week will address the investigative interview. Teaching will be partly didactic but also will include a range of participatory activities and role plays. The role plays will be video recorded to allow for detailed debriefing and assessment. Survivors of child abuse will contribute to the course.

Module programme

The joint investigation of child abuse
Day 1: Understanding child abuse
Day 2: Indicators of abuse. Procedures and good practice
Day 3: Multi-agency assessment, investigation and intervention. Legal frameworks
Day 4: Sexual abuse of children
Day 5: Safer care and survival skills

The investigative interviewing of children
Day 1: Achieving Best Evidence Guidance
Day 2: The phased interview approach
Day 3: Planning and preparation
Day 4: Role Plays
Day 5: Debrief

Assessment tasks

Essay

Provide an account of your experience or knowledge of a Section 47 (CA1989) investigation with particular emphasis on the child's perspective and inter-professional working (3,500 words).

Role Play

Role Play of an investigative child interview. The video must be of a quality suitable for presentation in court and in line with evidential requirements. The video will be assessed by course tutors (Pass/fail).

Marking and assessment

The module assessment will be weighted as follows:
Essay 100 per cent Pass mark 40 per cent
Role Play: Pass/Fail

MSc Module Handbook

LONDON
metropolitan
university

LONDON NORTH CAMPUS

Department of Applied Social Sciences

MSc Specialist Social Work (working with children)

The joint investigation of child abuse and investigative interviewing of children

Module Code: SWP021N

Module Handbook 2007–2008

Introduction to the Module

This Module, the joint investigation of child abuse and investigative interviewing of children, is within the MSc Specialist Social Work (working with children). This handbook will provide you with information specifically regarding this Module, and needs to be read in conjunction with the course handbook. The main source of information for this module is available on Weblearn. We hope you will enjoy studying with us.

The module will teach the skills required for the investigation of child abuse according to the statutory guidance *Working Together to Safeguard Children* (DfES, 2006) and the investigate interviewing of children according to the statutory guidance *Achieving Best Evidence in Criminal Proceedings: Guidance for Vulnerable or Intimidated Witnesses, including Children* (CJS, 2007). It will require the demonstration of competence and criticality in both these areas of advanced level child protection work.

Prerequisite: Agencies will be responsible for the initial selection of candidates. Candidates must be social work qualified and currently registered with the GSCC. Completion of the Protecting Children course or equivalent.

Location and staff contact

The course is located in North Campus, London Metropolitan University, 62–66 Highbury Grove, Ladbroke House, London, N5 2AD. Telephone: 020 7423 0000. Fax: 020 7753 5763.

The module is led by the Module Convenor, Liz Davies (e.davies@londonmet.ac.uk, 020 7133 5110) who is responsible for the day-to-day organisation of the course. The Academic Director, Stephen Fox, has overall responsibility for the programme, and teaching staff and tutors including Debbie Townsend are responsible for providing the workshops, tutoring of candidates, and liaison with the Module Convenor and Academic Director to ensure course quality.

Aims and learning outcomes of the module

This module aims to provide students with the knowledge and skills required to promote competence and criticality in the multi-agency investigation of child abuse and the investigative interviewing of children. The course will require analysis of current legislation, policy and practice guidance. The course will be presented in the context of the paramountcy of the child's welfare and partnership working with families and carers. Students will be expected to adopt a child rights approach to course content. There will also be emphasis on the professional as a specialist practitioner and the involvement of service users in the delivery.

By the end of this module students should be able to:

- Have knowledge of how to analyse the investigation of child abuse under Section 47 CA1989 and to seek justice for children within a context of current legislation, policy and practice guidance.

297

- Reflect on the processes of multi-agency work to effectively protect children from actual or likely significant harm and to demonstrate competence and a critical approach in the preparation, planning and conduct of a child interview.
- Analyse and evaluate child protection investigations and interventions, drawing on a critical appraisal of relevant research evidence and learning from the outcomes of child abuse inquiries.
- Plan and set objectives for a child interview, to communicate effectively with children of different ages and backgrounds and have the technical capability to ensure accurate and effective recording of a child interview.
- Work within and reflect upon practice in which key principles are the child's best interests being paramount, partnership with families and carers and anti-oppressive practice.
- Recognise and reflect upon the emotional impact of the work and the importance of safe working environments.

Syllabus

The syllabus includes:

- A child's right to seek justice – the child's perspective and childism
- Knowledge and skill in investigation of child abuse including complex forms of abuse
- Child protection legislation and policy – analysis of current trends
- Effective intervention through inter-agency 'working together' to protect children
- Communication with vulnerable children and partnership working with families
- The professional response – safe practice issues

Credits and learning time

Module level: H
The module attracts 20 CATS points at level 3.
The module consists of 10 days of University based learning
London Metropolitan University recommends that employers provide a minimum of 3 days study leave to complete the module.

Module structure

The course will delivered by a two week course. The first week will focus on the joint investigation of child abuse and the second week will address the investigative interview. Teaching will be partly didactic but also will include a range of participatory activities and role plays. The role plays will video recorded to allow for detailed debriefing and assessment. Survivors of child abuse will contribute to the course.

Module programme

The joint investigation of child abuse
Day 1: Understanding child abuse
Day 2: Indicators of abuse. Procedures and good practice
Day 3: Multi-agency assessment, investigation and intervention. Legal frameworks
Day 4: Sexual abuse of children
Day 5: Safer care and survival skills

The investigative interviewing of children
Day 1: Achieving Best Evidence Guidance
Day 2: The phased interview approach
Day 3: Planning and preparation
Day 4: Role Plays
Day 5: Debrief

Assessment tasks

Assessment is by essay, an assessed video role play of a formal child interview and a reflective account of the interview process from a range of perspectives.

Essay

A critical account of a Section 47 (CA1989) investigation drawing on knowledge, skills and values and based on direct work or a case example. (3,500 words) 90 per cent marks

Role Play

A video role play of an investigative child interview. The video must be of a quality suitable for presentation in court and in line with evidential requirements. The video will be assessed by course tutors. (pass/fail)

Reflective review

Reflection on role play from both your own perspective as lead interviewer and that of the child. (1000 words) 10 per cent marks

Marking and assessment

The module assessment will be weighted as follows:
Essay 90 per cent Pass mark 50 per cent
Role Play: Pass/Fail
Reflection on the role play 10 per cent Pass mark 50 per cent

Electronic supply of the handouts from Joint Investigation in Child Protection

If you would like to receive a PDF of the handouts from this book, please complete the form below, tear out this page, and return it to us. Please note that photocopies are not acceptable, nor are applications made through e-mail, phone or fax.

Please keep a copy of the completed form for your own records.

This PDF is free.

Please note

RHP reserves the right to withdraw this offer at any time without prior notice.

RHP reserves the right to qualify or reject any application which it is not completely satisfied is on an original torn-out page from the back of a purchased book.

Terms and conditions for use of the handouts from Joint Investigation in Child Protection

1. Buying a copy of *Joint Investigation in Child Protection* and completing the form at the back of this book gives the individual who signs the form permission to use the materials in the PDF that will be sent from RHP for their own use only.
2. The hard copies that they then print from the PDF are subject to the same permissions and restrictions that are set out in the 'photocopying permission' section at the front of this book.
3. Under no circumstances should they forward or copy the electronic materials to anyone else.
4. If the person who signs this form wants a licence to be granted for wider use of the electronic materials within their organisation, network or client base, they must make a request directly to RHP fully detailing the proposed use. All requests will be reviewed on their own merits.
   - If the request is made when submitting this form to RHP, the request should be made in writing and should accompany this form.
   - If the request is made later, it should be made in an email sent to help@russellhouse.co.uk, and should not only fully detail the proposed use, but also give the details of the person whose name and contact details were on the original application form.

RHP and the author expect this honour system to be followed respectfully, by individuals and organisations whom we in turn respect. RHP will act to protect authors' copyright if they become aware of it being infringed.

I would like to receive a free PDF of the handouts from *Joint Investigation in Child Protection*.

*Name _____

*Address _____

_____

_____

_____

*Post code _____

*Contact phone number _____

*e-mail address _____ (to which the PDF will be e-mailed).

I have read, and accept, the terms and conditions. I understand that RHP may use this information to contact me about other matters and publications, but that RHP will not make my details available to other organisations.

*Signed: _____   *Date _____

* All sections marked with an asterisk **must be completed**, or the form will be returned to the postal address given here.

Please return to: Russell House Publishing Ltd, 4 St Georges House, The Business Park,
Uplyme Road, Lyme Regis, Dorset DT7 3LS.